READING RESEARCH

Advances in Theory and Practice

Volume 1

EDITORIAL CONSULTANTS

FUTURE VOLUMES

Volume 2: Theme: Learning to read

Contributors:

READING RESEARCH

Advances in Theory and Practice

Volume 1

T. GARY WALLER
Department of Psychology
University of Waterloo
Waterloo, Ontario, Canada

G. E. MACKINNON
Department of Psychology
University of Waterloo
Waterloo, Ontario, Canada

ACADEMIC PRESS   New York   San Francisco   London   1979
A Subsidiary of Harcourt Brace Jovanovich, Publishers

ACADEMIC PRESS, INC.
111 Fifth Avenue, New York, New York 10003

United Kingdom Edition published by
ACADEMIC PRESS, INC. (LONDON) LTD.
24/28 Oval Road, London NW1 7DX

ISSN 0191–0914

ISBN 0–12–572301–6

PRINTED IN THE UNITED STATES OF AMERICA
79 80 81 82   9 8 7 6 5 4 3 2 1

CONTENTS

READING THAT COMES NATURALLY:
THE EARLY READER
Jane W. Torrey

THE CHILD'S SOCIAL ENVIRONMENT
AND LEARNING TO READ
Doris R. Entwisle

REHABILITATION OF ACQUIRED
DYSLEXIA OF ADOLESCENCE
Carole Ann Wiegel-Crump

COGNITION AND READING:
AN APPROACH TO INSTRUCTION
Hildred Rawson

LIST OF CONTRIBUTORS

Numbers in parentheses indicate the pages on which the authors' contributions begin.

MAX COLTHEART (1), *Department of Psychology, Birkbeck College, University of London, London WC1E 7HX, England*

LINNEA C. EHRI (63), *Department of Education, University of California, Davis, Davis, California 95616*

DORIS R. ENTWISLE (145), *Department of Social Relations, The Johns Hopkins University, Baltimore, Maryland 21218*

JOANNE R. NURSS (31), *Department of Early Childhood Education, Georgia State University, Atlanta, Georgia 30303*

HILDRED RAWSON (187), *20 Prince Arthur Avenue, Toronto, Ontario, Canada M5R 1B1*

JANE W. TORREY (115), *Department of Psychology, Connecticut College, New London, Connecticut 06320*

CAROLE ANN WIEGEL-CRUMP (171), *Vrij Universeitt, P.C. Hooftstraat 72, Amsterdam-DZ, The Netherlands*

PREFACE

In the last decade or so the quantity of research on reading has increased rapidly. The people concerned with such research represent diverse orientations, backgrounds, and interests; i.e., psychologists, linguists, neurologists, classroom teachers, and those concerned with the assessment and remediation of reading difficulty. The extensive research which is being published on reading, and which this variety of people is trying to follow, appears in an ever-increasing and bewildering array of scholarly publications. It has become difficult for the researcher, the student, and the consumer of research on reading to keep abreast of developments in the field. In essence, both the reading community and reading research are fragmented into diverse subgroups. Communication and interaction among these subgroups are seriously lacking.

With this background in mind, this series, "Reading Research: Advances in Theory and Practice," has been created. Its major purpose is to provide a publication outlet for systematic and substantive reviews and syntheses, both empirical and theoretical, and for integrative reports of programmatic research. The expectation is that such contributions will appeal to a broad, multifaceted, interdisciplinary audience, will help professionals keep abreast of growing knowledge in the various areas of reading research, will help serious students of reading come to terms with the diverse and complex field, and will help researchers by providing fresh viewpoints on areas close to their own.

The Editors have attempted deliberately to organize each volume in the series around a particular theme or topic. The chapters in Volume 1 are directed to the question, "What does a child have to know (or, be able to do) in order to learn to read?" The contributors treat the question in various ways. The book begins with an in-depth logical analysis in historical perspective of the concept of reading readiness by M. Coltheart. Chapters then follow which address: the current state of the art of assessing reading readiness (J. Nurss); the relationship between early linguistic insight and reading (L. Ehri); the factors which produce precocious readers (J. Torrey); the importance of the social environment in learning to read (D. Entwisle); and readiness for relearning to read following brain injury (C. Wiegel-Crump). The volume concludes with a discussion by H. Rawson of a program of instruction in reading predicated on the concept that readiness is a continuous and cumulative process of preparing children for successive advances in cognitive development.

The Editors would like to thank Marion Tapley for her assistance in the preparation of this volume. We also would like to thank the editorial consultants for their advice and enthusiastic support.

T. GARY WALLER
G. E. MACKINNON

WHEN CAN CHILDREN LEARN TO READ—AND WHEN SHOULD THEY BE TAUGHT?

MAX COLTHEART

Department of Psychology
Birkbeck College
London, England

I. SOME EARLY IDEAS

At what age is a child capable of learning to read? At what age should a child be taught to read? Educational theorists have been expressing their views on these questions for a long time. Twenty centuries ago, Quintilian observed that "some hold that boys should not be taught to read till they are seven years old, that being the earliest age at which they can derive profit from instruction" (Page, 1921, p. 27). Plato took a different view: "For reading or writing three years or so, from the age of ten, is a fair allowance of a boy's time" (Taylor, 1966, p. 194). There was considerable discussion of these issues in England in the seventeenth century: for example, Brinsley advocated in 1612 that reading instruction should begin at the age of five (Brinsley, 1612, p. 9) and Hoole in 1660 expressed the view that "betwixt three and four years of age a child has a great propensity to peep into a book, and then is the most seasonable time . . . for him to begin to learn" (Hoole, 1660, pp. 1–2).

1

More recently, Patrick (1899) asserted that reading was taught at much too early an age in the United States:

> So much has been said and written lately about the increase in myopia and other defects of the eye among school children that I shall merely refer to this subject here. Upon entering school children are practically free from these defects. Upon leaving school, a strikingly large percentage are suffering from them. . . . If pencils, pens, paper and books could be kept away from children until they are at least ten years of age, and their instruction come directly from objects and from the voice of the teacher, this evil could be greatly lessened.

Patrick gave a second reason for postponing the teaching of reading until children are 10 years old, namely, that there are some subjects younger children can learn successfully, and some they cannot, and that reading is one of the latter subjects:

> We have thus seen that there are certain branches of instruction for which the mind of the child from five to ten has ripened, and which therefore may be taught most economically and safely during this period. . . . there are subjects which are strikingly adapted to this period, namely, natural science, history, and morals.

These two claims—that young children are not ocularly equipped for the task of learning to read, and that they are also not mentally equipped—have been frequently reiterated throughout this century. In almost all discussions involving the concept of reading readiness one or the other, or both, of these claims is made by those who assert that young children are "not ready to read."

The view that teaching children to read before they are 10 damages their eyes, a view shared by Dewey (1898), was widespread in the early part of this century; Smith and Jensen (1935b, pp. 682–685) give numerous examples. However, expressions of this view in the early part of the century did not appeal to evidence, merely to the "experience" of teachers and ophthalmologists. When attempts were made in the 1930s to collect such evidence by investigating the relationships between the presence of various ocular defects and a child's progress in learning to read, the results were almost entirely negative (Witty and Kopel, 1935a,b; Fendrick, 1935; Dean, 1939; and others). Obviously a sufficiently severe and uncorrected astigmatism or hypermetropia or acuity defect might impair a child's reading progress, but it is clear from these studies that such defects are relatively infrequent in young children, and that the minor ocular defects which are often present are irrelevant as far as reading is concerned. Thus I will not be discussing reading readiness in terms of the readiness of young children's eyes for the task of learning to read.

Patrick's views concerning mental readiness for reading are more significant. He was by no means the first person to think of cognitive development as a process of "ripening"—Mulcaster used precisely the same term when dealing with cognitive development in 1581 (Mulcaster, 1581, p. 19)—but Patrick was the first to use the term "readiness" in this context:

> It is a well-known fact that a child's powers, whether physical or mental, ripen in a certain rather definite order. There is, for instance, a certain time in the life of the infant when the motor mechanism of the legs ripens, before which the child cannot be taught to walk, while after that time he cannot be kept from walking. Again, at the age of seven, there is a mental readiness for some things and an unreadiness for others.

This extraordinary analogy between learning to walk and learning to read crops up in very many discussions of reading readiness, for example: "Just as the normal child learns to walk and talk when he reaches the proper development for these activities, so he arrives at readiness for reading in his own time" (Adams, Gray, and Reese, 1949); "Reading, like walking, can be mastered only after a long process of growing and learning has taken place" (Harris, 1961).

Patrick's article appears to have had a strong and immediate effect—it is quoted with approval by Huey (1908) who agrees (p. 337) that an 8-year-old child "has not at this stage developed the logical and ideational habits that most printed language demands," and Hall (1911), although disputing the particular age at which children are ready to read, took the view that "there appears to come to many children a period, lasting perhaps many months, between the ages of five and eight, when both interest and facility in learning to read culminate, and if this period passes unutilised, they learn it with greater difficulty and at a certain disadvantage."

An educational zeitgeist thus became established in the first two decades of this century, a general opinion that a child could not be taught to read until he had passed a certain critical level of neurological maturity—a certain level of "ripeness" or "readiness," to use Patrick's terms. This prevailing opinion was just that, an opinion; it completely lacked empirical justification. In spite of this, educational research workers became interested in the concept of reading readiness in the 1920s, and so eventually research on this topic did begin.

II. THE INTRODUCTION OF THE TERM "READING READINESS"

Although Patrick was clearly referring to reading as well as to other school subjects when he used the term "mental readiness" in 1898, the term "readiness" was first explicitly applied to reading in 1925, on page 232 of the Report of the National Committee on Reading, published in the 24th Year Book of the United States National Society for the Study of Education. This report reflected the maturational viewpoint: "Buswell (1922) found that the span of recognition increases rapidly in the case of most pupils during the first four years. Similar periods favourable to rapid growth have been found for other phases of reading. Good instruction recognized the importance of those growth periods." A solely maturational view of the concept of reading readiness implies that instruction cannot be used to accelerate readiness, and indeed such a view has often been taken: "By taking the simple precaution of not giving children formal reading instruction until they are ready for it, much of the present retardation in reading can be prevented" (Harris, 1940); "All the evidence says: readiness comes as a healthy child grows and matures. Time is the answer—not special drills or special practice" (Hymes, 1958). The National Committee's report, however, did not adopt this approach, since the authors of the report were of the opinion that lack of readiness for reading could be dealt with by appropriate instruction: "Many pupils enter the first grade who are not adequately prepared for reading. . . . Appropriate instruction should be provided before formal work in reading is introduced." This view, too, has its adherents: "That the school has a definite responsibility in a program designed to develop a readiness for reading is commonly accepted. Merely waiting for such development is not sufficient" (Kibbe, 1939).

For those who wish to use the concept "reading readiness," the question of whether or not a child's state of readiness can be influenced by instruction is of crucial importance. If the answer to this question is yes, then the whole idea of readiness as an outcome of a maturational process begins to look rather odd. Either a child is failing to make progress in reading because he has not matured enough: or he is failing to make progress because he has not been taught or has not picked up certain skills which are needed for beginning to learn to read. There seems something rather self-contradictory in asserting both of these accounts of the processes underlying impaired acquisition of reading. Furthermore, if it is argued that those children who appear "unready to read" would be ready to read if they had had appropriate prereading instruction, then why do we need the maturational concept of reading readiness at all?

On the other hand, there are serious difficulties for the view that reading readiness can *not* be accelerated by appropriate instruction. If this were so, then the ease with which a child acquires the elements of reading could not be influenced by any form of prereading instruction. There is abundant evidence that prereading instruction *does* assist reading progress (discussed later in this chapter). Those proponents of the concept of reading readiness who assumed that any group of children in a first grade in the United States who had not made progress in learning to read had done so because they were not "ready" in the maturational sense seemed to have failed to consider the simple fact that the age at which children are first given reading instruction is different in different countries. This age is 5 years in Great Britain, Israel, India, Hong Kong, the Lebanon, and Uruguay; it is 6 in the United States, France, Argentina, Japan, and Australia; and it is 7 in Denmark, Finland, Iceland, Sweden, Afghanistan, and Ecuador (Downing, 1973). If one explained failures to learn to read in the first grade in the United States as due to inadequate maturity of a kind which cannot be accelerated by instruction, then such failures should be extremely common in those countries where reading tuition begins at 5, and extremely rare in those countries where reading tuition begins at 7. Even in the 1920s, it was clear that this was not so.

The explicit reference to reading readiness in the 1925 report of the National Committee of Reading was parallelled by the inclusion of a Reading Readiness Committee in the International Kindergarten Union in 1925. This Committee cooperated with the United States Bureau of Education in carrying out "an investigation of pupils' readiness for reading instruction upon entrance to first grade" (Holmes, 1927). This investigation consisted of sending a questionnaire to 560 teachers of first grade classes in September 1925. One of the questions was "What in your opinion constitutes 'reading readiness'?" Among the factors cited by teachers in response to this question were: appropriate comprehension, thinking, and judgment; sufficient command of English; good speaking vocabulary; wide and varied experiences; desire; interest; mental efficiency; physical efficiency; appropriate social attitudes (courtesy, cooperation, responsibility); correct pronunciation; and appropriate psychological traits and characteristics. The very wide variety of responses to this question showed that the term had no commonly accepted meaning among first-grade teachers at that time. A questionnaire circulated among teachers in England in 1958–1961 produced exactly the same result: an extraordinary heterogeneity in the definitions offered by teachers for the term "reading readiness" (Goodacre, 1967). One notable feature of the responses to both questionnaires is that neither group of teachers showed any tendency to think of reading readiness as corresponding to the attainment of some critical level of maturational development. The other early paper on reading readiness (Hooper, 1926) also showed no evidence of adopting this maturational viewpoint.

As far as I know, the term "reading readiness" was used during the 1920s in only these three publications; but from 1930 onward it appears frequently in the literature. During the 1930s, a large number of papers appeared on the topic, but only two of these were of much influence—the paper by Morphett and Washburne (1931) and that by Dolch and Bloomster (1937). I would like to consider them in a little detail, because almost all of the empirical basis for the concept of reading readiness derives from these two papers.

III. THE WORK OF MORPHETT AND WASHBURNE

In September 1928, all the first-grade children in Winnetka, Illinois, a total of 141 children, were given the Detroit First-Grade Intelligence Test. Their Stanford–Binet IQs were also obtained. After 4 months of reading tuition in the first grade, the amount of progress these children had made in learning to read was determined as follows: the reading materials used by the children were divided into steps (the beginning materials used by the children consisted of 21 of these steps, for example), and reading progress was measured in terms of number of steps the child had completed by February 1929. A second measure of reading was also used: the number of words from a maximum of 139 words which a child could read aloud correctly when each word was presented to him individually on a flash card.

Next, the term "satisfactory progress in reading" was defined, as follows:

> The first-grade teachers, all of whom had had several years of experience with the reading materials, agreed that children who seemed ready for reading from the beginning of the year had usually completed at least thirteen progress steps and knew at least thirty-seven sight words by February. Therefore, thirteen progress steps and thirty-seven sight words were accepted as a measure of the minimum degree of satisfactory progress. (Morphett and Washburne, 1931, p. 497)

Each child was therefore classified as having made satisfactory reading progress or not, and also as having made satisfactory sight-word progress or not. Then, for each half-year mental age range, the percentage of the children having an MA in this range who made satisfactory progress was calculated. Table I shows the results for reading progress; Table II shows the results for sight-word progress.

What impressed Morphett and Washburne about these data was that reading performance and sight-word performance increased steeply as a function of mental age category up to the category 6:6–6:11, and then remained fairly constant with further increases in mental age. They were led by this to the following conclusions:

> Children with mental ages of six years and six months made progress practically as satisfactory as that of children with higher mental ages. . . . The mental age of six years and six months is . . . the point beyond which there is very little gain in postponing the teaching of reading. . . . It pays to postpone beginning reading until a child has attained a mental age of six years and six months. . . . The children who had a mental age of six years and six months made far better progress than did the less mature children and practically as satisfactory progress as did the children of a higher mental age. . . . By postponing the teaching of reading until children reach a mental age level of six and a half years, teachers can greatly decrease the chances of failure and discouragement and can correspondingly increase their efficiency.

There are two reasons why these conclusions are not warranted by the data. The first is that the definition of "satisfactory progress" was completely arbitrary. The choices of 13 reading units and 37 sight words as the cutoff points below which reading progress is deemed to have been unsatisfactory were made on the obscure basis that first-grade teachers expected those levels to be reached by those children who, upon entering the first grade, "seemed ready for reading." In fact, any definition of satisfactory progress would have to be arbitrary, because progress in reading is a continuous variable, and so there is no amount of progress that could be rationally selected as the cutoff value between "unsatisfactory" and "satisfactory" progress. One might just as well choose 10 reading

TABLE I

Number of Children of Each Mental Age and Percentage Making Satisfactory Reading Progress

Mental age in years and months	Number of children		Percentage making satisfactory reading progress	
	Detroit Test	Stanford–Binet Test	Detroit Test	Stanford–Binet Test
4:5 to 4:11	1	1	—	—
5:0 to 4:5	12	1	0	—
5:6 to 4:11	12	12	0	8
6:0 to 6:5	17	22	47	41
6:6 to 6:11	23	38	78	68
7:0 to 7:5	29	31	79	68
7:6 to 7:11	16	15	75	87
8:0 to 8:5	7	11	—	82
8:6 to 9:0	8	2	—	—

units, or 43 sight words. This is a serious problem, because the choice of larger values for the cutoff points would increase the value of the mental age at which reading can be "taught satisfactorily," and smaller cutoff points would reduce the value of this critical mental age. In other words, since the definition of "satisfactory progress" was arbitrary, so must the choice of 6½ years as the

TABLE II

Number of Children of Each Mental Age and Percentage Making Satisfactory Sight-Word Scores

Mental age in years and months	Number of children		Percentage making satisfactory reading progress	
	Detroit Test	Stanford–Binet Test	Detroit Test	Stanford–Binet Test
4:5 to 4:11	1	1	—	—
5:0 to 5:5	12	1	0	—
5:6 to 5:11	12	12	0	8
6:0 to 6:5	17	25	71	52
6:6 to 6:11	23	43	87	77
7:0 to 7:5	31	35	84	89
7:6 to 7:11	23	18	83	94
8:0 to 8:5	10	11	90	91
8:6 to 9:0	12	3	100	—

critical mental age be arbitrary. Nevertheless, as the quotations cited further on in this section show, it has been claimed over and over again in the literature that Morphett and Washburne showed that a child cannot learn to read until he reaches a mental age of 6½.

Any attempt to apply a dichotomy to what is essentially a continuous variable will be misleading here, and so no statements about the minimum mental age necessary for reading can ever be derived from these kinds of results. All that the results can show is that there is a positive correlation between a child's mental age and how much he learns from 4 months of instruction in reading.

Morphett and Washburne not only concluded that, in their sample of children, only those with a mental age of 6½ or more made "satisfactory progress" in learning to read; they concluded furthermore that such satisfactory progress could be achieved for children with lower mental ages by postponing reading instruction until the child reached the critical mental age. This does not follow from their results either. It assumes that the degree to which a child profits from a given amount of reading instruction depends upon his mental age but is independent of his IQ; that if three children aged 5, 7, and 9 all have mental ages of 7, they will learn to read at the same rate. Why should this be so? It might instead be the case that a child who reaches the mental age of 6½ relatively late in life (and therefore has a relatively low IQ) would learn to read more slowly than a child who reaches this mental age early in life (and therefore has a relatively high IQ), even if for both children reading instruction begins as soon as they attain the "critical" mental age. Unless the relationship between IQ and reading progress with mental age partialled out is zero, one cannot conclude that those children in Morphett and Washburne's study who had mental ages lower than 6½ and made slow progress would have made the same amount of progress as did the brighter children if only reading instruction had been delayed for the duller children until their mental ages had reached 6½.

In fact, work by Davidson (1931) suggested that Morphett and Washburne's assumption was not only unjustified but incorrect. Davidson studied the reading abilities of five bright 3-year-olds, four 4-year-olds of average intelligence, and four dull 5-year-olds. Each of the three groups had the same average mental age, namely, 4 years. After less than one school term of reading instruction, the mean number of isolated sight words which could be pronounced by the three groups was 129.4, 55.2, and 40.0, respectively. Bliesmer (1954) confirmed this result. He studied two groups of children with equivalent mental ages (range 10:8 to 12:6 years). The younger group (CA range 8:7–9:10, IQ range 116–138) were superior to the older group (CA range 14:2–16:3, IQ range 72–84) on reading comprehension subtests from the Iowa Tests of Basic Skills.

On Morphett and Washburne's assumption that it is mental age that determines rate of progress in learning to read, Davidson's three groups should have made equal progress, since they had equal mental ages; the same applies to Bliesmer's two groups. Instead, the data indicate that a given mental age does not determine a given rate of progress in reading; rather, at any mental age, younger (therefore brighter) children make faster progress. Thus Morphett and Washburne were wrong to conclude that the problems of the duller children in their sample would not have occurred if reading had been delayed until a mental age of 6½ years had been reached.

I have argued, then, that Morphett and Washburne's work suffers from two defects. First, their conclusions rest on a definition of "satisfactory progress in learning to read" which is inescapably arbitrary. Second, even if this were not so, they were not justified, and in fact were wrong, in claiming that delaying reading instruction for duller pupils would eliminate their difficulties.

Unfortunately, these defects seem not to have been apparent to many educational practitioners and theorists, since Morphett and Washburne's conclusions were immediately taken up and quoted with uncritical enthusiasm, often being distorted and made more extreme in the process. A small selection from the many examples of such quotations follows.

> It has been found that in order to make any progress in reading a child must have attained a mental age of at least six years, and that a mental age of six and one half years more nearly insures success. (Harrison, 1936)

> Numerous studies of the relation between mental age and reading progress have led to the conclusion that children whose reading instruction begins before they have attained the mental age of six years and six months have little chance of making normal progress. (Keister, 1941)

> We ought perhaps to conclude that there is but one age to begin to learn to read, the age of six and a half. (Watts, 1944)

> The consensus of the results from educational research indicates that for normal pupils the more formal approach to reading should not begin before a mental age of six is reached. (Schonell, 1945)

> The literature in the readiness field has popularized a minimum MA of 6½ years as one criterion for reading readiness. (Kottmeyer, 1947)

> Morphett and Washburne are doubtless correct in asserting that a minimum mental age of 6½ is required for adequate progress in reading. (Inglis, 1948)

> The minimum mental age for success in first-grade reading is six years and four months. Reading taught by conventional methods cannot be learned by the typical child just six years old. (Hildreth, 1950)

> A child should be mentally at least six years and six months old before formal work on reading is attempted. (Carter and McGinnis, 1953)

> Children with a mental age of 6½ are not ready for the printed word. (de Hirsch, 1957)

> We have a mountain of evidence to prove that a perfectly "normal" child—IQ 100— cannot learn to read until he is about six years six months old. (Heffernan, 1960)

Morphett and Washburne's stated conclusions were merely that children with a mental age of less than 6½ made slower progress at learning to read than did children with this mental age, whereas progress was no faster for children with a mental age above 6½ than for children with this mental age. Some of the citations of their work express a much more extreme view—no child can learn to read *at all* until he attains a mental age of 6½, and when he does reach this mental age, he will learn to read normally. Such a view is absurd, since it assumes:

1. The state of being able to read is all-or-none.

2. The progress a child makes in learning to read is independent of such extrinsic variables as the method by which he is taught, the size of his class, and the abilities of his teacher.

3. Individual differences in the relationship between mental age and ability to learn to read do not exist.

If any one of these three assumptions is false, then it makes no sense to say that children cannot learn to read until they have a mental age of 6½; and, of course, all three assumptions are false. Whether or not a given child can learn to read is a matter of degree, since the amount of progress made in response to a given amount of instruction is a continuous variable, not a dichotomous one; the rate at which a child makes progress in learning to read is influenced by extrinsic variables; and even Morphett and Washburne's own data showed that children with the same mental age varied in their reading achievement. Thus, although it strains one's credulity to believe that there exist people who are willing to claim that no child with an MA below 6½ can learn to read, and all children with an MA above 6½ can learn to read, the quotations I have given, and other similar ones, indicate that such claims have been made. In fact Morphett and Washburne's paper had a strong influence on educational practice in the United States. Four years after the paper appeared, Smith and Jensen (1935a) noted that "here and there educators, psychologists, medical men, and other authorities are advising postponements of reading, suggesting six years and six months up to as late as the tenth year as the proper ages for beginning reading"; and Thackray (1971) remarks that the textbooks of Betts and Dolch "provide evidence that many school systems in America have accepted these statements (concerning the minimum mental age for learning to read) and put the underlying ideas into practice."

It is very difficult to understand why the Morphett–Washburne work was taken up so enthusiastically and had such a long-lasting influence. Presumably this occurred because their conclusions, especially when distorted by subsequent commentators, provided what seemed like a simple answer to the question of why some children fail to read in first grade: they fail to read because they are not ready to read, and the cure is simply to wait until they become ready. This analysis was attractive enough to induce people to overlook its circularity (the evidence that a child is not ready to learn to read is that he has not learned to read), its unsatisfactory empirical basis (the Morphett–Washburne study) and the dubious assumptions upon which this concept of readiness was based, in particular the assumption that a child's failure to learn to read has causes which are all intrinsic to the child. Gates (1937) showed that the mental age at which a given level of reading was achieved varied from 5 to 7 years across four classes which used differing teaching methods and had differing numbers of pupils. He therefore concluded that ''statements concerning the necessary mental age at which a pupil can be entrusted to learn to read are essentially meaningless.'' This much-needed statement of the obvious, that how well a child will profit from reading instruction cannot depend solely on his mental age or state of reading readiness, fell on deaf ears. The concept of reading readiness retained its popularity, reinforced by the other major paper on the topic, Dolch and Bloomster's paper, ''Phonic Readiness,'' published in 1937.

IV. THE WORK OF DOLCH AND BLOOMSTER

The work of Dolch and Bloomster was concerned specifically with children's phonic ability; the authors' conclusion was:

A mental age of seven years seems to be the lowest at which a child can be expected to use phonics (Dolch and Bloomster, 1937)

and this conclusion, like the conclusions of Morphett and Washburne, has been widely cited:

Dolch and Bloomster provide evidence that few children with mental ages below 7 show ability in phonic analysis. (Schonell, 1961)

Children do not begin to profit from an analytic (i.e., phonic) approach to reading much before they are seven years mentally. (Sheldon, 1962)

The consensus of opinion . . . is that children below the mental age of seven show insufficient ability (of analysis) to benefit from systematic phonic instruction. (Bruce, 1964)

Studies had indicated that children could not make the best use of formal phonics instruction until they had arrived at a mental age of seven years. In the light of these studies, phonics was generally delayed until the second grade. (Smith, 1964, describing educational practice in the United States in the decade 1940–1950)

This view appears even to have spread to the United Kingdom; according to Gardner (1967) ''It is quite common for teachers of Infants classes to shun 'phonics'. The frequent assertion that 'children are not ready for phonics until they have a mental age of six-and-a-half years' is the justification.''

One can object to these conclusions from Dolch and Bloomster's work on the grounds that such conclusions ignore individual differences and treat the ability to carry out phonic tasks as an all-or-none variable, as one can object to any statement concerning a minimum mental age for learning any task. A further objection (discussed further on), is that other work has shown that young children do possess reasonable phonic abilities to a substantial degree.

The task given to children by Dolch and Bloomster required them to choose, from a row of four printed words, the one which was identical to the word spoken by the tester. These tasks were Tests 1 and 2 of the Word-Attack Series of the Dolch–Gray Readings Tests. The actual test items are not listed in Dolch and Bloomster's paper, and the tests themselves are, according to Buros (1968), now out of print, so one cannot learn anything about the items used beyond what is given in Dolch and Bloomster's paper. It was assumed that the pronunciations of the printed words had not been learned on a whole-word basis, since these words did not appear on lists of words common to primary reading books. Therefore to perform the task presumably a child must obtain the pronunciation of each printed word via the operation of grapheme–phoneme correspondence rules, followed by selection from among these four pronunciations of the one which matches the word spoken by the tester. In this sense, the test tapped phonic ability. It did so in a rather rigorous way, however, because each of the three incorrect alternatives differed from the correct item by a single letter. It is unclear why the task was arranged in this way. Dolch and Bloomster explained it as follows: "the word wholes look so much alike that the method of pure sight is difficult for a beginner . . . sight knowledge is rendered largely useless by the great similarity of the word forms." This is unclear for two reasons. First, the words were supposed never to have been seen before by the child (otherwise, the task would not require phonic ability) and so it is hard to know what is meant here by "sight knowledge." Second, since the incorrect items all looked similar to the correct item, they would also have sounded similar to it, so this "great similarity" should cause just as much difficulty for performing the task phonically as for performing it visually.

Dolch and Bloomster reported no data except for correlations between mental age and performance on this task (correlations which ranged from +.41 to +.52) but they comment that "Children with mental ages below seven years made only chance scores"; it is this single sentence which gave rise to the quotations of their work given earlier, and to the concept of "phonic readiness." It is clear from subsequent work, however, that Dolch and Bloomster seriously underestimated the phonic ability of young children.

Chall, Roswell, and Blumenthal (1963) used the Roswell–Chall auditory blending test to study young children's phonic ability. In this test, the tester speaks the component parts of the word (usually, though not always, the individual phonemes of the word) at intervals of about half a second. The child's task is to "blend" these components, i.e., to repeat the word having integrated it into a phonological whole, and then to write down the answer. A group of 62 first-grade Negro children in New York, primarily of lower to lower-middle socioeconomic class, scored an average of 76.1% correct with two-letter words,

47.6% correct with four-letter words divided into two components, and 20.6% correct responses with CVC words divided into three components. This test has also been administered to 6-year-old children of average intelligence in Australia, by Firth (1972), and they too performed well. In addition, Firth administered a second test of phonic ability, requiring "phoneme elision." A typical item here included "What word is made if I take the 'f' away from 'fall'?''. The children averaged 11.66 correct out of 20, again demonstrating substantial phonic ability.

The particular phonic abilities required by tests employed by Chall *et al.* and by Firth include the synthesis of a spoken word from phonemic or near-phonemic components, and the analysis of a spoken word into its phonemic components. These abilities are only part of what is needed when a child is being taught to read by a phonic method. In addition to the synthesis and analysis of spoken words, the child needs to learn how to map letters or letter groups onto phonemes. A pure test of his ability to achieve this is to ask him to pronounce words he has never seen before. He cannot have learned their pronunciation in a whole-word fashion, since he has never seen these whole words; thus if he can pronounce them correctly, he must be able to perform the phonic task of letter-to-sound translation. The best way to ensure that such a test uses only words that a child has never seen as wholes before is to use nonwords which follow the normal English conventions of spelling and hence are as pronounceable as genuine English words. Firth (1972) gave his 6-year-old children such a test, early in their first grade at school. The test consisted of 70 two-letter or three-letter pronounceable nonwords, all with an unambiguously correct pronunciation. Each child was asked to speak each nonword aloud. The mean number correct out of 70 was 27.27. Thus many 6-year-old children who have had only a few months of reading tuition can succeed reasonably well in this test of phonic ability.

Read's work on preschool spellers (Read, 1971, 1972) provides further evidence that very young children can possess substantial phonic ability. The children he studied had learned to spell before they had learned to read. Each had independently invented his own spelling system. Their system was quite consistent from child to child and, though bizarre to adult eyes (*country* is spelled CWNCHRE, *dragon* is JRAGIN), was highly regular in terms of letter–sound correspondences. Most important, the invention of such a system demonstrated that these children possessed a refined and acute understanding of the phonological constituents of speech and of how each of these can be represented in print by a letter or letter cluster. The youngest of these children was only 3½ years old.

Fox and Routh (1975) studied children's ability to elide phonemes by speaking two- or three-phoneme syllables to the children and asking them to repeat the syllables minus a phoneme; for example, the child's response to "Pete" should be "Pe." Even children as young as 3 years of age were correct on 25% of occasions, and 6-year-old children averaged nearly 100% correct.

In the phoneme-counting task devised by Liberman, Shankweiler, Liberman, Fowler, and Fischer (1977), 70% of 6-year-old children succeeded. Calfee (1977, Table 5) also provides evidence of the existence of substantial phonetic-segmentation ability at this age.

All of this evidence demonstrates that children of the age at which reading instruction normally begins possess phonic abilities to a considerable degree. The poor performance of the children in Dolch's and Bloomster's experiment may perhaps be attributed to the fact that in that experiment every test item required not only the derivation of a pronunciation for four different (and highly visually similar) words but the comparison of all four pronunciations to a spoken word, and the decision as to which of these comparisons produced the greatest degree of similarity. All four comparisons would produce considerable similarity, since all four items would sound something like the spoken word. Problems arising at this difficult stage, problems unrelated to what we normally think of as phonic tasks, may have produced the poor performance. In straightforward tests which call upon phonic ability and little else, such as phoneme elision, nonword pronunciation, or segmentation of syllables into phonemes, even very young children perform well. It is thus clearly quite wrong to believe that there exists a stage of "phonic readiness" which children do not reach until some time after a stage of "reading readiness."

V. MEASURING READING READINESS

According to Smith (1964), in United States schools in the 1940s "the readiness concept had . . . been widely accepted; practically all schools had readiness programs. The subject was seldom mentioned in research reports or in periodical writings. Reading readiness books were widely used." This does appear to have been the case; in publications that originally appeared in the 1930s and 1940s one frequently comes across such statements as "Reading readiness means the maturation of all the mental, physical, and emotional factors involved in the reading process. Regardless of the chronological age of the child, the point at which the child's growth and development have brought about proper maturation of these factors should be the point at which the reading process begins" (Smith and Jensen, 1935a). Even in 1958, according to Durkin (1966b, p. 68): "There appeared to be fairly general acceptance of a mental age of 6.5 as a prerequisite for beginning reading." Teachers who believed that children should not be taught to read until they had attained the stage of reading readiness naturally wished to know, for each pupil, whether this stage had been reached; and the psychometric industry came to their aid. Reading readiness tests, for measuring how ready a child was for reading, proliferated.

Numerous studies of the validity of these tests were carried out. Such studies took the form of applying the tests to a group of children before reading instruction began, measuring reading achievement after a period of instruction, and determining the correlation between scores on the readiness test and scores on the reading achievement test. These correlations were always rather low when the contribution of IQ was partialled out (see e.g., Kottmeyer, 1947; Karlin, 1957; Wilson and Burke, 1937; Lee, Clark, and Lee, 1934; Henig, 1949; Barrett, 1965). Furthermore, those studies which compared the validity of teachers' predictions as to how well a child would learn to read with the validity of predictions from reading readiness tests found that teachers' predictions were at least as good as, and often superior to, the results of readiness tests (Lee *et al.,* 1934; Wilson and Burke, 1937; Carr and Michaels, 1941; Kottmeyer, 1947; Henig, 1949). This was so despite the fact that many reading readiness tests achieved a spuriously high validity coefficient by incorporating items which actually measured *reading,* such as naming letters and digits, reading words aloud, and choosing from printed words the one spoken by a tester. If children who can actually read a little before formal teaching begins are likely to do well in the first grade at learning to read, as would surely be the case, then the results of those reading readiness tests that incorporate items which actually require reading would correlate with subsequent reading achievement, even if these tests were completely unable to predict how well *nonreaders* would learn to read.

These studies of validity showed that reading readiness tests could not be used to predict with any accuracy the success with which a nonreader would learn to read, and that certainly such tests did not produce more accurate predictions than did teachers' ratings. Nevertheless, many reading readiness tests were developed; Buros (1968) listed 20 different tests of reading readiness, and there are many others not present in this list. Those who advocated the use of such tests overlooked the fact that no reading readiness test was available in the United Kingdom; British children learned to read without their readiness first being measured.

VI. A RESUMÉ

The fact is that some children make rapid progress when given elementary reading instruction and some do not, and this is so even when there are no obvious reasons for the slow progress of the latter group. The purpose of the concept of reading readiness is to provide an answer to the question of why some children fail to make progress in learning to read, the answer being that these children are not "ready" to learn to read.

The concept of "readiness" had a fairly clear logical status if a completely maturational view is taken. Three-month-old children are not "ready" to learn to walk because the necessary muscular apparatus has not matured. This maturation will occur without the necessity of any treatment designed specifically to bring it about, and when it does, the child will quickly master the skill of walking, without needing tuition. Quotations given earlier in this chapter reveal that some authors have thought of reading in the same way: it cannot be learned until a certain maturational level is reached, and then can be learned quickly. Those who make slow progress have not reached this maturational level; that is why their progress is slow.

Although this account of backwardness in reading is logically coherent, it lacks any empirical support, and in fact is inconsistent with what we know about reading. Reading does not appear spontaneously, as walking does; if a child is not taught to read, he will never be able to do it, no matter how mature he is. The putative maturational stage at which a child will suddenly be able to respond to reading instruction has never been identified; no method for determing whether or not a given child has reached this stage has ever been developed. Claims that this stage is reached when a child attains a "critical" mental age (usually specified at 6½) are unjustified extrapolations from the Morphett and Washburne study, and ignore the existence of individual differences and the influence of various environmental factors upon the rate at which a child learns to read. Individual differences and environmental effects are much less marked with physical skills such as walking, and one can say what it is that must mature before walking can occur. These differences between physical skills and such mental skills as reading are so marked that the concept of maturational readiness cannot be plausibly applied to the development of the ability to read.

Consequently, one might expect the concept of reading readiness which emerged from the solely maturational viewpoints of Dewey, Patrick, and others at the turn of the century to have withered away when it became clear that reading was not like walking. This, however, did not happen. The exclusively maturational viewpoint was abandoned, but, curiously, the concept of readiness remained. The view was taken that a state of reading readiness would be brought about by appropriate instruction. This is a complete departure from the idea that originally produced the concept of readiness, since now slowness in learning to read is attributed, not to immaturity, but to lack of certain prereading skills, skills which can be taught; they are not skills which simply develop through maturation. There is no need for the concept of readiness here; it is redundant. If we say that certain kinds of prereading instruction will produce a state of readiness, and once a state of readiness is reached a child can begin to learn to read, why not simply restate this without reference to readiness by saying that when certain kinds of prereading skills have been mastered by instruction, a child can begin to learn to read, since he has been equipped with the necessary skills?

Not only is the concept of readiness no longer necessary; it may even be harmful. The statement that X has not yet learned to read because he is not "ready" sounds like an explanation, but is not. First, it is circular, since the only evidence for the lack of readiness is the failure to learn to read. Second, it disguises the fact that we do not know anything at all about the characteristics of this state of readiness, and so do not know what it is the lack of which is preventing X from learning to read. If we were to dispense with the concept of readiness, we would be more clearly confronted by the fact that we often simply do not know why X is having such difficulty in learning to read while Y is making rapid progress.

In short, then, the concept of reading readiness developed originally from an untenable identification of physical skills with mental skills. When it became clear that these two forms of skills are fundamentally different, the concept of reading readiness should then have been abandoned. Instead it was retained, although the acknowledgment that the absence of a state of readiness could be caused by the lack of prereading instruction was an implicit acknowledgment that "readiness" was being used in a completely different sense, the concept of readiness as a consequence of maturation having been abandoned. The retention of this concept could not have occurred without the quite unjustified and incorrect use which so many educational theorists made of the work of Morphett and Washburne and of Dolch and Bloomster.

The question "When can children learn to read?" has often been answered by "When they are ready." If, as I have argued, this answer is completely unsatisfactory, what other answer might be given? It seems to me that the problem lies with the question, not the answer. Whether a child will respond well to initial reading tuition will depend upon the child and the tuition. Therefore, if the question "When can children learn to read?" does not specify a particular child and a particular method of tuition, it can no more be answered than can the question "How far is up?" The situation is different with physical skills such as walking; it is even different with the psychological skill of speech acquisition. Individual differences in the ease with which children learn to speak are much less marked than individual differences in the ease with which they learn to read; and learning to speak is not as dependent upon appropriate experience and tuition as reading is. Thus the concept of "critical period" might plausibly be used in connection with learning to speak, but scarcely in connection with learning to read. I conclude that there can be no answer to the question "When can children learn to read?" and hence no reason to ask this question.

The second question with which this chapter is concerned is "When should children be taught to read?," and I turn now to a discussion of this issue.

VII. WHEN SHOULD CHILDREN BE TAUGHT TO READ?

Let us suppose that it made sense to say that certain young children are "ready to read" at an early age, and so will make rapid progress if given reading instruction, whereas other young children are not ready, and will not be able to profit from reading instruction for some time yet. The usual conclusion from this statement is that children who are ready to read should be taught, and those who are not should not.

Not every one has accepted this conclusion. It has sometimes been argued that learning to read is so difficult that it should be introduced, not as soon as it becomes **possible,** but later, when it becomes **easy.** Others have argued that learning to read is not the most important task for the young child, there are other things he should be doing in school, and tuition in reading ought not to dominate the curriculum. However, the assumption made by most parties to the dispute about whether children should be taught to read when very young is that this early tuition, desirable or not, will at least be effective in the long run. The assumption is a far from secure one.

It is by no means certain that teaching reading to a child who, although very young, can learn to read well, has any effect on how well he will be reading in a few years' time. This issue needs to be clarified if we are discussing reading readiness, since it may be necessary to distinguish between "ready to make rapid progress in response to learning instruction" and "ready to learn something about reading which will have long-term effects on reading skills." Thus I would like to conclude this chapter by discussing whether an early introduction to reading, for those children who can cope with it, makes any difference to their reading abilities in the long term.

Few of the studies in this area meet even the most elementary methodological requirements; in general I will consider only those studies which approach methodological adequacy. An early example is the work of Keister (1941). He took advantage of the fact that in the 1940s in Nebraska, children normally entered grade 1 at the age of five; elsewhere in the United States they entered grade 1 at 6. These children made considerable progress in learning to read throughout grade 1, and their reading achievement scores measured at the end of grade 1 were substantial. These scores were, however, much lower when measured at the beginning of grade 2. Thus in the 4 months between the end of grade 1 and the beginning of grade 2 much of what had been learned about reading during grade 1 had been lost. These children were of average intelligence, and hence it is difficult to argue that Keister's result would not be generalizable to children outside Nebraska; nor can one argue that the methods used to teach these children to read were inadequate, since the children were attaining high scores on reading tests at the end of grade 1. This work suggests, then, that teaching 5-year-old children to read by conventional methods in a normal classroom setting, while it has considerable short-term success, may have rather meager long-term effects, there being substantial loss of what was learned in grade 1 during the summer between the end of grade 1 and the beginning of grade 2.

Bradley (1955) compared two groups, each containing 31 children. The groups were matched on sex, age, IQ, and father's socioeconomic status. Group A began reading instruction at the beginning of grade 1. Group B children began instruction when judged to be "ready"; there were in fact three subgroups, who were introduced to reading after 5, 8, or 10 months of schooling. Early in grade 2, Group A was significantly superior to Group B in each of the three subtests of the Philadelphia Reading Test (word recognition, phrase recognition, paragraph comprehension). At the end of grade 2, the two groups were indistinguishable in terms of reading ability on the Chicago Reading Test's three subtests (word comprehension, phrase comprehension, and story comprehension). At the end of grade 3, the two groups were equal on the silent comprehension subtest of the Iowa Test of Basic Skills. Group B scored significantly higher on the vocabulary subtest of this test, a result which is not relevant here since it does not concern reading.

Bradley's work suggests that reading achievement at the end of grade 2, and at the end of grade 3, is not influenced by whether reading tuition was introduced at the beginning of grade 1, the middle of grade 1, or the beginning of grade 2; in other words, that grade 1 reading instruction leaves very little long-term residue even though it has strong short-term effects. An important feature of this study was that it extended to the end of grade 2. Many studies are of too limited a time scale to detect the presence or absence of long-term effects. One example of such a study is that of Hillerich (1965), which showed that reading scores at the end of grade 1 were higher for children who had had formal training in prereading skills in kindergarten than those who had not had such training; whether this difference would remain in subsequent grades is the important question, and it cannot be answered from Hillerich's data.

The studies of Keister and Bradley were small-scale ones, although that is not a reason for discounting their results. Problems of representativeness can be solved more easily in large-scale studies, however. Two such large studies on the effect of early reading were carried out in the United States in the early 1960s: Durkin's longitudinal study (Durkin, 1966a, b) and the Denver study reported by Brzeinski (1964a, b).

Durkin identified a number of California children and a number of New York children who could read before they went to school. Many references to Durkin's work are concerned with the mere existence of such children—sometimes their existence is used (Downing and Thackeray, 1971) as a disproof of the Morphett–Washburne claim that children cannot learn to read until they have a mental age of 6½. However, there have been many previous reports of precocious readers (Dolbear, 1912; Terman, 1918; Fowler, 1962; Terman and Oden, 1947; Lynn, 1963; and others). What is of interest for the present discussion is whether the early readers in Durkin's study achieved any long-term benefits from an early introduction to reading. We thus need to compare these children with a group of nonearly readers.

The best way to do this is to select a group of children and assign them at random to early-reader and nonreader subgroups. The former children are taught to read at an early age; the latter are not. However, Durkin approached the problem differently: she identified a group of children who had **already** learned to read at an early age. This is a characteristic approach in educational research, but it presents serious methodological problems. If the research worker wishes to investigate what effects are generated by early tuition in reading, this can only be done by comparing a group of children who had such early tuition with a group of children who did not. It must be demonstrated that these two groups of children do not differ systematically in any other way than with respect to the independent variable (presence versus absence of early reading). This is why the best way to do this kind of study is to assign children at random to the two groups. If this is not done, and the early readers are chosen because they have **already** learned to read at an early age, the problem then is to choose a group of nonreaders who differ systematically from the early readers in only one way: the presence versus absence of early reading.

It could be argued that this is impossible. One cannot know of every variable which influences reading progress, and therefore one cannot ever show that the post-hoc-selected nonreader group was comparable to the early reader group on every relevant variable except the independent variable of interest. Thus if the early reader group is superior in reading progress to the nonreader group, one cannot be sure that this is due to early tuition in reading. It might be due to some variable which **independently** produces early reading **and** good subsequent progress in reading. Thus I doubt if this research strategy is **ever** worth employing. In general, suppose one discovers a group of children who possess characteristic X, and one wishes to discover how the presence of X influences the subsequent development of characteristic Y. One therefore selects a group of children who do **not** possess characteristic X. The two groups are then compared with respect to their subsequent development of characteristic Y. Suppose the group of children who possessed X developed Y better than did the group who did not possess X. The aim of this kind of research design is to be able to make a causal statement of the form "The presence of X assists the subsequent development of Y." Such a conclusion does not follow here, because one cannot demonstrate that there are not **other** differences between the two groups (e.g., in intelligence or socioeconomic status) which **independently** produce both the presence of X and the rapid development of Y. Only if one knew every variable that influenced Y would one have any chance of overcoming this problem. Since such knowledge is simply not possible, this research design is inherently defective (although, of course, very widely used in educational research).

The problem is sometimes at least partially recognized. Research workers often attempt to **match** the two groups on at least **one** obviously relevant and potentially confounded variable, such as IQ. This is what Durkin did: she selected a group of 30 nonearly readers who were matched on IQ pairwise with a group of 30 early readers. Each group thus had the same median IQ (132). This matching technique is typical in these research situations. The idea is that, since the two groups have identical median IQs, any differences which emerge in subsequent investigations of the children cannot be caused by IQ differences. This research design, however, does not permit such a conclusion; the matching technique is of no use at all as an attempt to overcome the problem of selecting a "control group" against which one's "experimental group" can be compared.

The impotence of the matching technique can conveniently be illustrated with reference to Durkin's own data. She found that the reading achievement of the group of early readers was superior to the reading achievement of the IQ-matched group of nonearly readers at the end of grades 1, 2, and 3. She thus concluded that early reading confers long-term benefits, assuming that the achievement differences between the groups could not have occurred because of a confounding between IQ and early reading, since the two groups were matched on IQ.

The fallacy in this reasoning arises because of the statistical phenomenon of regression to the mean; hence a brief discussion of this phenomenon is in order.

Suppose one measured the IQs of a group of N subjects, and then retested the same subjects with the same test a short time later. Assume that the test is not susceptible to any carry-over effects, so that the two testing occasions are comparable. If so, M_i, the mean IQ produced by the initial testing, will differ from M_f, the mean IQ produced by the final testing, in an unsystematic way. The probability that M_f will exceed M_i is equal to the probability that M_f will be less than M_i.

Although this is true for the group means, it is not true for individual scores. A score on the first testing which was **above** M_i is more likely to be reduced on subsequent testing than to be increased. A score which was **below** M_i on original testing is more likely to be increased on subsequent testing than to be reduced. Thus individual scores regress toward the mean on retesting.

McNemar (1962, pp. 158–159) provided a simple algebraic proof that regression to the mean must occur. If we denote by g the gain between first testing and retesting (i.e., the algebraic difference between a person's retest score and his original score), we denote by i a person's original score, and we denote by r_{tt} the reliability of the test, then McNemar shows that

$$r_{ig} = \frac{r_{tt} - 1}{\sqrt{2 - 2r_{tt}}}$$

Unless the test has a reliability coefficient of 1.0, the value of r_{ig} must be negative. Thus high initial scores will have low gains and low initial scores will have high gains. The regression equation relating X'_f, the predicted final-testing score, to X_i, the original-testing score, is

$$X'_f = r_{tt} X_i + M_f - r_{tt} M_i$$

Assuming $M_f = M_i = M$

$$X'_f = r_{tt} X_i + M(1 - r_{tt})$$

When $X_i = M$, this gives $X'_f = X_i$. Thus a score which is at the group mean on original testing will show no regression effect. When $X_i > M$, $X'_f < X_i$, so that a score above the mean on original testing will move down on final testing. When $X_i < M$, $X'_f > X_i$; hence a score below the mean on original testing will move up on final testing.

Durkin's early readers were not selected with reference to their IQs. Thus their median IQ will not be a biased estimate of the mean IQ of the entire population of early readers. If their IQs were tested, one would expect the median still to be 132; some IQs would move up, some down, but the median would remain the same.

This is not true for the so-called "control group." They *were* selected with reference to their IQs. These children nearly all possessed IQs in excess of the population mean, 100. Thus if these children were retested, most of their scores would move down toward the population mean, 100; this would be a simple case of regression toward the mean.

Therefore, although the early readers and the nonearly readers were matched for IQ on a pairwise basis, and the two groups had identical median IQs, it still cannot be claimed that the groups were of equal IQ. The "control" group would almost certainly show a lower median IQ than the "experimental" group if all the children were retested. Consequently, any differences in reading achievement which occurred cannot confidently be ascribed to the effects of early reading; these differences could instead simply be due to IQ. One cannot interpret Durkin's finding of a superiority of early readers as evidence that early reading assists subsequent reading achievement.

It is surprising that the matching fallacy is so widely committed, since elementary statistics textbooks such as McNemar's identify the fallacy so explicitly, and since statistical methods for avoiding it are also set out explicitly. One simply calculates regressed IQ scores using the regression equation previously given. It is these **regressed** scores which should be used as the basis for pairing. When this is done, any differences which emerge between the two groups cannot be due to IQ differences.

Durkin's New York study cannot provide an unequivocal conclusion concerning the effects of early reading on subsequent reading achievement, because of this matching fallacy. Her California study did not employ the matching technique. Instead, she selected a sample of 636 nonearly readers. The mean IQ of this sample would of course be considerably lower than the median IQ of the California early readers, which was 121. Consequently, Durkin derived a regression equation for predicting reading achievement from IQ, using the data of the 636 nonearly readers (for whom these two variables correlated .76). She then used this equation to predict the reading achievement of 37 early readers from their IQs. The predicted reading achievements were compared to obtained reading achievements; the t-value here was 1.80, which is significant, if a one-tailed test is used.

Methodological problems arise here too. First, the procedure assumes linearity of regression of reading achievement on IQ. Durkin did not test the assumption, nor present any data enabling it to be tested. Nonlinear regression of reading scores on IQ is frequently found (e.g., Morphett and Washburne, 1931; Firth, 1972) and if it occurred in Durkin's data her method for comparing early readers to nonearly readers would not be legitimate. Second, the assumption of homogeneity of regression, also needed if this method is to be legitimate, was not tested. In subsequent work (Durkin, 1974) involving early and nonearly tuition groups, this assumption was tested, and this testing showed significant in-homogeneity of regression on several occasions. Third, there is Durkin's incon-sistent attitude toward one-tailed testing. She treats a t-value which is significant only on a one-tailed test as significant in this study, but a similar value obtained in a subsequent study is treated as insignificant (Durkin, 1974, p. 26). Fourth, and most important, Durkin's procedure assumes that the only extraneous variable which might influence reading achievement and be confounded with early/nonearly reading is IQ. There are many other possible confounding factors (socioeconomic status and family size are two examples) which could cause both early reading and superior long-term reading achievement. All such factors would need to be included, in a multiple regression equation, if the procedure adopted by Durkin were to be legitimate; and they were not. This point also applies to the use of analysis of covariance using IQ as the covariate; Durkin (1974) used this technique when analyzing reading achievement differences be-tween a group of children who had had an extensive pre-first-grade language–arts program and a group who had not. A further problem with this latter study is that, even when tests for homogeneity of regression showed significant in-homogeneity, analyses of covariance were still carried out and their results discussed.

It is evident that neither the matching technique used for the New York data nor the regression-equation technique used for the California data allow legiti-mate comparison to be made between the reading achievement of early readers and nonearly readers; and hence Durkin's work does not allow us to reach any conclusions concerning the possible long-term effects of an early introduction to reading.

My comments on the Denver study can be only brief, since early reports of this work (Brzeinski, 1964a, b) lack sufficient detail to permit an evaluation, and the completed study has not been published in any easily accessible form. However, criticisms of this work by Mood (1967) appear to be serious enough to raise considerable doubt as to the value of the work. A group of children who were taught to read in kindergarten was superior to a group who were not taught to read in kindergarten, even as late as grade 5. According to Mood, these two groups received different forms of reading programs after kindergarten; and of course if this were so the differences present at grade 5 could not be ascribed to the reading tuition received in kindergarten. A further problem is a large difference in attrition rates between the two samples: according to Mood there were originally 1250 children in the experimental group and 750 in the control group because a higher attrition rate was expected in the experimental group. The reverse occurred; at the end of the study, 61% of the experimental children and only 30% of the control children were still available. In the absence of further information about this significant difference in attrition rates, comparisons between the two groups at the end of the study must be suspect.

Tanyzer, Alpert, and Sandert (1966) compared the performance of children who were given instruction in reading in kindergarten with those who were not. The two groups showed equivalent reading achievement at the end of grade 1, and this was also the case at the end of grade 2 and grade 3. Furthermore, this failure to find any effect of whether or not reading instruction was given in kindergarten occurred both with teaching via **ita** (initial teaching alphabet) and teaching via traditional orthography. A brief paper by Shapiro and Willford (1969) does, however, report an advantage at the end of grade 2 of children who were introduced to **ita** in kindergarten over children who were introduced to **ita** in the first grade.

Durkin (1974) compared the reading achievement through grades 1 to 4 of two groups. The experimental group had participated in a 2-year pre-first-grade language–arts program. The control group children had not attended this program, but had attended kindergarten classes in which some reading tuition had been given. There was a large superiority of the experimental group over the control group in reading achievement at the end of grade 1. The advantage of the experimental group was smaller at the end of grade 2, but still statistically significant. These differences were no longer statistically significant by the end of grade 3 and they remained insignificant at the end of grade 4.

Durkin's children were predominantly from the middle class with above-average IQs. Gray and Klaus (1970) carried out a similar study, but with black children from lower-income families and with predominantly below-average IQs. Gray and Klaus describe their results as follows:

> One might interpret this as showing that the intervention program did have measurable effects upon test performance at the end of first grade, but by the end of the fourth grade, the school program had failed to sustain at any substantial level the initial superiority.

Thus, despite the major differences between the types of children studied by Durkin and by Gray and Klaus, the two investigations produced precisely the same pattern of results.

This brief review of work on the longer-term effects of an early introduction to reading suggests strongly that, under normal classroom conditions with typical teaching methods, few children learn much about reading during kindergarten or first grade that is of enduring benefit, despite the fact that most children can make rapid progress in acquiring the elements of reading even during kindergarten. If this is so, then the term "reading readiness" becomes even more obscure: a child who makes satisfactory progress in response to initial tuition in reading, thereby demonstrating that he was "ready" to learn to read, may not be acquiring any skills or any knowledge upon which he will be drawing a few years later. If so, the concept of a child being "ready to read," in the sense of being able to make rapid progress in reading, is not only obscure, as I have argued earlier, but irrelevant.

VII. CONCLUSIONS

Many of the views about reading discussed in this chapter have been distorted by an excessive emphasis on factors intrinsic to the child. The very existence of a concept of "reading readiness" makes this clear. Comparisons of reading with walking, or even of reading with the acquisition of speech, are misleading, because experiential factors are much more influential in learning to read than in learning to speak or walk. Durkin (1974) continually suggests that the failures to find any long-term advantages of an early start in reading occur because subsequent reading tuition fails to capitalize on this early start, and that an early start would produce permanent advantages if subsequent tuition were appropriately modified, although she provides neither evidence nor argument to support these claims. Even if she were correct, however, the fact is that the reading teacher's practices are what they are. All readers, early or nonearly, pass through a school curriculum, and if this curriculum is such that it eliminates the advantages that early readers initially had, that is that: early reading is simply not beneficial. It may be true that a different curriculum would allow this early advantage to remain. (However this very idea is an odd one. Will this advantage be present in adult life? If children of normal aptitude are taught via this new curriculum, what would the nature of the early reader's permanent advantages be, when all the children have grown up?) We know that redesigning of school curricula rarely occurs simply because psychologists recommend it or because evidence suggests that it would be beneficial. Ideological influences are much stronger than rational ones, and it is certainly unlikely at present that schools will make changes especially to accommodate the brightest of their pupils. It can therefore be argued that research on learning to read ought to address itself to how children respond to existing curricula, rather than speculating as Durkin does about what would happen if other curricula were operating.

Various answers are possible to the question "When should children be taught to read?" The kinds of answers one gives depend upon whether one regards learning to read as of paramount importance in the education of young children. If one does not, then views about when children should be taught to read will be dictated by value judgments concerning the relative importance of the various activities in which young children can engage in school. If, on the other hand, one considers learning to read to be a highly important aspect of early education, answers to the question of when children should be taught to read can be somewhat more objective. The main issue here has been whether an early introduction to reading has more than short-term effects. The evidence suggests that it does not; but why it does not cannot be determined. One could take the view that 5-year-old children, even though capable of learning to read, are not capable of acquiring permanent reading-related skills, and hence whether they are taught anything about reading or not will make no difference to their long-term level of achievement. Alternatively, one could take the view that something permanent is learned during an early introduction to reading, but that reading instruction in its present form does not utilize this early learning; it is not uncommon to find able readers being neglected by reading teachers, and Durkin (1974, p. 30) described one classroom situation thus:

> ... the teacher worked separately with 2 groups of children over a period of 60 minutes. Ten minutes went to the highest achievers whereas the remaining 50 were spent with 5 children who were below grade level in reading. Asked about this later, the teacher commented "They [the highest achievers] seem to get everything pretty well. I like to spend more time with the slower ones."

I suggest that extrinsic factors of this kind are important determinants of children's progress in acquiring the ability to read, and that attention is directed away from this by questions which emphasize intrinsic influences upon learning to read—questions such as "When can children learn to read?" and "When should they be taught?."

REFERENCES

Adams, F., Gray, L., and Reese, D. *Teaching children to read.* New York: Ronald, 1949.
Barrett, T. C. The relationship between measures of prereading visual discrimination and first-grade reading achievement: A review of the literature. *Reading Research Quarterly,* 1965, **1,** 51–76.
Bliesmer, E. P. Reading abilities of bright and dull children of comparable mental ages. *Journal of Educational Psychology,* 1954, **45,** 321–331.
Boney, C. W., and Agnew, K. Periods of awakening or reading readiness. *Elementary English Review,* 1937, **14,** 183–187.
Bradley, B. E. An experimental study of the readiness approach to reading. *Elementary School Journal,* 1955, **56,** 262–267.
Bremer, N. Do readiness tests predict success in reading? *Elementary School Journal,* 1959, **59,** 222–224.
Brinsley, J. *Ludus literarius: or, the grammar schoole.* London: Printed for Thomas Man, 1612.
Bruce, D. J. The analysis of word sounds by young children. *British Journal of Educational Psychology,* 1964, **34,** 158–170.
Brumbaugh, F. Reading expectancy. *Elementary English Review,* 1940, **17,** 153–155.
Brzeinski, J. E. Reading in the kindergarten. In W. B. Cutts (Ed.), *Teaching young children to read.* Washington, DC: U.S. Office of Education, 1964. (a)

Brzeinski, J. E. Beginning reading in Denver. *The Reading Teacher,* 1964, **18,** 16–21. (b)

Buros, O. K. (Ed.), *Reading tests and reviews.* Highland Park: Gryphon Press, 1968.

Calfee, R. C. Assessment of independent reading skills: Basic research and practical applications. In A. S. Reber and D. L. Scarborough (Eds.), *Toward a psychology of reading.* Hillsdale, N. J.: Lawrence Erlbaum Associates, 1977. Pp. 289–323.

Carr, J. W., Jr., and Michaels, M. O. Reading readiness tests and the grouping of the first grade entrants. *Elementary English Review,* 1941, **18,** 133–138.

Carroll, M. W. Sex differences in reading readiness at the first grade level. *Elementary English Review,* 1948, **25,** 370–375.

Carter, H. L. H., and McGinnis, D. J. *Learning to read: A handbook for teachers.* New York: McGraw-Hill, 1953.

Chall, J., Roswell, F. G., and Blumenthal, S. H. Auditory blending ability: A factor in success in beginning to read. *Reading Teacher,* 1963, **17,** 113–118.

Davidson, H. P. An experimental study of bright, average and dull children at the four-year mental level. *Genetic Psychology Monographs,* 1931, **9,** 119–289.

Dean, C. D. Predicting first-grade reading achievement. *Elementary School Journal,* 1939, **39,** 609–616.

de Hirsch, K. Tests designed to discover potential reading difficulties at the six-year-old level. *American Journal of Orthopsychiatry,* 1957, **27,** 566–576.

Deputy, E. C. Predicting first grade reading achievement. *Contributions to Education No. 426.* New York: Teachers' College, Columbia University, 1930.

Dewey, J. The primary-education fetich. *Forum,* 1898, **25,** 315–328.

Dolbear, K. E. Precocious children. *Pedagogical Seminary,* 1912, **19,** 461–491.

Dolch, E. W., and Bloomster, M. Phonic readiness. *Elementary School Journal,* 1937, **38,** 201–205.

Downing, J. Is a 'mental age of six' essential for reading readiness? *Educational Research,* 1963, **6,** 16–28.

Downing, J. Reading readiness examined. In J. Downing (Ed.), *The first international reading symposium.* London: Cassell, 1966.

Downing, J. Should today's children start reading earlier? In J. Downing and A. L. Brown (Eds.), *The third international reading symposium.* London: Cassell, 1968.

Downing, J. *Comparative reading.* New York: Macmillan, 1973.

Downing, J., and Thackray, D. *Reading readiness.* London: University of London Press, 1971.

Durkin, D. *Children who read early.* New York: Teachers' College Press, 1966. (a)

Durkin, D. The achievement of pre-school readers: Two longitudinal studies. *Reading Research Quarterly,* 1966, **1** (4), 5–36. (b)

Durkin, D. A six year study of children who learned to read in school at the age of four. *Reading Research Quarterly,* 1974, **10,** 9–61.

Fendrick, P. Visual characteristics of poor readers. *Teachers' College Contributions to Education,* 1935, No. 656.

Firth, I. *Components of reading disability.* Unpublished Ph.D. thesis, University of New South Wales, 1972.

Fowler, W. Teaching a two-year-old to read: An experiment in early childhood learning. *Genetic Psychology Monographs,* 1962, **66,** 181–283.

Fox, B., and Routh, D. K. Analyzing spoken language into words, syllables, and phonemes: A developmental study. *Journal of Psycholinguistic Research,* 1975, **4,** 331–342.

Gardner, K. Early reading—some personal thoughts. In A. L. Brown (Ed.), *Reading: Current research and practice.* Edinburh: W. & R. Chambers, 1967.

Gates, A. I. The necessary mental age for beginning reading. *Elementary School Journal,* 1937, **37,** 497–508.

Gates, A. I., and Bond, G. L. Reading readiness: A study of factors determining success and failure in beginning reading. *Teachers' College Record,* 1936, **37**, 678–685.

Gjessing, H. The concept of reading readiness in Norway. In M. D. Jenkinson (Ed.), *Reading instruction: An international forum.* Newark, Del.: International Reading Association, 1967.

Goodacre, E. J. *Reading in infant classes.* Slough: NFER, 1967.

Gray, S. W., and Klaus, R. A. The early training project: A seventh-year report. *Child Development,* 1970, **41**, 909–924.

Gunderson, D. V. *Research in reading readiness.* Bulletin, 1964, No. 8. Washington, DC: U. S. Department of Health, Education and Welfare.

Hall, G. S. *Educational problems,* Vol. II, New York, 1911. (Cited in Matthews, M. M., *Teaching to read historically considered.* Chicago: University of Chicago Press, 1966, p. 134).

Harris, A. J. *How to increase reading ability.* New York: Longmans Green & Co., 1940. Cited in Betts, E. A., *Foundations of reading instruction.* New York: American Book Co., 1946.

Harris, A. J. *How to increase reading ability.* New York: McKay, 1961 (4th ed.).

Harrison, M. L. *Reading readiness.* Boston: Houghton Mifflin, 1936.

Heffernan, H. Significance of kindergarten education. *Childhood Education,* 1960, **36**, 313–319.

Henig, M. S. Predictive value of a reading readiness test and of teachers' forecasts. *Elementary School Journal,* 1949, **50**, 41–46.

Hildreth, G. *Readiness for school beginners.* Yonkers, N. Y.: World Book, 1950.

Hillerich, R. L. Pre-reading skills in kindergarten: A second report. *Elementary School Journal,* 1965, **65**, 312–317. (a)

Hillerich, R. L. Kindergarteners are ready. Are we? *Elementary English,* 1965, **42**, 569–574. (b)

Hillerich, R. L. An interpretation of research in reading readiness. *Elementary English,* 1966, **43**, 359–364.

Holmes, J. A. When should and could Johnny learn to read? In J. A. Figurel (Ed.), *Challenge and experiment in reading.* New York: Scholastic Magazines, 1962.

Holmes, M. C. Investigation of reading readiness of first grade entrants. *Childhood Education,* 1927, **3**, 215–221.

Hoole, C. *A new discovery of the old art of teaching schoole.* London: Printed by J. T. for Andrew Crook at the Green Dragon in Paul's Church-yard, 1660.

Hooper, L. What constitutes readiness for reading? *Childhood Education,* 1926, **2**, 228.

Huey, E. B. *The psychology and pedagogy of reading.* First published in 1908, reprinted by MIT Press, 1968.

Hymes, J. L., Jr. *Before the child reads.* New York: Row, Peterson, 1958.

Inglis, W. R. The early stages of reading: A review of recent investigations. In *Studies in reading, Vol. 1.* University of London Press, 1948.

Karlin, R. The prediction of reading success and reading-readiness tests. *Elementary English,* 1957, **34**, 320–322.

Keister, B. V. Reading skills acquired by five-year-old children. *Elementary School Journal,* 1941, **41**, 587–596.

Kibbe, D. E. *Improving the reading program in Wisconsin schools.* Madison, Wisconsin Department of Public Instruction, 1939. Cited in Betts, E. A., *Foundations of reading instruction.* New York: American Book Co., 1946.

Kottmeyer, W. Readiness for reading. *Elementary English,* 1947, **24**, 355–360.

Lee, J. M., Clark, W. W., and Lee, D. M. Measuring reading readiness. *Elementary School Journal,* 1934, **34**, 656–666.

Liberman, I. Y., Shankweiler, D., Liberman, A. M., Fowler, C., and Fischer, F. W. Phonetic segmentation and recoding in the beginning reader. In A. S. Reber and D. L. Scarborough, (Eds.), *Toward a psychology of reading.* Hillsdale, N. J.: Lawrence Erlbaum Associates, 1977. Pp. 207–225.

Lynn, R. Reading readiness and the perceptual abilities of young children. *Educational Research,* 1963, **6**, 10–15.

McNemar, Q. *Psychological statistics*. New York: John Wiley, 1962 (3rd. ed.).

Mood, D. W. Reading in kindergarten? A critique of the Denver study. *Educational Leadership*, 1967, **24**, 399–403.

Morphett, M. V., and Washburne, C. When should children begin to read? *Elementary School Journal*, 1931, **31**, 496–503.

Mulcaster, R. *Positions wherein those primitive circumstances be examined, which are necessary for the training of children, either for skill in their booke, or health in their bodie*. Imprinted at London by Thomas Vautrollier dwelling in the blacke Friers by Ludgate, 1581.

National Society for the Study of Education. *Report of the National Committee on Reading*. 24th Year Book of the National Society for the Study of Education. Bloomington, Indiana: Public School Publishing Co., 1925.

Page, T. E. (Ed.), *The institutio oratoria of Quintilian*. London: Heinemann, 1921.

Patrick, G. T. Should children under ten learn to read and write? *Popular Science Monthly*, 1899, **54**, 382–392.

Read, C. Pre-school children's knowledge of English phonology. *Harvard Educational Review*, 1971, **41**, 1–34.

Read, C. *Children's categorization of speech sounds in English*. Urbana, Ill.: National Council of Teachers of English, Monograph No. 17, 1972.

Sanderson, A. E. The idea of reading readiness: A re-examination. *Educational Research*, 1963, **6**, 3–9.

Schonell, F. J. *The psychology and teaching of reading*. London: Oliver & Boyd, 1945 (1st ed.).

Schonell, F. J. *The psychology and teaching of reading*. Edinburgh: Oliver & Boyd, 1961 (4th ed.).

Shapiro, B. J., and Willford, R. E. i.t.a.—kindergarten or first grade? *Reading Teacher*, 1969, **22**, 307–311.

Sheldon, W. D. Teaching the very young to read. *Reading Teacher*, 1962, **16**, 163–169.

Sinks, N. B., and Powell, M. Sex and intelligence as factors in achievement in reading in grades four through eight. *Journal of Genetic Psychology*, 1965, **106**, 67–79.

Smith, C. A., and Jensen, M. Educational, psychological and physiological factors in reading readiness. I. *Elementary School Journal*, 1935, **36**, 583–594. (a)

Smith, C. A., and Jensen, M. Educational, psychological and physiological factors in reading readiness. II. *Elementary School Journal*, 1935, **36**, 682–691. (b)

Smith, N. B. Readiness for reading. *Elementary English*, 1950, **27**, 21–39, 91–106.

Smith, N. B. Trends in beginning reading since 1900. In W. G. Cutts (Ed.), *Teaching children to read*. Washington, DC: U.S. Office of Education, 1964.

Tanyzer, H., Alpert, H., and Sandert, L. Beginning to read—the effectiveness of i.t.a. and t.o. *Report to the Commissioner of Education*. Washington, DC: U.S. Office of Education, 1966.

Taylor, A. E. (Ed.) *Plato: The laws*. London: Dent, 1966.

Taylor, C. D. The effect of training on reading readiness. In *Studies in reading, Vol. II*. London: University of London Press, 1950.

Terman, L. M. An experiment in infant education. *Journal of Applied Psychology*, 1918, **2**, 219–228.

Terman, L. M., and Oden, M. The gifted child grows up: Twenty-five-year follow-up of a superior group. *Genetic Studies of Genius*, 1947, **4**, 1–448.

Thackray, D. B. The relationship between reading readiness and reading progress. *British Journal of Education Psychology*, 1965, **35**, 252–254.

Thackray, D. B. *Readiness to read with i.t.a. and t.o.* London: Geoffrey Chapman, 1971.

Watts, A. F. *The language and mental development of children*. London: Harrap, 1944.

Williams, G. H. What does research tell us about readiness for beginning reading? *Reading Teacher*, 1953, **6**, 34–40.

Wilson, F. T., and Burke, A. Reading readiness in a progressive school. *Teachers College Record*, 1937, **38**, 565–580.

Wilson, F. T., and Sartorius, I. C. Early progress in reading: Not reading readiness. *Teaching College Record,* 1939, **40,** 485–694.

Wilson, F., Flemming, C. W., Burke, A., and Garrison, C. G. Reading readiness in kindergarten and primary grades. *Elementary School Journal,* 1938, **38,** 442–449.

Witty, P. A., and Kopel, D. Heterophoria and reading disability. *Journal of Educational Psychology,* 1936, **27,** 222–230. (a)

Witty, P. A., and Kopel, D. Studies of eye-muscle imbalance and poor fusion in reading disability: An evaluation. *Journal of Educational Psychology,* 1936, **27,** 663–671. (b)

Witty, P., and Kopel, D. Preventing reading disability: The reading readiness factor. *Educational Administration and Supervision,* 1936, **28,** 401–418. (c)

ASSESSMENT OF READINESS

JOANNE R. NURSS

Department of Early Childhood Education
Georgia State University
Atlanta, Georgia

I. INTRODUCTION

The concept of readiness for reading and the measures to assess readiness have changed considerably over the past 40 years. Readiness is generally used as a psychological construct meaning preparedness for what comes next. In the 1920s and 1930s, psychological measurements began to be applied to educational questions, including reading. Initially, readiness for reading was seen as cognitive or mental preparedness that developed as a result of maturity; thus readiness was determined in large part by mental age. Morphett and Washburne (1931) suggested that beginning reading instruction would not be successful until the child had attained a mental age of 6½ years.

A natural outgrowth of mental ability tests was the reading readiness test to assess a child's readiness for beginning reading instruction. Early readiness tests measured many of the same skills that aptitude tests measured, including vocabulary and verbal comprehension. The readiness measures usually yielded a total readiness score or readiness age that determined whether or not the child was ready to begin reading instruction. Those children judged not ready were given readiness instruction, usually with nonreading materials and activities.

As early as 1936, Gates questioned the mental age concept of readiness. He noted that the important variable in beginning reading success was not mental age, but rather the method and materials by which the child was to be instructed. In other words, the child's specific skills must be assessed and this information used to plan an instructional program. The educational climate was apparently not ready to make use of Gates' ideas, for they were largely ignored for the next 30 years. In 1969, MacGinitie suggested that the relevant questions were "readiness for what" and "readiness how" rather than "Is the child ready?" Ausubel (1959) made the same point by defining readiness as "the adequacy of existing capacity in relation to the demands of a given learning task" (p. 247). As a result of her longitudinal research on early readers and on beginning reading instruction, Durkin (1967, 1968) stated that readiness assessment and readiness instruction should be accomplished in the same task. She concluded that the important readiness information to be obtained is an assessment of the child's knowledge, not a single readiness age which results from maturation. Thus, the focus of readiness assessment is on the process of learning to read, not on a total readiness score.

Current literature defines readiness for reading as an assessment of the child's skills necessary for success in beginning reading, taking into account the particular method and materials to be used for instruction. No longer can readiness tests simply assess a child's level of development and give a total score labeling a child as "ready" or "not ready." The question to ask is "ready for what?"

The following sections of this chapter will consider current readiness tests, recent research on the assessment of readiness, and some future directions that assessment in readiness should consider.

II. CURRENT READINESS TESTS AND RELATED RESEARCH

There are many readiness tests currently in use. These tests do not measure the same skills although there are many similarities.

A. Description of Current Tests

Most definitions of reading include two components in the reading process, decoding and understanding. Several processes are included within each of these.

Decoding consists of a variety of visual skills, auditory skills, and auditory-visual integration skills. Understanding consists of knowledge of oral language structure, vocabulary, and comprehension or reasoning skills applied to reading. Success in beginning reading by any method requires skills in decoding and understanding simple reading material. The relative emphasis on visual as opposed to auditory skills, for example, depends upon the method of instruction. During the initial phases of reading instruction, reading methods usually emphasize decoding skills over comprehension skills.

Several norm-referenced readiness tests are currently and widely used to assess readiness for reading at the end of kindergarten and/or the beginning of first grade. As one surveys these measures, it becomes obvious that, although they all measure certain common skills, they do not assess exactly the same set of skills. Readiness test authors disagree as to which of these skills are the most important for beginning reading instruction and which should be included in a test of reading readiness. This disagreement is seen in a survey of five readiness test batteries containing 29 subtests completed by Rude (1973). He classified only eight of those subtests as measures of one of five specific prereading skills—grapheme perception, left-to-right visual scan, understanding of grapheme-phoneme relationships, and phoneme blending (Rude, p. 579). There is also variation in the format of the tests and in the extent to which they assess skills using letters, words, and language sounds as opposed to shapes, pictures, and environmental sounds.

Most readiness tests are group, paper-and-pencil tests designed to be given by the classroom teacher within a reasonable amount of time. These limitations considerably reduce the variety of test formats and content that might be included. Some commonly used readiness tests are the Clymer–Barrett Prereading Battery (1968), the Gates–MacGinitie Reading Skills Test (1968), the Metropolitan Readiness Tests (1976), and CIRCUS: A Comprehensive Program of Assessment Services for Preprimary Children (1974).

1. Clymer–Barrett Prereading Battery

The Clymer–Barrett Prereading Battery is designed to assess a child's readiness skills at the end of kindergarten or the beginning of first grade. The authors state "that readiness to learn to read occurs at different times for different children and that being in a state of readiness enables a child to learn to read without unwarranted strain or difficulty" (Directions Manual, p. 5). The test consists of six subtests measuring three aspects of reading: visual discrimination (letter recognition and word matching), auditory discrimination (hearing beginning sounds and hearing ending rhyming sounds), and visual–motor coordination (completing shapes and copying sentences). The authors cite studies in which visual discrimination of words, auditory discrimination of beginning and ending sounds in words, shape completion, and sentence copying predict early reading achievement (Directions Manual, pp. 7–8). These studies are given as the rationale for including these areas; no rationale is given for excluding the assessment of comprehension skills. Included in this battery, also, is an individual observation scale with which the teacher is to rate each child's oral language, reasoning, and affective skills. This addition to the paper-and-pencil test is designed to expand the test's "general assessment and diagnostic purposes" (Directions Manual, p. 9). The authors suggest giving a short form of the test (one visual discrimination test and one auditory discrimination test) as a screening measure, and the entire test as a diagnostic measure. Giving the long form of the test yields three subscores (Visual Discrimination, Auditory Discrimination, and Visual–Motor) as well as a total battery score.

2. Gates–MacGinitie Readiness Skills Test

The Gates–MacGinitie Readiness Skills Test assesses a somewhat different set of prereading skills. It consists of eight subtests to be used at the end of kindergarten or the beginning of grade one. The test measures auditory skills (discrimination of similar words and blending of sounds into whole words), visual skills (discrimination of words and recognizing letters), visual–motor skills (completing letters), comprehension skills (listening comprehension and following oral directions), and reading (recognizing words). The authors also suggest that the teacher should consider other measures of readiness such as attention span, emotional maturity, physical health, language background, motor coordination, prior training, home background, attitude toward reading, and ability to work with others and to work independently (Teachers' Manual, pp. 17–18). The test yields scores on each of the seven readiness subtests (excluding the Word Recognition subtest) as well as a total weighted readiness score.

3. Metropolitan Readiness Tests

The Metropolitan Readiness Tests, Level II, is designed for use at the end of kindergarten or the beginning of first grade. (Level I is designed for the beginning of kindergarten.) It assesses prereading skills in several areas including auditory and auditory–visual integration skills (discrimination of beginning consonants and sound–letter correspondences), visual skills (matching letters or numerals and locating letters or numerals within larger contexts), and comprehension skills (listening comprehension and understanding language structure). Also included are two premathematics tests (quantitative concepts and quantitative operations) and a visual–motor test (copying a sentence). No measure of ability to recognize words is included in this test. The Metropolitan Readiness Tests yield three prereading area scores (auditory, visual, and language) plus a quantitative area score and a prereading skills composite score. The authors state that "the test results provide valuable information for planning instructional activities that take into account the pupils' current level of skills development" (Teacher's Manual, Part II, p. 14).

4. CIRCUS: A Comprehensive Program of Assessment Services for Preprimary Children

In addition to the norm-referenced tests, several newer tests have been developed as criterion-referenced and/or diagnostic batteries of prereading skills. An example of this type of measure is CIRCUS: A Comprehensive Program of Assessment Services for Preprimary Children (1974). CIRCUS consists of 17 measures of which the teacher is urged to give a Core Package of five measures, plus any others which are appropriate for the children being assessed. The authors state that CIRCUS "provides information . . . about the competencies of preprimary children in a variety of cognitive and social areas in ways that make it possible to plan an instructional program from knowledge about their levels of competency" (Administering, Scoring, and Interpreting the Instruments, p. 5). Scores are either the number of items correct, reported with the percentages of nursery and kindergarten children in the national samples scoring at or below that raw score or with an accompanying sentence describing the child's performance on that subtest. Examples of such sentences for the subtest, What Words Mean, are: "Generally competent in receptive vocabulary skills but may need additional help with modifiers" and "Responded correctly to a number of receptive vocabulary items, but probably needs further instruction and practice" (Administering, Scoring, and Interpreting the Instruments, pp. 32–33). Scores can be obtained only for each subtest; no total test score can be obtained. The authors state that raw scores "can be used and interpreted by themselves without reference to an external norm or standard, because each test was developed to measure one or more specific skills and abilities" (Administering, Scoring, and Interpreting the Instruments, p. 189). The item information provides specific help to the teacher in knowing which skills the child has acquired and which have not yet been mastered. Each teacher sets his/her own criterion for each subtest. The authors state that CIRCUS is both criterion-referenced, "sentence reports were written on the basis of judgement about 'acceptable' performance" (Manual and Technical Report, pp. 32–33), and norm-referenced, "sentence reports are also based on results obtained in the national CIRCUS Administrations" (Manual and Technical Report, p. 33).

The subtests in CIRCUS include most of the usual prereading or readiness subtests as well as a number of other measures requiring individual administration. Included are measures of visual skills (visual discrimination, letter/numeral recognition, nonverbal visual memory), auditory skills (discrimination of real world sounds, discrimination of sounds in words), visual–motor skills (copying), comprehension (receptive vocabulary, listening comprehension, understanding language structure, problem solving, nonverbal divergent thinking), concepts (general information, quantitative concepts), oral language (expressive vocabulary, use of oral language structure, storytelling), and observational scales assessing the child's classroom behavior, test behavior, and educational environment.

If a teacher or school so chose, a criterion-referenced prereading skills battery assessing the skills traditionally measured by readiness tests could be assembled from the CIRCUS program. Such a battery would yield separate scores for each skill area measured.

The preceding descriptions illustrate the variety of readiness measures available to teachers and researchers. Since no precise taxonomy of prereading skills exists, it is impossible to say that any one of these tests does or does not measure the essential skills necessary for beginning reading success.

Table I shows the even wider variety of skills assessed by other readiness tests currently in use. All of the eight tests reviewed include at least two measures of visual skills. Seven of them include auditory skill measures, but only six have measures of language comprehension. The authors seem to agree that reading is a visual process and that beginning reading is generally taught using some type of sound–letter or phonics instruction. The omission of auditory measures from the Lee–Clark Reading Readiness Test limits its usefulness in connection with most current instructional programs. The absence of any language comprehension measures from two of the tests (Clymer–Barrett Prereading Battery and Murphy–Durrell Reading Readiness Analysis) suggests that those authors perceive beginning reading as simply decoding printed symbols rather than decoding in order to understand the author's message. These factors must be taken into account in selecting an appropriate readiness instrument.

Selection of an instrument appropriate for a given situation also requires consideration of the three basic requirements for all tests—utility, reliability, and validity—as well as the instructional methods and materials to be used.

B. Utility

Tests designed for young children need to be efficient in assessing as many skills as possible in a brief time. Young children need short testing sessions, and tests that are attractive, easy to handle, easy to mark, and have as few distractions as possible. Most test publishers are aware of these requirements and strive to meet them. More recently published tests such as CIRCUS and the Metropolitan Readiness Tests include practice booklets which help the children become familiar with the testing format and marking system. The length of time required for testing varies from test to test, but about 90 minutes divided into three or four testing periods is average.

Most readiness tests are hand-scored, although the Metropolitan Readiness Tests has a machine-scoreable edition (the pupil marks directly on the test booklet) and CIRCUS scores can be recorded on separate answer sheets for machine scoring. The local school situation will dictate whether machine scoring is required or available.

TABLE I. Skills Assessed by Current Readiness Tests[a]

Tests	Practice test	Visual skills							Auditory skills						Language comprehension skills								Quantitative skills		Observation scale
		Visual matching	Visual discrimination	Letter recognition	Visual memory	Figure-ground perception	Word recognition (reading)	Visual-motor coordination	Auditory matching	Auditory discrimination	Auditory memory	Rhyming	Auditory blending	Sound-letter correspondence	Word meaning	Listening	Language structure	Following directions	Productive language	Information	Problem solving	Divergent thinking	Quantitative concepts	Quantitative operations	
CIRCUS, 1974	X		X		X			X	X	X					X	X	X		X	X	X	X	X		X
Clymer–Barrett, 1968		X		X			X	X	X			X													X
Gates–MacGinitie, 1968		X	X	X			X	X		X			X			X		X							
Harrison–Stroud, 1956		X	X				X		X	X						X		X							
Lee–Clark, 1962		X	X												X										
Metropolitan Readiness, Level I, 1976	X	X		X				X		X	X					X	X						X		X
Metropolitan Readiness, Level II, 1976	X	X				X		X	X					X		X	X						X	X	X
Murphy–Durrell, 1965		X		X			X		X	X															

[a] X indicates that the test includes one, two, or three subtests measuring the skills indicated.

C. Reliability

An important requirement of any test is that it be reliable in what it measures. Not only the test as a whole, but also any part of the test for which a score may be obtained and interpreted, must be shown to be reliable. In general, reliability is affected by the length of the measure, so it can be expected that the total test score will be more reliable than will the part scores.

The reliability of the tests described in the preceding sections varies somewhat. The Clymer–Barrett Prereading Battery reliability coefficients (Spearman–Brown formula) range from $r = .82$ to $.94$ for the subtests for the first-grade norming group (Directions Manual, p. 27). The Kuder–Richardson formula #20 reliability coefficients for first graders' Gates–MacGinitie Readiness Skills Test scores range from $r = .65$ to $.86$ (Technical Supplement, p. 3). The Metropolitan Readiness Tests reliability coefficients (Spearman–Brown formula) are $r = .94$ for the prereading skills composite score and range from $r = .72$ to $.93$ for the area scores (Teacher's Manual, Part II, p. 24). For the CIRCUS battery only alpha coefficients of internal consistency are given. For the kindergarten population these range from $r = .49$ to $.87$ (Manual and Technical Report, p. 12).

Several of the subtests for which scores are given are very short and have low reliability. For example, the Metropolitan Readiness Tests Language Skills area score is composed of only 18 items and has a reliability of only $.72$, compared with the Auditory Skills area score which has 29 items and a reliability of $.93$ (Teacher's Manual, Part II, p. 24). The Gates–MacGinitie Readiness Skills Test has two subtests with 14 items each, Following Directions and Auditory Blending. They have reliabilities of $.69$ and $.67$, respectively (Technical Supplement, p. 3). Any subtest with a reliability of $.70$ or less accounts for only 50% or less of the variance and leaves a large margin for test error. Such scores may provide misleading information, particularly about an individual child's prereading skills. Users of readiness tests need to be aware of such problems and interpret scores with low reliability very cautiously.

D. Validity

Another consideration in evaluating and selecting a readiness measure is the validity of the test.

1. Face Validity

Are the illustrations, print, and format appropriate for kindergarten or first-grade pupils? Does the test appear to be related to reading? Most users expect that the tests will include reading-related tasks. Typically, alphabet recognition tests are included in order to meet this face validity requirement. All of the four readiness measures previously described include tasks related to learning to decode. The lack of any language comprehension measure in the Clymer–Barrett Prereading Battery raises a question about its validity as a reading-related test. Many of the CIRCUS subtests appear to have limited direct relationships to reading; for example, Noises, Do You Know . . .? and Make a Tree (a test of divergent thinking).

2. Construct Validity

Early readiness tests were constructed as measures of general verbal aptitude. Their validity was assessed by calculating the correlation between the readiness test and a commonly used verbal intelligence measure. Many readiness tests still report such validity. For example, the Clymer–Barrett Prereading Battery reports correlations between the part and total test scores and four intelligence tests. The correlations between the long form total score and IQ are .43 for an individual intelligence test and .55 for the three group intelligence tests. The authors explain that these modest correlations indicate "an area of agreement" but also "areas in which the two tests are measuring something different" (Directions Manual, p. 28).

3. Predictive Validity

It is more common, however, for readiness tests to report predictive validity data. Reading readiness tests derive their major purpose by providing information about a child's ability to succeed in beginning reading instruction. The most logical predictive measure, therefore, is the correlation of the child's performance on a readiness test with his/her performance on a reading achievement test at the end of first grade. The Clymer–Barrett Prereading Battery reports correlation coefficients of the readiness battery total score with the subtests of the Metropolitan Achievement Tests, Primary Form given at the end of grade one, ranging from $r = .60$ to .69 (Directions Manual, p. 29). The Gates–MacGinitie Readiness Skills Test reports correlation coefficients of the weighted total score with the Gates–MacGinitie Reading Tests, Vocabulary and Comprehension subtests of $r = .60$ and .59 (Technical Supplement, p. 3). Correlations of the subtest scores with Vocabulary and Comprehension range from $r = .29$ to .57. The Metropolitan Readiness Tests, Level II, report correlation coefficients of $r = .54$ to .70 with the Reading subtest of the Metropolitan Achievement Tests, given at the end of the first grade. The Metropolitan Readiness Tests, Level I, given at the beginning of kindergarten are also related to about the same extent to the Reading subtest on the Metropolitan Achievement Tests at the end of first grade (Teacher's Manual, Part II, p. 25).

These correlations are typical and lead to the conclusion that readiness tests do predict reading achievement at the end of the first grade to some extent, but by no means perfectly. When considering individual children, the prediction may be quite imperfect. Interestingly, most readiness batteries predict end-of-first-grade mathematics achievement about as well as they predict reading achievement (Engin, 1974). For the Metropolitan Readiness Tests, for example, the correlations with the mathematics subtest on the Metropolitan Achievement Tests vary from $r = .58$ to $.71$. Only the Auditory Skills area score predicts reading achievement better than it predicts math achievement. Use of the total readiness test score to predict end-of-first-grade achievement is not the best use of readiness test information. MacGinitie (1969) and Wanat (1976) have suggested that use of a single, total readiness score to predict achievement is inappropriate. Wanat states that "reading readiness assessment is a process of gauging the match between learner characteristics and task characteristics" (p. 103). Readiness tests, therefore, should be constructed and used for instructional, rather than predictive, purposes.

Many studies over the past 40 years have attempted to identify which specific learner characteristics (that is, which subtests) are the best predictors of reading success. In nearly every study completed, the test of letter recognition or letter knowledge is found to be the best single predictor. In fact, in many studies, letter recognition predicts as well as the remainder of the readiness test. Barrett (1965) reviewed the literature on visual discrimination and first-grade achievement and concluded that letter discrimination and letter naming are the most effective single predictors of reading achievement. Studies by Johnson (1969), Lowell (1971), Olson (1958), Weiner and Feldman (1963), and Zaruba (1968) are among those concurring that letter recognition is the best predictor of end-of-first-grade reading achievement. In a study of beginning first-grade skills as predictors of later reading achievement, Muehl and Nello (1976) found that letter naming predicted reading achievement best in grades 1 and 2, but that intelligence was a better predictor of achievement in grades 6 and 7.

Questions have frequently been raised as to why knowledge of letter names is such an effective predictor of reading success, when efforts to teach children letter names have generally not facilitated their success in reading (Linehan, 1958; Samuels, 1972; Speer and Lamb, 1976). In fact, Muehl (1962) states that learning letter names interferes with sight-word learning and Venezky (1975) concludes that "a heavy emphasis on letter-name learning in either prereading or initial reading programs has neither logical nor experimental support" (p. 19). It has been suggested that the significant, positive correlations between performance on the tests of letter-name knowledge and beginning reading may be due to the child's linguistic competence and prior interest in reading (Gibson and Levin, 1975). Samuels states that a survey of the research "leads one to suspect that correlational findings between letter-name knowledge and reading may be a product of uncontrolled organismic or environmental conditions" (p. 72).

Recent research indicates, however, that letter recognition may no longer be the best predictor of reading success. In a study completed in connection with the

1976 revision of the Metropolitan Readiness Tests, Mitchell (1974) reports that entering first-grade pupils have gained in their knowledge of letter recognition; therefore, an alphabet test is no longer appropriate in a readiness test designed for children at the end of kindergarten or the beginning of first grade. Children tested on the Metropolitan Readiness Tests (1964 edition) in 1973 received an average score of 15 on a 16-item test of letter recognition compared to an average score of 10 received by children on the same test in 1964. The quartile scores for the 1973 and 1964 samples, were 12 and 5, respectively for the twenty-fifth percentile, and 16 and 14 for the seventy-fifth percentile. A letter recognition test is now too easy for the average pupil entering first grade and, therefore, is no longer the best predictor of end-of-first-grade reading achievement.

The 1976 edition of the Metropolitan Readiness Tests, Level II, does not include a letter recognition test. Level I of the Metropolitan Readiness Tests does include a letter recognition test, and it does predict the reading and mathematics scores on the Metropolitan Achievement Tests, Primer Level at the end of kindergarten ($r = .64$ and $.61$, respectively). In other words, the letter recognition test is still a good predictor when given in kindergarten, but not in first grade.

This change in letter knowledge may be due to emphasis on earlier academic instruction at home and in nursery school. Educational television programs of the late 1960s and early 1970s have made deliberate efforts to teach most children to recognize letters and numerals prior to entering school. Such efforts have succeeded, according to the test results. Whether such efforts have improved the probability that all children will succeed in first-grade reading remains to be seen. Venezky (1975) suggests not, saying that "letter names are convenient but not indispensable labels" (p. 20). Research is needed to learn if programs designed to teach letter names have had any effect on young children's linguistic competence or interest in reading.

4. Content Validity

In addition to assessing face, construct, and predictive validity, efforts have been made to assess the content validity of readiness tests. Those beginning reading skills that the test authors believe to be most important to success in reading are included. This approach results in a variety of skills from one test to another with very little overlap.

CIRCUS provides measures of many skills involved in early school success and allows the school or teacher to choose those most relevant to the curriculum and to set the criterion level necessary for success in that instructional setting. The content validity of the Clymer–Barrett Prereading Battery is supported by citing studies which show positive correlations between beginning reading and a given skill, such as auditory discrimination of beginning sounds. Similarly, for the Metropolitan Readiness Tests, the authors reviewed relevant research, outlined a continuum of prereading/beginning reading skills, and empirically tested many of those skills with kindergarten and first-grade children.

Some publishers have developed tests to accompany a particular reading series. One would assume this would result in a test directly related to the instructional materials; that is, a criterion-referenced test that answers the question of "readiness for what." Unfortunately this is not the case. The Initial Survey Test (1972) published by Scott, Foresman is essentially a norm-referenced test with the same features as the Clymer–Barrett Prereading Battery or the Gates–MacGinitie Readiness Skills Test. The Initial Survey Test measures listening vocabulary and comprehension, auditory discrimination, visual discrimination, letter recognition, sound–letter correspondences, and mathematics concepts in general terms, not in relation to the Scott, Foresman instructional materials. The only reliability information given is for the total score ($r = .96$, Spearman–Brown formula), even though interpretative data are given for subtest scores (Manual and Directions, p. 46). No validity information is given in relation to either the prediction of reading success or the content of the reading program published by Scott, Foresman although the test is mentioned in the Scott, Foresman Manual as a related component.

Another example of a test designed to accompany a reading series is the Inventory of Pre-Reading Skills for Getting Ready To Read (1976) published by Houghton Mifflin. This is a criterion-referenced test in two parts. The Survey Test contains two subtests which measure the child's reading skills—Decoding Printed Words In Spoken Context and Understanding Rebus Sentences. If the child fails to achieve criterion (85% correct) on this test, the Diagnostic Test is to be given. It includes five subtests assessing oral context, letter recognition, auditory discrimination, sound–letter correspondences, and word recognition. Unfortunately no reliability or criterion validation data are given for this test. The inventory is to be given after the child has been instructed in a prereading program using Level A of the Houghton Mifflin program (Getting Ready To Read) so the test becomes an achievement test. If alternate forms of the test were available and if the reliability were known, it would be possible to recommend using this test before the instructional program and to differentiate subsequent instruction based upon the child's pretest performance.

In summary, the readiness tests designed to accompany reading instructional programs do not demonstrate any more instructionally relevant content validity than do norm-referenced standardized readiness tests.

A major weakness in assessing the content validity of all readiness tests is the lack of a definitive, empirically derived taxonomy of prereading/beginning skills. A number of different theoretical models of reading have been developed and are being studied at this time (Singer and Ruddell, 1976). As this work progresses, information should become available that will assist in assessing the content validity of readiness measures.

None of the norm-referenced tests reviewed adequately addresses the question raised by Gates in 1936. Because most attempt to be nationally standardized tests equally applicable to a variety of situations, none fully accounts for the questions "what methods" or "what materials" will be used for instruction. Interpretive materials and suggestions given in the Metropolitan Readiness Tests Teacher's Manual, Part II (pp. 14–20) raise questions for the teacher regarding the meaning of a given pupil's scores in relation to the reading materials and methods to be used in subsequent instruction, but only in a very general manner.

Another reason norm-referenced tests have not related test performance to instructional methods as closely as might be desired is the problem of the length of the subtests and the resulting low reliability of the subtest scores. Farr and Anastasiow (1969) reviewed five common readiness tests and concluded that none has subtests long enough to be used alone reliably. Dykstra (1967) similarly concluded that readiness tests as a whole are reliable, but they should not be used as diagnostic batteries. In many cases, the subtests can be grouped into area or part scores with high enough reliability to be used alone. Such part scores will generally be more useful to the teacher in planning instruction than will the total test score because they can legitimately be used in a more diagnostic manner owing to their higher reliability. If, as Wanat (1976) states, the aim of readiness tests is to modify the learning environment as well as the learner (p. 122), these part scores can give the teacher information on ways to adjust the learning activities to the child in order to facilitate her/his learning to read. It is the responsibility of the test authors to provide this kind of interpretive information for the classroom teacher.

III. WHAT READINESS TESTS DO MEASURE

As has been stated, there is no general agreement as to what readiness is or what readiness tests should measure. Researchers and test authors disagree on the assumptions about readiness upon which tests should be based. Some define reading, at least implicitly, as decoding while others measure decoding and understanding. None seems to deal adequately with attitudes, interests, and environmental factors as they affect beginning reading. As a result each test measures somewhat different aspects of readiness, and no one test has perfect correlation with achievement. In fact, the best information is obtained by combining the results from several tests (Pikulski, 1974). In addition, readiness tests can measure only a limited number of readiness skills, generally chosen to enhance the predictive, rather than diagnostic, quality of the measure. This emphasis on prediction creates two problems for the readiness test user. First, it fosters a reliance on the total score which gives a label that can be used inappropriately to set teacher, pupil, and parent expectancy. If the tests were perfectly accurate in their prediction, this would be no problem. However, the less than perfect reliability and validity, even of the total score, and the failure of the tests to take account of instructional variables means that the expectancy is often too high or, what is more serious, too low, creating a cycle of low expectation and low achievement. Second, predictive correlations often reflect a relationship, not causation. An example of this is the fact that a test of letter recognition predicts, but apparently does not cause, end-of-first-grade reading achievement. The solution to a prediction of low reading achievement is apparently not to teach the alphabet earlier. The question then is what do reading readiness tests actually measure.

A. General Readiness versus Specific Skills

Factor analytic studies of readiness tests published in the late 1960s typically yield one general readiness factor similar to general cognitive ability (Lowell, 1970; Olson and Fitzgibbon, 1968). Such studies suggest that regardless of the subskills included, the tests are measuring a general skill of verbal/perceptual aptitude which is, in most instances, predictive of academic success in reading and mathematics at the end of the first grade. Generally, readiness tests show significant correlations with reading achievement even with chronological age and IQ score removed (Karlin, 1957). If only a general factor were measured and, hence, only a total readiness score could be used, teachers would be just as successful in grouping and instructing pupils by giving a letter recognition test and/or using teacher observation and judgment. However, this general grouping and subsequent extended readiness instruction period for the "low group" is not an appropriate use of readiness test information. There is little evidence that a prolonged readiness period improves pupils' subsequent reading achievement (Dykstra, 1967). What is needed is specific information about the child's pre-reading skills so instruction can be specific.

More recently published readiness tests have drawn heavily on research relating specific skills to success in reading, in some cases giving attention to specific reading methods and materials. Such tests are more likely to be measuring separate skills or groupings of skills needed for success in the reading process. Telegdy (1974a) gave ending kindergarteners four school readiness tests, Screening Test of Academic Readiness (1966), First Grade Screening Test (1966), Bender–Gestalt Test for Young Children (1964), and Metropolitan Readiness Tests (1965). A factor analysis of the scores yielded three principal factors: (1) Visual–Perceptual–Motor Function (largely the Bender–Gestalt Test and the Copying, Matching, Numbers, and Letters subtests of the Metropolitan Readiness Tests); (2) Language Comprehension (the First Grade Screening Test, the Picture Vocabulary and Relationships subtests of the Screening Test of Academic Readiness, and the Word Meaning and Listening subtests of the Metropolitan

Readiness Tests); (3) Abstraction of Essential Characteristics (the Picture Completion, Picture Description, and Human Figure Drawing subtests of the Screening Test of Academic Readiness). Evanechko, Ollila, Downing, and Braun (1973) tested beginning first graders with 13 readiness subtests covering the concept of the reading task, perceptual ability, linguistic competence, and cognitive functioning. They factor analyzed the scores and obtained a general readiness factor accounting for almost 50% of the variance and three other specific factors, Listening (15% of variance), Conceptualizing (11% of variance), and Literacy Behavior (10% of variance). However, 6 of the 13 subtests used had low reliabilities (.50 to .68) raising questions about the findings of the factor analysis. Schueneman (1975) did a factor analysis of the 1976 revision of the Metropolitan Readiness Tests and obtained the following results for Level II. The first factor was a general perceptual language factor, accounting for 55% of the variance; the second and third factors were auditory and visual-versus-language factors, accounting for 5% and 4% of the variance, respectively. These data seem to support the area scores provided on the Metropolitan Readiness Tests, Level II, although there is a strong general factor present throughout the tests. In summary, factor analysis of readiness measures suggests that some specific reading-related skills are being measured.

Another way to look at the general versus subskills question is to examine the subtest intercorrelations within several readiness measures. For the Clymer–Barrett Prereading Battery the intercorrelations among the three-part scores (Visual Discrimination, Auditory Discrimination, and Visual–Motor) range from $r = .41$ to .56, and the correlations of these scores with the total battery score range from $r = .78$ to .91 (Directions Manual, p. 28). On the Gates–MacGinitie Readiness Skills Test the subtest intercorrelations range from $r = .23$ to .58 (Technical Supplement, p. 3). For the Metropolitan Readiness Tests, Level II, the intercorrelations among the auditory, visual, language, and quantitative skill area scores for first graders range from $r = .57$ to .72 (Teacher's Manual, Part II, p. 23). No intercorrelation data are provided for CIRCUS, but the authors state that "there is evidence of a general ability factor contributing to performance on many of the CIRCUS measures" (Manual and Technical Report, p. 26). Tests listed as seeming to measure separate factors, to a greater extent than some of the others, are the measures of visual discrimination, visual–motor coordination, auditory discrimination, productive language, nonverbal visual memory, and nonverbal divergent thinking (Manual and Technical Report, p. 27). Most of these intercorrelations are low enough to suggest that the subtests are measuring somewhat different skills.

The factor analytic and correlational studies of current readiness tests indicate that the skill scores provided can be used as separate scores which lend themselves to instructional interpretation. For example, a child scoring high on language comprehension measures, but low on auditory measures, could be started on a language-experience reading instructional program and an auditory discrimination prereading instructional program. Thus, readiness tests are moving toward being able to provide the user with information to answer the questions, "readiness for what and how."

B. Reading Skills

In addition to information about the learner (gained from readiness tests), the teacher must have information about the reading task. What skills have been shown to be empirically related to beginning reading success? Which can be easily tested in a readiness measure? The studies described in the following sections form the rationale used by test authors for including or excluding certain measures in their readiness tests. A survey of these reading and nonreading skills will suggest what specific skills readiness measures can and do test.

1. Decoding Skills

Reading is a visual process so it is natural that visual skills would be included in readiness measures. Visual skills which have been shown to be related to success in beginning reading include visual discrimination of letters and words, visual memory, and letter recognition (Barrett, 1965). To read fluently, discriminations must be made rapidly so that letter and word discrimination becomes automatic (Paradis, 1974). Goins (1958) described two other visual factors related to first-grade reading success. One is figure–ground perception or the ability to keep a figure in mind against distraction; the other is visual closure or the ability to complete an image visually. Marchbanks and Levin (1965) found that kindergarten and first-grade children use initial and final letters rather than whole-word configurations to recognize or match words. These results emphasize the need to assess visual skills using letters or letterlike symbols. All the readiness tests described in Table I have at least one visual or letter subtest included in their batteries.

Most beginning reading programs today use some form of word analysis or phonics instruction. Such instruction requires auditory and auditory–visual integration skills for success in learning to read. This change in beginning reading instruction over the past 20 years is reflected in readiness tests. Both auditory discrimination of sounds (Dykstra, 1966) and discrimination of rhyming sounds (Gates, Bond, and Russell, 1939) are related to beginning reading success. McNinch and Richmond (1972) found that an auditory screening battery accounted for 41% of the variance of end-of-first-grade word-reading scores. The auditory battery assessed auditory memory, auditory discrimination, auditory blending, and auditory–visual integration. This last task, based upon earlier work of Birch and Belmont (1964), assesses the child's skill in matching a visual pattern of dots to a group of spoken words. It is an attempt to measure the skill required in sound–letter correspondence, the essence of the decoding process. Muehl and Kremenak (1966) and Jorgenson and Hyde (1974) both suggest a relationship between auditory–visual integration and beginning reading success. Studies of older retarded readers suggest that verbal mediation may be a factor in successful auditory–visual integration and that temporal–spatial integration may be a more important indicator of perceptual learning in young children (Blank and Bridger, 1966; Bryden, 1972; Sterritt, Martin, and Rudnick, 1971). Both auditory–visual integration and sound–letter correspondence measures appear to be subtests that will be included in future readiness measures, especially if instructional methods and materials continue to stress word analysis or phonics approaches to decoding.

2. Understanding Skills

Beginning reading instruction, regardless of the theoretical orientation of the instructional materials, emphasizes decoding skills; that is, relating the auditory symbol to the graphic symbol. Therefore, any measure of prereading skills that is to be helpful to the teacher in beginning reading instruction must provide an assessment of the child's visual, auditory, and visual–auditory integration skills. However, decoding is not reading. Reading involves attaching meaning to the visual symbol and understanding the message communicated by the combination of symbols presented in the sentence or paragraph. Thus, a successful beginning reader must also have certain language and understanding skills. Prereading measures usually assess these comprehension skills by paper-and-pencil tests of the child's language understanding, aural vocabulary, listening, and following of orally given directions.

The use of language subtests has been suggested by a number of researchers. Hildreth (1950) stated that "the connecting link between concrete experiences and abstract word symbols is to be found in oral language, which is actually symbolical but has become meaningful to the child through use in daily experience. It is this link which makes language the basic skill needed as preparation for reading" (p. 251). Fillion, Smith, and Swain (1976) suggested some language universals important to school success, including reading achievement: among these are the relation of language meaning and language function both of which are learned as language is learned. They state that education is largely a matter of learning school language, both meaning and function. Failure to learn school language is likely to affect the child's success in school, including reading achievement. Smith (1975) also observed that reading is prediction of meaning from visual information. Denner (1970), using Farnham–Diggory's symbol tests (1967), concluded that vocabulary knowledge does not guarantee reading success. Measures of visual and perceptual skills are better predictors of early reading (decoding), but measures of syntax are better predictors of later reading (comprehension). Gibson and Levin (1975) stated that "learning to read is learning a system of rules and strategies for extracting information from the text'' (p. 332).

It appears that readiness tests attempting to assess skills needed in learning to read should include in addition to measures of meaning, measures of syntactic comprehension and of school or instructional language. Assessment of vocabulary is both too narrow and too culturally bound a measure to be of much instructional use, and assessment of higher order abstract reasoning and thinking skills is not useful as these skills are generally not used in beginning reading materials.

3. Reading

Another task included in several tests is word recognition or word learning; in other words, reading words. In the Gates–MacGinitie Reading Skills Test (1968), this subtest assesses the child's success in recognizing and marking the word read by the examiner. In the Murphy–Durrell Reading Readiness Analysis (1965) the pupils are taught to recognize nine words, using a sight-word, meaning-emphasis method. One hour later they are tested on their ability to remember, recognize, and mark these same words, giving a measure of their rate of learning words. Both of these tests help identify children who may already be reading or who have some reading skills. This knowledge will increase the confidence of the children and their teachers in the children's ability to succeed in beginning reading and, in so doing, will greatly increase the probability that they will succeed (MacGinitie, 1969).

Lambert (1970) suggested that the use of a paired-associate learning task improves the prediction of beginning reading success. She gave first graders a paired-associate learning task with four conditions. The paired associate task did increase the multivariate prediction of end-of-first-grade reading achievement when added to socioeconomic status, IQ, age, and general readiness test scores. The four conditions of presentation were control (spoken words with pictures— knife, cake), action elaboration (spoken words with pictures showing action— knife cutting cake), sentence elaboration (words in sentence context with pictures—The knife is cutting the cake), and sentence-action elaboration (words in sentence context with pictures showing actions). As the elaboration increased, the subjects' learning rate increased, but the correlation with reading achievement decreased. There was a significant correlation between the paired-associate task control condition and later reading achievement. Lambert concludes that "those children who evidence better associative memory or some strategy for recalling the pairs of words perform best on the control condition . . . (and) the reading lesson as well'' (p. 579).

4. Other Related Skills

There are a number of other skills that are frequently included in readiness assessment batteries. In several instances, they are also of assistance in planning beginning reading instruction. Several tests assess visual–motor coordination. Typically, these measures relate to reading achievement about as well as measures of visual discrimination. Visual–motor coordination is one component in an integrated language–arts program which provides instruction in spelling, writing, speaking, and listening, along with reading. Several test authors mention this as a rationale for including visual–motor skills in a reading test. Hall (1976) suggested that readiness instruction which includes early writing activities is especially effective in helping children succeed in beginning reading, and Durkin (1974–75) found that many early readers learned to read through an early interest in writing. Assessment of early writing skills might also be useful in a readiness battery.

Measures of quantitative concepts, quantitative operations, verbal reasoning, expressive language, and problem solving are included in CIRCUS and the Metropolitan Readiness Tests in order to measure more than just prereading skills. As has been mentioned, readiness tests predict first-grade achievement in mathematics about as well as in reading.

C. Nonreading Skills

There also appear to be some non-reading-related tasks which are being measured and some reading-related tasks which are not being measured by the common readiness tests.

1. Test-Taking Skills

One set of nonreading skills that all tests measure is the child's proficiency and experience in taking tests. Most readiness tests give one or two sample items at the beginning of each subtest to teach the format and marking scheme for that subtest. Recently, readiness tests have begun to include a practice test to assist the child with the vocabulary of the test (page, row, top, same, different, and so on) as well as the format of the various items within the test (CIRCUS, 1974; Metropolitan Readiness Tests, 1976). The score on any test which does not include such practice material will reflect on the child's proficiency or lack of proficiency in the required test-taking skills rather than her/his proficiency in the skills supposedly measured by the test (Osborn and Osborn, 1976). This is particularly true for young children in kindergarten or first grade who may have had no previous school experience with a structured, academic setting requiring marking with pencils, working independently, and following precise directions.

Shapiro (1976) has shown that reflective children score better on a multiple-choice readiness measure than do impulsive children. Presumably, a practice test would help eliminate that personality-related difference. It goes without saying that children from low socioeconomic backgrounds with fewer verbal and written experiences in their homes will be more disadvantaged by such a test than will children from middle-socioeconomic backgrounds who have had ample verbal and written experiences at home.

2. Nonverbal Symbols

A number of reading readiness tests measure visual and/or auditory discrimination skills using nonverbal symbols. Visual tests often assess proficiency with geometric shapes or pictures and auditory tests with environmental sounds. Proponents of such measures argue that perceptual measures using actual symbols (letters and/or numerals) assess the child's familiarity with the symbols rather than her/his ability to discriminate or match symbols. This argument, however, ignores the fact that the purpose of a reading readiness test is to assess the child's prereading skills. What the teacher needs to know is whether the child can discriminate among letters, not among shapes. Barrett (1965) concludes his survey of studies considering visual discrimination and reading by stating that "visual discrimination of letters and words has a somewhat higher predictive relationship with first grade reading achievement than does visual discrimination of geometric designs and pictures" (p. 51).

Supplementary tests used in addition to standard readiness batteries for the purpose of predicting reading failure or identifying learning-disabled children usually include visual discrimination and/or visual–motor coordination tests of geometric and other nonverbal designs (deHirsch, Jansky, and Langford, 1966). Children who are unable to discriminate and match letters should be assessed on this lower level skill. Cox (1976) has suggested that a child's acquisition of conservation might facilitate learning to discriminate letters. For instance, a child who can see transformations might be better able to distinguish among b, d, p, and q. Further investigation of conservation as it relates to prereading is needed to determine whether measures of transformation and conservation would be useful in a readiness battery.

The 1976 Metropolitan Readiness Tests include visual matching of artificial letterlike symbols patterned after earlier work done by Gibson, Gibson, Pick, and Osser (1962). These artificial letters have the element of novelty, hence, measure visual matching rather than letter recognition; they also have the distinctive features of letters, hence, measure the child's skill in making discriminations unique to graphic symbols. These items correlate about as well with end-of-first-grade reading achievement as do items using actual letters and numerals.

3. Pupil Background

As with other standardized tests, prereading tests measure other variables in the child's background in addition to her/his prereading skills. These include socioeconomic level, cultural and/or ethnic group membership, native language and/or home dialect, regional/geographic environment, sex, and previous school experience. Standardized test publishers and authors have given serious consideration to these matters in developing and standardizing their tests. Before using any test, however, the teacher or school should examine the teacher's and/or technical manual carefully to determine if efforts have been made to eliminate as much systematic bias as possible. Use of the "Checklist for Evaluating Readiness Tests for Young Children" (Nurss, 1976) should assist in this process. This checklist evaluates the readiness test and its development, considering test content, illustrations, vocabulary, language, standardization, review, scores, and other materials provided for the user.

Studies considering the relationship of some pupil background variables to prereading assessment include those by: Mortenson (1968), showing that there were significant socioeconomic-level and sex differences on all subtests of the Clymer-Barrett Prereading Battery (1968) favoring upper-middle-socioeconomic-level children and favoring girls; Telegdy (1974b), finding a significant socio-economic-status difference favoring middle-socioeconomic-status pupils on four readiness tests, Screening Test of Academic Readiness (1966), First Grade Screening Test (1966), Bender-Gestalt Test for Young Children (1964), and Metropolitan Readiness Tests (1965), but finding no sex difference on the tests given; Kaufman and Kaufman (1972), indicating that physical maturity (as assessed by teething) was not as good a predictor of first-grade reading achievement as was the Gesell Development Tests of School Readiness (1965); Hirst (1970), showing that school entrance age was not related significantly to Metropolitan Readiness Tests (1965) performance or to first-grade achievement; Mitchell (1976), indicating that girls score significantly higher on the Metropolitan Readiness Tests (1976) at the beginning and end of kindergarten than do boys with greater differences in the auditory and visual area scores than in the language area scores.

Previous experiences with school, with books, with school language, and with letters, sounds, and words influence the child's performance on readiness tests. Henderson and Long (1968) found that preschool education predicted Metropolitan Readiness Tests (1965) scores better than did teachers' ratings or chronological age. Sprigle (1971) found that a kindergarten program of instruction on letters, language, and listening prepared a group of Head Start children for the Metropolitan Readiness Tests (1965) better than did comparable time spent watching Sesame Street. One wonders, however, if watching Sesame Street did not prepare the children for the readiness test better than a play school experience or no school experience would have.

4. Verbal Memory

Jones (1970) found that readiness tests have a very high memory load so that a score on a readiness measure might simply reflect the child's verbal memory span rather than his/her language or comprehension skills. Subtests that assess listening comprehension and ability to follow oral directions are particularly susceptible to memory overload.

In summary, readiness tests may assess a number of prereading skills, but they also may assess a number of "hidden" nonreading variables. These include the pupil's test-taking skills, environmental exposure to letters and books, socioeconomic status, sex, preschool education, and/or verbal memory. Users of readiness tests need to look for these variables when selecting and interpreting prereading tests.

IV. WHAT READINESS TESTS DO NOT MEASURE

There are a number of prereading skills and variables related to success in beginning reading that are not measured by group, paper-and-pencil tests. In some cases, it is because the variable can not be easily measured in that format. In other cases, it is because the variable has been overlooked by readiness test authors.

A. Observation of Pupils

Prereading variables that cannot be measured in a group, pencil-and-paper testing situation are often tapped by an observational checklist designed to accompany the readiness test. Sanacore (1974) suggests such a checklist should include an assessment of auditory discrimination, visual discrimination, left-to-right orientation, oral (expressive) language, concept development, social and emotional development, and motor coordination. The Prereading Rating Scale included in the Clymer–Barrett Prereading Battery assesses the child's facility in oral language, concept and vocabulary development, listening abilities, critical and creative thinking skills, social skills, emotional development, attitude toward and interest in reading, and work habits. Both CIRCUS and the Metropolitan Readiness Tests, Levels I and II, include observational checklists, and CIRCUS has several individually administered, oral subtests. Readiness textbooks usually suggest that the teacher should also obtain information on the child's visual and auditory acuity, speech, general health, physical development, home background, and school attendance. Certainly, a child's interest in books, stories, writing, and letters indicates a degree of motivation toward and interest in learning to read, both of which are major factors in success. Use of a readiness test without any additional pupil observation will result in an incomplete picture of the child's skills. In order to plan an appropriate instructional program, the teacher must have attitudinal and behavioral information necessarily omitted from the readiness tests.

Questions have been raised regarding the utility of teacher judgment in assessing a child's readiness for reading. Is such judgment valid? Does it predict as well as or better than readiness tests? Lederman and Blair (1972) found that teachers' ratings of children's readiness accounted for about 50% of the variance on a readiness test, while mothers' ratings of their children's readiness using the same rating scale accounted for about 25% of the variance on the test. Shinn (1969) reported that teacher judgment predicted first-grade reading achievement better than did a readiness test. Children were given the Metropolitan Readiness Tests (1965) at the end of kindergarten. At the same time teacher judgments were obtained using the rating scale accompanying that readiness test. According to correlational data teacher judgment rating was a better predictor of end-of-grade-one reading achievement than was the readiness test.

B. Concepts of Language and Reading

Recent research on early reading behavior has called attention to a group of variables not traditionally assessed by readiness measures. These include such factors as: the child's concept of reading and of words, letters, and sounds; the child's ability to segment oral or written language into phrases, words, and sounds or letters; and the child's familiarity with instructional language about reading. Carroll (1976), in discussing the nature of the reading process, emphasized the need for the child who is to be successful in reading to understand the relationship between spoken and written language. Mason (1967) stated that the first step in learning to read is learning that one does not know how to read! Downing, Ollila, and Oliver (1975) reported that children from cultures with little experience in reading and writing were confused about the concept of reading and did not understand the concepts of "word" or "letter." In fact, Oliver (1975) found that over half of the 3-year-olds and a third of the 4-year-olds interviewed said they knew how to read (they were not able to do so). Only a few 5-year-olds said they could read, indicating a developmental progression with this concept. Young children often do not understand the purpose of written language and do not understand the language used by teachers to discuss reading (Downing, 1969; Francis, 1973). If this is the case, it can be assumed that children will be equally confused by the language used in readiness tests (Downing, 1976; Hardy, Stennett, and Smythe, 1974; Sabaroff, 1970).

Young children also have difficulty in segmenting language into words, sounds, or letters (Christina, 1971; Huttenlocher, 1964). Holden and MacGinitie (1972) asked kindergarten children to tap at the end of words presented in an oral or written context. The children seemed to devise their own system of segmentation and could identify groups of speech or print by their own system. Only a few could do so using conventional word boundaries, however. Ehri (1975) showed that readers were more proficient in picking out embedded words from verbal contexts than were prereaders. It might be that this task, similar to Goins' figure–ground visual discrimination task, could be added to readiness measures. Ehri (1976) also indicated that the ability to read may be the factor which makes children conscious of words in both written and spoken contexts. Evans (1975) suggested that learning to read helps children focus on the structure of the sentence rather than its units of meaning. Whether competence in this area would help children learn to read, particularly if they are being taught by a language experience or sight-word method, is a question that should be investigated. If such competence is useful, it is an area that could be included in prereading assessment batteries.

Downing and Oliver (1973–74) found that children of ages 5.6 to 6.5 years could correctly segment short words, although they did not consider long words to be words. One wonders if extensive experience with three- and four-letter words in reading and phonics instructional material gives beginning readers an incorrect concept of words. Goldstein (1976) states that oral language analysis–synthesis skills (segmenting and blending spoken words) predict success in initial reading instruction using a synthetic method. This finding suggests that readiness test authors might give more attention to measuring visual–auditory blending or integration skills. Goldstein also learned that this skill improved with instruction, suggesting that the initial assessment should provide a baseline for instruction but not a reason for withholding reading instruction.

The findings of this group of studies suggest that prereading skills tests should include measures of the child's concepts of reading, language, words, letters, and sounds. Readiness test authors should devise and try out appropriate subtests to tap these skills in future test development efforts. Both Ehri and Goldstein suggest that these skills will improve with instruction, lending further support to the merger of readiness assessment and instruction.

Merging readiness assessment and instruction has been proposed by both Durkin (1967) and Wanat (1976). Durkin suggested that "an assessment of readiness . . . will be most reliable when it comes from the combination of (a) a situation offering varied opportunities to learn to read; and (b) knowledge of what individual children are able to learn from opportunities offered" (p. 31). Wanat concludes that one principle for readiness testing is "Try to teach the student a particular reading skill" (p. 117). As has been discussed earlier only a few readiness tests measure even a child's word-recognition skills. One way test authors might do so is to create beginning trial lessons which would serve as a measure of the child's ability to profit from specific prereading and/or reading instruction.

V. FUTURE DIRECTIONS FOR READINESS ASSESSMENT

The assessment of prereading or readiness skills in young children has changed in the past 40 years reflecting many of the research findings in the field of beginning reading. Some of these changes are: the inclusion of visual, auditory, and language measures in most prereading tests; a trend toward reporting part scores rather than a total score, thus allowing the child's performance to be related to instruction; and efforts to eliminate cultural, sex, economic, racial, or regional bias from the test content and the standardization process.

In spite of these improvements one might still ask the question, why give a readiness measure if it does not provide diagnostic, instructional information for the teacher. From an instructional viewpoint, the response is that such tests do provide some information about each child's prereading skills allowing the teacher to form initial instructional groupings, select initial reading instructional materials and methods, and focus on appropriate skill areas for further diagnosis, teaching, and evaluation.

From a measurement viewpoint, the response is a question: What would be used instead? Any teacher-made or, for that matter, basal-reader-supplied, readiness test is likely to be both less reliable and less valid than a standardized carefully developed readiness test. The assessment instrument designed by any one or two teachers is less likely to be carefully tested for cultural, ethnic, sex, or regional bias and less likely to take account of past and current research on what skills really are essential to success in reading. In other words, current readiness tests are, at least, good measurement instruments. It seems reasonable then to suggest that, instead of doing away with them, we should strive to improve them.

Readiness tests do need further modification to keep abreast of current research findings, to become more instructionally related, and to become more diagnostic. Additional research is also needed to answer other questions about the reading process and how it relates to assessment.

A. Changes Needed in Readiness Tests

Readiness tests need to be modified to include some recent research findings.

1. Language Concepts

Prereading skills tests should provide the teacher with information about each child's understanding of the reading task, words, sounds, and letters as basic to any other information provided about the child's visual, auditory, language, and comprehension skills.

Recent work suggests that young children often do not understand the reading task and cannot segment words, letters, and sounds. Sawyer (1975) states that beginning reading instruction assumes that children recognize the relationship between syllables and single letters inherent in phonics (decoding) instruction. Neither assumption is generally true. Teachers need information about each child's level of skill development in this area.

2. Readinglike Tasks

Prereading assessment in the future should be based on "readinglike" tasks using actual letters, sounds, and words.

As has been discussed earlier, letter recognition seems to have been acquired by most children entering first grade in the 1970s. It, therefore, seems appropriate to omit this measure from readiness tests designed for the beginning of first grade and to assess other prereading skills. These might include visual–auditory integration, analysis and synthesis of visual and auditory stimuli, word recognition, and word learning. A test in which the pupil is taught a few words, phrases, or symbols and later asked to recall and comprehend them might be the most feasible way to relate prereading assessment and instruction (Durkin, 1967; MacGinitie, 1969, 1976).

3. Relation to Instructional Methods and Materials

Readiness tests should assess instructional skills that can be related to specific reading methods and materials.

Such tests will be of use to the classroom teacher in planning instruction and will increase the probability that the teacher can use the readiness test information to teach each child to read and, thus, "ruin the prediction" of the test score. In order to use scores for instructional diagnosis, the prereading measure must provide part scores based upon sufficient items to be both reliable and independent and must provide the teacher with appropriate prereading and reading activities to follow up the diagnosis.

Prereading skill batteries could include subtests assessing those skills found to be necessary for success in reading using a variety of methods and materials. The teacher would assemble into a skill battery those subtests shown to be reliable and to be related to the reading methods being used. In other words, the child's reading instructional tasks could be matched to his/her specific skills.

4. Content Validity

Prereading measures should focus upon content validity related to instruction rather than upon predictive validity.

The concept of a reading readiness test as a task given to children at the end of kindergarten or beginning of first grade in order to obtain a single score with which to predict their success in reading at the end of first grade must be discarded. Emphasis should be placed on assessing skills needed for reading instruction at any level.

5. Assessment of Beginning Reading Skills

The focus of prereading assessment should shift from readiness to beginning reading skills.

As prereading measures become more closely related to instruction, the typical readiness period and readiness materials will be replaced by instruction in prereading and beginning reading skills. Thus the test and subsequent instructional assessment should emphasize the skills, materials, and instruction of beginning reading. No longer will the readiness score be used to identify children who are not "ready" for instruction. Rather the skill scores should be related to beginning reading so they can be used to suggest which beginning instructional steps should be tried for each child.

B. Research Needed

Additional research is needed in several areas in order to implement the preceding suggestions and further to improve readiness assessment.

1. Language Skills

Further research is needed to determine which language concepts are necessary for success in beginning reading instruction (considering the various methods and materials in use) and which will be learned as the child learns to read. Current enthusiasm about this area of linguistic development could falsely suggest that the child must have readiness instruction in language concepts when, in fact, what the child needs is reading instruction.

2. Empirically Validated Assessment Tasks

Developers of tests should investigate reading methods, materials, and current readiness tests to determine if there is a set of agreed-upon tasks that can be shown to be empirically related to reading success. If so, a criterion-referenced, standardized prereading assessment battery could be developed and used nationally.

This research must also consider the teacher variable. How can the assessment instrument account for variation in teacher competence and style?

3. Beginning Reading Model

In order to develop a prereading measure related to specific instructional methods and materials, taxonomies and hierarchies of beginning reading skills are needed. Toward this end, Samuels (1976) has defined some hierarchical skills in reading acquisition defining specific steps required to be able to pronounce a word. He also has pointed out (1973) that more research needs to be done to determine to what the reader gives his/her attention in the reading process. Ruddell (1968) stated that reading consists of mastery of: (a) decoding processes (grapheme–phoneme correspondence and morphographemic–morphophonemic correspondence); (b) comprehension processes (relational meaning, lexical meaning, short- and long-term memory); (c) affective mobilizers; and (d) cognitive strategies. Further research on these and other models of reading, leading to a comprehensive theory and description of beginning reading, is essential for successful prereading skills assessment.

VI. CONCLUSION

The questions of readiness "for what," "taught how," "by whom" must be answered. Only when these have been considered will prereading tests provide information that is of value to the teacher and is of maximum help to the young child learning to read. Surveying the literature on readiness assessment makes it clear that most researchers and test developers have considered ways to assess the child. Tests provide developmental or diagnostic information about the child's growth and learning in skills related to beginning reading. Only recently have researchers considered the equally important issue of analyzing the learning task—the instructional materials, the instructional methods, the teacher and his/ her teaching style, and the learning environment. To be valid and effective, assessment must allow a match between the learner and the instructional task in such a way that the chances for successful learning are optimized. Readiness assessment is just beginning to address ways to match learners and instruction. In the future it must do so in a reliable, valid, practical way.

ACKNOWLEDGMENT

Appreciation is expressed to Ms. Kathleen Telepak for her assistance in the preparation of this manuscript.

REFERENCES

Ausubel, D. P. Viewpoint from related disciplines: Human growth and development. *Teachers College Record,* 1959, **60,** 245–254.

Barrett, T. C. The relationship between measures of prereading visual discrimination and first grade reading achievement: A review of the literature. *Reading Research Quarterly,* 1965, **1,** 51–76.

Birch, H. G., and Belmont, L. Auditory-visual integration in normal and retarded readers. *American Journal of Orthopsychiatry,* 1964, *34,* 852–861.

Blank, M., and Bridger, W. H. Deficiencies in verbal labeling in retarded readers. *American Journal of Orthopsychiatry,* 1966, **36,** 840–847.

Bryden, M. P. Auditory-visual and sequential-spatial matching in relation to reading ability. *Child Development,* 1972, **43,** 824–832.

Carroll, J. B. Nature of the reading process. In H. Singer and R. B. Ruddell (Eds.), *Theoretical models & processes of reading* (2nd ed.). Newark, Del.: International Reading Assoc., 1976. Pp. 8–18.

Christina, R. Replication study: Word boundaries. In M. Early (Ed.), *Language face to face.* Syracuse: Syracuse Univ. Press, 1971. Pp. 115–119.

Cox, M. B. The effect of conservation ability on reading competency. *Reading Teacher,* 1976, **30,** 251–258.

deHirsch, K., Jansky, J. J., and Langford, W. S. *Predicting reading failure.* New York: Harper, Row, 1966.

Denner, B. Representational and syntactic competence of problem readers. *Child Development,* 1970, **41,** 881–887.

Downing, J. How children think about reading. *Reading Teacher,* 1969, **23,** 217–230.

Downing, J. The reading instruction register. *Language Arts,* 1976, **53,** 762–766; 780.

Downing J., and Oliver, P. The child's conception of "a word". *Reading Research Quarterly,* 1973–74, **9,** 568–582.

Downing, J., Ollila, L., and Oliver, P. Cultural differences in children's concepts of reading and writing. *British Journal of Educational Psychology,* 1975, **45,** 312–316.

Durkin, D. Informal techniques for the assessment of prereading behavior. In T. C. Barrett (Ed.), *The evaluation of children's reading achievement.* Newark, Del.: International Reading Assoc., 1967. Pp. 26–34.

Durkin, D. When should children begin to read. In H. M. Robinson (Ed.), Innovation and change in reading instruction. *Yearbook for the National Society for the Study of Education,* 1968, **67,** Part II, 30–71.

Durkin, D. A six-year study of children who learned to read in school at the age of four. *Reading Research Quarterly,* 1974–75, **10,** 9–61.

Dykstra R. Auditory discrimination abilities and beginning reading achievement. *Reading Research Quarterly,* 1966, **1,** 5–34.

Dykstra, R. The use of reading readiness tests for prediction and diagnosis: A critique. In T. C. Barrett (Ed.), *The evaluation of children's reading achievement.* Newark, Del.: International Reading Assoc., 1967. Pp. 35–51.

Ehri, L. C. Word consciousness in readers and prereaders. *Journal of Educational Psychology,* 1975, **67,** 204–212.

Ehri, L. C. Word learning in beginning readers and prereaders: Effect of form class and defining contexts. *Journal of Educational Psychology,* 1976, **68,** 832–842.

Engin, A. W. The relative importance of the subtests of the *Metropolitan Readiness Tests* in the prediction of first grade reading and arithmetic achievement criteria. *Journal of Psychology,* 1974, **88,** 289–298.

Evanechko, P., Ollila, L., Downing, J., and Braun, C. An investigation of the reading readiness domain. *Research in the Teaching of English,* 1973, **7,** 61–78.

Evans, M. C. Children's ability to segment sentences into words. In G. H. McNinch and W. D. Miller (Eds.), Reading: Convention & Inquiry. *24th Yearbook of the National Reading Conference,* 1975, 177–180.

Farnham-Diggory, S. Symbol and synthesis in experimental reading. *Child Development,* 1967, **38,** 223–231.

Farr, R., and Anastasiow, N. *Tests of reading readiness and achievement: A review and evaluation.* Newark, Del.: International Reading Assoc., 1969.

Fillion, B., Smith, F., and Swain, M. Language "basics" for language teachers: Towards a set of universal considerations. *Language Arts,* 1976, **53,** 740–745, 757.

Francis, H. Children's experience of reading and notions of units in language. *British Journal of Educational Psychology,* 1973, **43,** 17–23.

Gates, A. I. Necessary mental age for beginning reading. *Elementary School Journal,* 1936–37, **37,** 497–508.

Gates, A. I., Bond, G. L., and Russell, D. H. *Methods of determining reading readiness.* New York: Bureau of Publications, Teachers College, Columbia Univ., 1939.

Gibson, E. J., and Levin, H. *The psychology of reading.* Cambridge, Mass.: MIT Press, 1975.

Gibson, E. J., Gibson, J. J., Pick, A. D., and Osser, H. A developmental study of the discrimination of letter-like forms. *Journal of Comparative and Physiological Psychology,* 1962, **55,** 876–906.

Goins, J. T. Visual perceptual abilities and early reading progress. *University of Chicago Supplemental Educational Monographs,* 1958, No. 87.

Goldstein, D. M. Cognitive–linguistic functioning and learning to read in preschoolers. *Journal of Educational Psychology,* 1976, **68,** 680–688.

Hall, M. A. Prereading instruction: Teach for the task. *Reading Teacher,* 1976, **30,** 7–9.

Hardy, M., Stennett, R. G., and Smythe, P. C. Development of auditory and visual language concepts and relationship to instructional strategies in kindergarten. *Elementary English,* 1974, **51,** 525–532.

Henderson, E. H., and Long, B. H. Correlations of reading readiness among children of varying backgrounds. *Reading Teacher,* 1968, **22,** 40–44.

Hildreth, G. H. *Readiness for school beginners.* New York: World Book Co., 1950.

Hirst, W. E. Entrance age: A predictor variable for academic success. *Reading Teacher,* 1970, **23,** 547–555.

Holden, M. H., and MacGinitie, W. H. Children's conceptions of word boundaries in speech and print. *Journal of Educational Psychology,* 1972, **63,** 551–557.

Huttenlocher, J. Children's language: Word–phrase relationship. *Science,* 1964, **143,** 264–265.

Johnson, R. E. The validity of the *Clymer–Barrett Prereading Battery. Reading Teacher,* 1969, **22,** 609–614.

Jones, M. H. *The unintentional memory load in tests for young children.* (Center for the Study of Evaluation, Report No. 57.) Los Angeles: Univ. of California at Los Angeles, 1970.

Jorgenson, G. W., and Hyde, E. M. Auditory–visual integration and reading performance in lower social-class children. *Journal of Educational Psychology,* 1974, **66,** 718–725.

Karlin, R. Prediction of reading success and reading readiness tests. *Elementary English,* 1957, **34,** 320–322.

Kaufman, A. S., and Kaufman, N. L. Tests built from Piaget's and Gesell's tasks as predictors of first grade achievement. *Child Development,* 1972, **43,** 521–535.

Lambert, N. M. Paired associate learning, social status, and tests of logical concrete behavior as univariate and multi-variate predictors of first grade reading achievement. *American Educational Research Journal,* 1970, **7,** 511–527.

Lederman, E., and Blair, J. R. Comparison of the level and predictive validity of *Preschool Attainment Record* ratings obtained from teachers and mothers. *Psychology in the Schools,* 1972, **9,** 392–395.

Linehan, E. B. Early instruction in letter names and sounds as related to success in beginning reading. *Journal of Education,* 1958, **140,** 44–48.

Lowell, R. E. A factor analysis of reading readiness tests. *Journal of the New England Reading Association,* 1970, **5,** 28–30.

Lowell, R. E. Reading readiness factors as predictors of success in first grade reading. *Journal of Learning Disabilities,* 1971, **4,** 563–567.

MacGinitie, W. H. Evaluating readiness for learning to read: A critical review of evaluation and research. *Reading Research Quarterly,* 1969, **4,** 396–410.

MacGinitie, W. H. When should we begin to teach reading? *Language Arts,* 1976, **53,** 878–882.

Marchbanks, G., and Levin, H. Cues in word recognition. *Journal of Educational Psychology,* 1965, **56,** 57–61.

Mason, G. E. Preschoolers' concepts of reading. *Reading Teacher.* 1967, **21,** 130–132.

McNinch, G., and Richmond, M. Auditory perceptual tasks as predictors of first grade reading success. *Perceptual and Motor Skills,* 1972, **35,** 7–13.

Mitchell, B. C. *Changes over an eight- and a nine-year period in the readiness level of entering first-grade pupils.* Paper presented at the meeting of the National Council on Measurement in Education, Chicago, April, 1974.

Mitchell, B. C. *Sex differences in readiness at kindergarten entrance.* Unpublished report, Psychological Corp., 1976.

Morphett, M., and Washburne, C. When should children begin to read? *Elementary School Journal,* 1931, **31,** 496–503.

Mortenson, W. P. Selected prereading tasks, socio-economic status, and sex. *Reading Teacher,* 1968, **22,** 45–49.

Muehl, S. The effects of letter-name knowledge on learning to read a word list in kindergarten children. *Journal of Educational Psychology,* 1962, **53,** 181–186.

Muehl, S., and Kremenak, S. Ability to match information within and between auditory and visual sense modalities and subsequent reading achievement. *Journal of Educational Psychology,* 1966, **57,** 230–239.

Muehl, S., and Nello, M. C. Early first-grade skills related to subsequent reading performance: A seven-year follow-up. *Journal of Reading Behavior,* 1976, **8,** 67–81.

Nurss, J. R. An attempt to reduce test bias in readiness tests. In R. C. Granger and J. C. Young (Eds.), *Demythologizing the inner-city child.* Washington, D.C.: National Association for the Education of Young Children, 1976. Pp. 33–36.

Oliver, M. E. The development of language concepts of pre-primary Indian children. *Language Arts,* 1975, **52,** 865–869.

Olson, A. V. Growth in word perception abilities as it relates to success in beginning reading. *Journal of Education,* 1958, 140, 35–36.

Olson, A. V., and Fitzgibbon, N. H. Factor analytic investigation of two readiness tests. *Perceptual and Motor Skills,* 1968, **27,** 611–614.

Osborn, J. D., and Osborn, K. D. Testing procedures and auditory discrimination. *Childhood Education,* 1976, **52,** 284–286.

Paradis, E. E. Appropriateness of visual discrimination exercises in reading readiness materials. *Journal of Educational Research,* 1974, **67,** 276–278.

Pikulski, J. J. Assessment of pre-reading skills: A review of frequently employed measures. *Reading World,* 1974, **13,** 171–197.

Ruddell, R. B. Psycholinguistic implications for a systems of communication model. In K. Goodman and J. Fleming (Eds.), *Psycholinguistics and the teaching of reading.* Newark, Del.: International Reading Assoc., 1968. Pp. 61–78.

Rude, R. T. Readiness tests: Implications for early childhood education. *Reading Teacher,* 1973, **26,** 572–580.

Sabaroff, R. E. Improving achievement in beginning reading: A linguistic approach. *Reading Teacher,* 1970, **23,** 523–527.

Samuels, S. J. The effect of letter-name knowledge on learning to read. *American Educational Research Journal,* 1972, **9,** 65–73.

Samuels, S. J. Success and failure in learning to read: A critique of research. *Reading Research Quarterly,* 1973, **8,** 200–239.

Samuels, S. J. Hierarchical skills in the reading acquisition process. In J. T. Guthrie (Ed.), *Aspects of reading acquisition.* Baltimore: Johns Hopkins Univ. Press, 1976. Pp. 162–179.

Sanacore, J. A checklist for the evaluation of reading readiness. *Elementary English,* 1974, **50,** 858–860, 870.

Sawyer, D. Readiness factors for reading: A different view. *Reading Teacher,* 1975, **28,** 620–624.

Scheuneman, J. *Maximum likelihood factor analysis.* Unpublished report, Harcourt, Brace, Jovanovich, 1975.

Shapiro, J. E. The relationship of conceptual tempo to reading readiness test performance. *Journal of Reading Behavior,* 1976, **7,** 338–340.

Shinn, B. M. A study of teacher judgment and readiness tests as predictors of future achievement. *Illinois School Research,* 1969, **6,** 12–15.

Singer, H., and Ruddell, R. B. (Eds.). *Theoretical models and processes of reading.* Newark, Del.: International Reading Assoc., 1976.

Smith, F. *Comprehension and learning: A conceptual framework for teachers.* New York: Holt, Rinehart & Winston, 1975.

Speer, O. B., and Lamb, G. S. First grade reading ability and fluency in naming verbal symbols. *Reading Teacher,* 1976, **29,** 572–576.

Sprigle, H. J. Can poverty children live on "Sesame Street?" *Young Children,* 1971, **25,** 202–216.

Sterritt, G. M., Martin, V., and Rudnick, M. Auditory-visual and temporal-spatial integration as determinants of test difficulty. *Psychonomic Science,* 1971, **23,** 289–291.

Telegdy, G. A. A factor analysis of four school readiness tests. *Psychology in the Schools,* 1974, **11,** 127–133. (a)

Telegdy, G. A. The relationship between socio-economic status and school readiness. *Psychology in the Schools,* 1974, **11,** 351–356. (b)

Venezky, R. L. The curious role of letter names in reading instruction. *Visible Language,* 1975, **9,** 7–23.

Wanat, S. F. Reading readiness. *Visible Language,* 1976, **10,** 101–127.

Weiner, M., and Feldman, S. Validation studies of a reading prognosis test for children of lower and middle socio-economic status. *Educational and Psychological Measurement,* 1963, **23,** 804–814.

Zaruba, E. Objective and subjective evaluation at grade one. *Reading Teacher,* 1968, **22,** 50–54.

TEST REFERENCES

Bender–Gestalt Test for Young Children. Koppitz, E. M. New York: Grune & Stratton, 1964.

CIRCUS: A Comprehensive Program of Assessment Services for Preprimary Children. Anderson, S., *et al.* Princeton: Educational Testing Service, 1974. Manual and Technical Report, Teacher's Edition. Administering, Scoring, and Interpreting the Instruments.

Clymer–Barrett Prereading Battery. Clymer, T., and Barrett, T. C. Lexington, Mass.: Personnel Press, 1968. Directions Manual, Form A, with Norms for Kindergarten & Grade 1.

First Grade Screening Test. Pate, J. E., and Webb, W. W. Circle Pines, Minn.: American Guidance Service, 1966.

Gates–MacGinitie Reading Tests: Readiness Skills. Gates, A. I., and MacGinitie, W. H. New York: Teachers College Press, 1968. Teacher's Manual. Technical Supplement.

Gates–MacGinitie Reading Tests. Primary A. Gates, A. I., and MacGinitie, W. H. New York: Teachers College Press, 1968.

Gesell Developmental Tests of School Readiness. Ilg, F. L., and Ames, L. B. Lumberville, Pa.: Programs for Education, 1965.

The Harrison–Stroud Reading Readiness Profiles. Harrison, M. L., and Stroud, J. B. Boston: Houghton Mifflin, 1956. Teacher's Manual.

Initial Survey Test. Monroe, M., Manning, J. C., Wepman, J. M., and Gibb, E. G. Glenview, Ill.: Scott, Foresman & Co., 1972. Manual and Directions.

Inventory of Pre-Reading Skills for Getting Ready to Read. Harrison, M. L., and Brzeinski, J. E. Boston: Houghton Mifflin, 1976. Test Manual, Survey Test and Diagnostic Test.

Lee–Clark Reading Readiness Test. Kindergarten and Grade 1, 1962 Revision. Lee, J. M., and Clark, W. Monterey, Calif.: CTB/McGraw–Hill, 1962. Manual.

Metropolitan Achievement Tests. 1970 edition. Durost, W. H. *et al.* New York: Harcourt, Brace, Jovanovich, 1971.

Metropolitan Readiness Tests. Hildreth, G. H., Griffiths, N. L., and McGauvran, M. E. New York: Harcourt, Brace & World, 1965.

Metropolitan Readiness Tests Assessment Program. Levels I & II. Nurss, J. R., and McGauvran, M. E. New York: Harcourt, Brace, Jovanovich, 1976. Teacher's Manual Part I: Directions for Administering. Teacher's Manual Part II: Interpretation and Use of Test Results.

Murphy–Durrell Reading Readiness Analysis. Murphy, H. A., and Durrell, D. D. New York: Harcourt, Brace, & World, 1965. Manual of Directions.

Screening Test of Academic Readiness. Ahr, E. A. Skokie, Ill.: Priority Innovations, 1966.

LINGUISTIC INSIGHT: THRESHOLD OF READING ACQUISITION

LINNEA C. EHRI

University of California, Davis
Davis, California

I. INTRODUCTION

If the light were not so gradual in dawning, the relationship between speech and print might count as one of the most remarkable discoveries of childhood. At a point when the youngster has achieved substantial competence with spoken language, he learns that this highly traveled terrain contains parts he never noticed before. This insight comes as a consequence of learning how it is that language can be represented in an entirely different modality, one designed for eyes rather than ears. In the process of learning to decode written language, the child's basic view of spoken language undergoes a transformation. He develops a clear conception of language as having separate words and sounds, and he learns that these units combine together at two levels—sounds to form words, and words to form sentences—and that they participate in wholes which are worth much more than the sum of their parts. The purpose of this chapter is to consider the development of various linguistic insights about written and spoken language and to review and evaluate evidence for their emergence and their relationship to reading acquisition.

Several linguistic capabilities which stand at the threshold of learning to read have received attention from researchers: word consciousness; syllable and phoneme consciousness; metalinguistic strategies; terminology, concepts, and structural features of written language. Available evidence regarding their relationship to reading acquisition is primarily correlational and so does not really clarify whether the process of learning to read might benefit from advance instruction in any of these prereading skills. Given evidence that a capability is positively correlated with beginning reading achievement or that it distinguishes beginning readers from prereaders or nonreaders, four alternative interpretations for this relationship are possible. The capability might stand as a **prerequisite** in which case a beginning reader finds it impossible to make progress unless he has full possession of this skill or knowledge. Prereading instruction would be mandatory here.

Alternatively, the skill might act as a **facilitator,** meaning that learners who possess it move along faster than those who do not, but that those lacking the skill are not thereby prevented from learning to read. Furthermore, in the process of learning, beginning readers might pick up the skill even though it is not taught separately and explicitly. Prereading instruction in facilitator skills appears justified because it speeds up or otherwise eases the reading acquisiton process, but it is not essential.

The third possibility is that a particular capability is merely a **consequence** of learning to read. That is, the child inevitably acquires the knowledge or skill as a result of his experiences in learning to read, and this happens without any direct instruction. In this case, advance instruction would be a waste of time.

The final possibility is that the capability emerges independently of reading but appears to bear a direct relationship because both capabilities are tied to a common source. In this case, the skill is an incidental **correlate** of reading ability. Obviously, instruction would have little impact on reading here.

In evaluating the instructional implications of research on prereading capabilities, it is important to consider the alternative relationships which each might bear to reading acquisition, particularly in cases where available evidence does not settle the matter. During the course of the following discussion, some of these possibilities will be examined.

II. WORD CONSCIOUSNESS AND ITS CORRELATES

It has generally been assumed that words are natural units and that young children who can speak fluently are also aware of the separate words they are combining and recombining in their speech. More careful consideration of children's experiences with words and the relationship between words and meanings, however, raises doubt about this assumption. Young children experience most words in the context of other words, and their attention is centered upon the meanings conveyed by these spoken combinations, not upon their linguistic structure. Moreover, there are no auditory signals segmenting speech into word units. Hence, words as components of speech are neither salient nor clearly marked. Second, many words such as auxiliaries, past tense verbs, prepositions, and conjunctions, depend for their meaning upon the presence of other words. If heard as isolated sounds without contexts, these words may not be recognized because they evoke no independent meaning. Third, more frequent words are semantically ambiguous and tend to have multiple meanings (Carroll, 1971). The fact that the same sounds perform many functions in the youngster's language may make him especially immune to the link between single word sounds and their linguistic function. Fourth, the phonological forms of some words, especially functors lifted out of context and pronounced separately (e.g., *of* versus "gimme a piece *a* candy") may change, eluding detection and recognition. Fifth, the prereader has had little experience with concrete word forms. It may be that children achieve clear awareness of words as units only when they become familiar with language which endures, that is, speech represented as clusters of printed letters separated by empty spaces.

There is substantial evidence challenging the assumption that children are conscious of separate words. Karpova (1955) was among the first to examine children's ability to segment sentences into words. Although his findings yield some interesting generalizations about the course of emergence of word consciousness, the tasks may have been too complex for his younger subjects. Karpova employed Russian children aged 3½ to 7. First, he trained them to count pictures and orally presented words. This was done to convey the idea of enumerating objects and word units. Then he asked them to repeat each of several sentences, to count the words, and to identify the first, second, third . . . word in each sentence. On the basis of children's performances, Karpova distinguished several stages. The youngest children regarded the sentence as a unified message and divided it into semantic rather than lexical units. For example, a 4-year-old asserted that the sentence "Galya and Vova went walking," had two words, "Galya went walking and Vova went walking." At the next stage, following repeated questioning, children began to isolate nouns and to make simple binary divisions of the sentence into subject and predicate. In the third stage, older children were able to identify component words but they tended to leave out prepositions and conjunctions and occasionally they divided words into syllables. These findings suggest a slow development in word consciousness beginning with semantically salient units and culminating in words which perform syntactic-relational functions in sentences but lack much independent semantic identity.

In another study conducted with English-speaking children Hatch (1969) reported data indicating that Karpova's tasks were very difficult for preschoolers. Not only the counting operation but also the intangible nature of the stimulus created unnecessary complexity. Hatch adopted Karpova's procedures in order to examine preschoolers' awareness of various types of words whose status as single or multiple lexical units might be less obvious: compound nouns (e.g., *baseball*), two-word verbs (e.g., *call up, ate up*), pronouns, negatives (e.g., *unhappy*). To her disappointment, she found that no child in her sample (ages 3:11 to 5:8) was able to answer any of Karpova's questions about orally presented sentences (i.e., ''How many words are there? What is the first word?''). Adding a motor component to the sentence segmentation task by having the child move checkers as each word was spoken enabled some of the subjects to distinguish noun phrase from verb phrase, but half still failed to segment the sentences at all. She concluded that either a better task or more extensive training was needed in order to investigate lexical awareness in young children.

An easier task was adopted by Huttenlocher (1964) who shortened the sequences of units and simplified the segmentation response. She examined 4- and 5-year-old's ability to divide pairs of items of various classes: digits and letters, like parts of speech (e.g., *black–white*), common reversible and nonreversible grammatical word sequences (e.g., *I–do, Man–runs*), and grammatical but semantically anomalous sequences (e.g., *table–goes*). The task was to reverse the order of the units or to await a tap between units. She found that 35% of the children could not divide any pairs while 11% could do them all. For the remaining children, common English grammatical pairs proved more difficult than the others. These results confirm that segmenting speech, even very short utterances, is hard for many preschoolers, particularly when the words form a sentence which is familiar and makes sense.

Huttenlocher's findings, however, conflict with those obtained by Fox and Routh (1975) using a different task. They too wanted to simplify the sentence segmentation operation to see whether young preschoolers might display more success. Each child was given a sentence and told to say ''just a little bit of it.'' If he responded with a multiple-word phrase, the examiner repeated it back saying ''tell me a little bit of (phrase).'' This continued until all the words in a segment had been isolated, either by being asserted separately or dropped from a previous assertion. In contrast to Huttenlocher (1964), Fox and Routh found that 3-

year-olds were successful on a mean of five out of eight sentences, and by age 4, children were able to perform perfectly. However, there are some problems with this study limiting its conclusions. So much experimenter prompting was employed that it is questionable whether successful performance on the segmentation task can be considered evidence of lexical awareness. Not the child but the experimenter determined when lexical analysis was complete. If the child's response still contained multiple words, the experimenter continued to ask for little bits until one word remained. Also, the children were far above average socioeconomically and intellectually with a mean IQ of 117. How many of the younger subjects had some acquaintance with the reading process is not clear. These uncertainties cast doubt on the conclusion that preschoolers as young as 3 or 4 are aware of words as units of language.

Holden and MacGinitie (1972) explored slightly older children's segmentation ability with a wide variety of meaningful phrases and sentences, and their results are consisistent with those of Huttenlocher's indicating that words are not salient units for youngsters. In this study, kindergarteners, of ages 5 and 6, were given the task of pointing to a poker chip as they uttered each word in sentences containing several words. Holden and MacGinitie found that the children were able to break apart the sentences although they did not often do so correctly. Words having greater lexical meaning were sometimes isolated accurately, but function words were frequently combined with adjacent units. Whether function words were isolated or compounded appeared to depend upon the rhythmic pattern children imposed on the sentences ("The book/is in/the desk." "Snow / is / cold.") rather than on awareness of separate words. In discussing their results, Holden and MacGinitie point out that use of printing conventions as a standard for correct segmentation is somewhat arbitrary, particularly in the case of compound words. Even linguists cannot agree about the definition of a word. Holden and MacGinitie suggest that children may have trouble segmenting sentences "correctly" because their notion of word units and boundaries is discrepant with conventional boundaries. However, on the basis of the data of Holden and MacGinitie, it is questionable whether children can be regarded as possessing a definitive notion of word units at all, discrepant or otherwise. Subjects' haphazard divisions of sentences, influenced more by rhythm than by lexical identities, suggest an alternative possibility, that children lack a clear notion of words as units, and that when forced to distinguish units in a sentence segmentation task, they respond on the basis of the most salient cues in the sound track. Some words get marked correctly by accident because stress and pause location happen to isolate these words.

In order to examine how children might segment sentences stripped of any suprasegmental rhythm or intonation, Ehri (1975) employed a tapping and a poker-chip word-marking task and had children utter each sentence in a monotone with stress on each word. Also, she had them mark each sentence twice, once before and once after the correct behavior was modeled. Results revealed that despite monotone sentence production and modeling, children still mismarked words, either slighting them or marking them more than once. Function words were ignored more often than semantically salient content words although children were inconsistent in marking or ignoring particular words across sentences. This suggests that lack of a clear awareness of words as units rather than possession of a discrepant notion of word units may more appropriately characterize these children.

Ehri (1975) investigated some other aspects of word consciousness in her study, and she tested the hypothesis that beginning readers would outperform prereaders in the various tasks. Results revealed that readers were substantially more advanced than prereaders in their awareness of words and also syllables as units of language. Readers were better at creating sentence contexts for single words, at segmenting sentences into words and shifting segmentation bases from words to syllables, at picking out the single word distinguishing two otherwise identical sentences (e.g., ''The teacher is wearing a pretty dress. The teacher is wearing a **very** pretty dress.''), with stress placed on a nontarget word, and at identifying the word with a particular final unstressed syllable (e.g., *drinking* containing the syllable -*king*). In contrast, prereaders revealed several difficulties with these tasks. Function words proved more elusive than content words. The younger prereaders often displayed semantic rather than lexical analyses of words and sentences. For example, when asked to identify the single word distinguishing the two sentences—''The fat king ate the whole apple pie. The king ate the whole apple pie.''—one child said, ''The king doesn't have a fat stomach.'' Prereaders appeared to have trouble pulling single words out of meaningful sentence contexts. Often they would repeat the sentence stressing the key word (e.g., *fat* or *very* in the above examples) but they could not seem to extract and utter it alone. It may be that some lexical-analytic tasks are troublesome not only because word consciousness is required but also because the child must violate and analyze good Gestalt forms (i.e., meaningful sentences).

Ehri (1976) conducted an additional study to verify that the experience of learning to read is associated with superior lexical awareness. In the previous investigation, readers had been older than prereaders, and so it was possible that other factors associated with age rather than reading experiences produced the observed differences. To check on this, Ehri obtained some kindergarten readers and prereaders who were matched in age, and also some first-grade readers. Rather than employing any of the preceding lexical-analytic tasks, she designed a new one requiring subjects to recognize and store single words in memory. Each child was given a paired associate learning task in which he associated five orally pronounced words with five highly discriminable visual nonsense figures. Two types of words served as responses, context-free words (nouns and adjectives) and context-dependent words (past-tense verbs, prepositions, other functors).

Children were taught one of the three words from each of five form classes: (1) *milk, box, fish;* (2) *fast, hot, small;* (3) *came, helped, ran;* (4) *of, at, on;* (5) *and, could, were.* It was reasoned that if word consciousness distinguishes readers from prereaders, then readers should be able to learn the words much faster. Furthermore, prereaders should have special difficulty learning context-dependent words whose existence as separate units in speech is quite unfamiliar. Comparison of performances revealed that, as expected, prereaders required significantly more trials to criterion per word ($\overline{X}$ = 7.1 trails) than kindergarten readers ($\overline{X}$ = 2.5 trials) or first-grade readers ($\overline{X}$ = 1.7 trials) whose means did not differ statistically. Context-dependent words proved harder than context-free words for readers as well as prereaders. However, only the prereader group had subjects who were unable to learn the context-dependent words at all in 22 trials. In a second task, Ehri observed that readers were also better able to perceive and extract these words from spoken sentence contexts than a subgroup of prereaders who had been able to learn the words. She concluded that learning to read rather than age and its correlates is the significant factor accounting for the emergence of word consciousness.

One other purpose of Ehri's word-learning study was to examine whether prereaders might benefit from the presence of defining sentences in learning the words, particularly the context-dependent words. Some of the children heard either semantically rich or impoverished contexts following the presentation of each word during the learning trials (e.g., *helped*—''The teacher **helped** the girl draw the picture'' or ''He **helped** her get it''—with the target word stressed), and some heard the word simply repeated. It was reasoned that the sentence contexts might help children recognize the linguistic identity of the words and thus enhance the words' memorability. However, neither rich nor empty contexts exerted any influence on learning. Inspection of prereaders' errors indicated that children given sentences along with the context-dependent words were having trouble extracting and remembering the single correct word from the sentences. Often they would persist in recalling another word from the sentence or a phrase containing the word or the entire sentence. Such behavior is not unexpected given Ehri's (1975) finding that children who lack word consciousness have trouble picking single words, particularly function words, out of meaningful sentences.

One other type of response difficulty was also common, that of failing to recall any word when the stimulus was presented. This was the most frequent error among children who heard the words without contexts but was also prevalent among children given contexts with the words. Response omission occurred more frequently than the usual error type observed in paired associate learning studies, that of mismatching responses to stimuli. Apparently prereaders were having much trouble just keeping the context-dependent words in mind as responses. There are two reasons why this might be so. It may be that prereaders failed to recognize the isolated sounds as real words in their language and so treated them as nonsense responses to be learned from scratch. Goodman (1973), for one, has claimed that contexts are essential for making words meaningful, and that without them, beginning readers learning single printed words merely "bark at print." Alternatively, it may be that prereaders recognized the words but since function words are relatively meaningless, the children lacked any mnemonic device for distinguishing and preserving the words in memory.

Downing and Oliver (1974) have provided some evidence for the first alternative mentioned, that prereaders have difficulty distinguishing between real words and nonsense sounds when the words are presented orally without contexts. They tested preschoolers, kindergarteners and first graders (ages 4½ to 8) to determine whether the children could classify various types of auditory stimuli as words and nonwords. First, pretraining experiences were provided. Pictures of one or several familiar objects were presented and each child learned to say "yes" to single objects, "no" to multiple sets. This was intended to convey the idea that only single units were correct. Then auditory stimuli such as bottle sounds and bells were presented, and the child learned to say "yes" to single sounds, "no" to more than one sound. This was intended to transfer the response to the auditory mode. The discrimination task followed. Various classes of auditory stimuli including nonverbal noises, phonemes, syllables, short words, long words, phrases, and sentences were presented. The child's task was to say "yes" to single words and "no" to all other stimuli. Analysis of performances revealed that none of the children succeeded. Although many said "yes" correctly to the words, they also said "yes" to other sounds, most notably syllables and phonemes. From these results it might be concluded that children cannot distinguish isolated words from nonsense sounds. However, the study has some shortcomings. It is not clear that the pretraining procedure or the instructions clarified the nature of the discrimination expected. The distinction *single* versus *multiple* received primary attention during pretraining while the distinction *word* versus *nonword* was ignored. Subsequently, the child was simply told to identify single words. Being less than certain about the meaning of the term "word," he may have inferred from the pretraining that his task was to distinguish single from multiple verbal sounds. In fact, errors suggest that this is what he did. For these reasons, Downing's and Oliver's task may not have tapped the child's competence at discriminating single words from nonwords.

To clarify whether prereaders can recognize isolated words as familiar units of their speech, Ehri (1977) conducted another study designed to ensure that subjects would understand the nature of the discrimination task and the basis for their response. A second purpose of this study was to see whether some classes of words might evade detection more than others. From results of Ehri's (1976) word-learning study, it was expected that context-dependent words would be much harder to identify as real words than context-free words having independent semantic status. One problem with Ehri's previous study was that only a limited variety of monosyllabic words was examined. In this study, both single and polysyllabic words were included, and words were drawn from several grammatical classes.

Ehri employed an oral word discrimination task referred to as the Sense and Silly Word Game. The game had two parts, a preparatory phase followed by a word–pseudoword discrimination test. Kindergarteners (age 5½ to 6 years) were introduced to drawings of two faces, one resembling a person called "Mr. Sense" who "likes to say a single word and then put that word in a story," and one resembling a hairy green animal called "Mr. Silly" who "can't talk right and says words that are silly gibberish." Each child heard 20 sounds accompanied by a sentence or nonsense context clue indicating whether the sound belonged to *Sense* or *Silly* (e.g., *after*—"A mouse is running **after** a cat." *keer*— "Heb gin **keer** surb.") His task was to point to the face belonging to each sound. Then the same sounds were re-presented without contexts and the child again classified them. The discrimination task followed. The child heard and classified 30 new words and 30 new pseudowords as *sense* or *silly*. No contexts were provided, and the experimenter reinforced correct responses. All words but the nouns were taken from the Dolch list of basic sight words. Of the 40 words, 8 were two-syllable words and the remaining were monosyllabic. Pseudowords were patterned after the real words, with 8 two-syllable forms and the others one-syllable forms. All were easily pronounced.

From performance on the preparatory phase of the task, it was evident that subjects understood the nature of the discrimination they were expected to perform. Out of 32 kindergarteners tested, 29 understood the difference between Mr. Sense and Mr. Silly. That is, they were able to point to the correct face when the sounds were presented with contexts. However, only some of these children were successful on the discrimination task. Moreover, as is evident in Fig. 1,

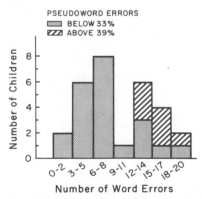

Fig. 1. Number of real words judged to be nonsense on the transfer task (maximum = 30).

word error scores were distributed bimodally. Among the 29 children, there were 7 whose sound discrimination performance was considered at a chance level. Errors were above 39% on the nonsense sounds and above 40% on the words. (Random guessing would yield error rates around 50%). The remaining 22 children did much better than chance with nonsense sounds (i.e., error rates at or below 33%), but their success at recognizing words was quite varied. These subjects were in fact distributed bimodally (see Fig. 1.) Such results suggest that there may be two populations of kindergarteners, those who can recognize at least some real words presented in isolation and those who find this quite difficult.

One possible factor accounting for this separation is reading ability, although the kindergarteners tested were thought to be prereaders since they had undergone no formal reading instruction in school. Inspection of their scores on printed word-recognition and spelling tests confirmed that most children knew relatively little about printed language (i.e., mean words recognized = 2.3 out of 10; mean words spelled = .7 out of 6). These scores were, however, positively correlated with success in discriminating between words and nonsense forms. The correlations ranged from .44 ($p < .05$) to .51 ($p < .01$). To determine whether variations in reading ability might account for the bimodal distribution in Fig. 1, subjects were sorted into high and low scoring groups on the basis of performances on the oral word-discrimination, printed-word-recognition, and spelling tasks. Results indicated that high scorers on the *sense–silly* task included most of those children who possessed some knowledge of printed language, as expected. However, a surprising number of children quite unfamiliar with print also comprised this group. In contrast, low scorers were exclusively those who knew little about printed language. These results suggest that reading ability is one factor which contributes to the separation between children in their word-detection ability. However, it is not the whole story. There are other factors as well.

The discovery of a bimodal distribution of word-discrimination scores, particularly among a group of prereaders, was quite unexpected. Previous studies ignored the possibility that children might be distributed bimodally in lexical awareness. Usually a presumption of normality is made, and researchers do not bother to inspect their distributions of scores. Calfee, Chapman, and Venezky (1972) are among the few who have noticed and mentioned such a phenomenon. According to Calfee, Fisk, and Piontkowski (1975), gross measures of nonspecific processes such as memory or intelligence yield normal distributions because a large number of skills are tapped and pooled in a haphazard way. "As statisticians know, the sum of a large number of independent binary events is a normal distribution" (p. 145). In contrast, the operation of single skills which underlie performance on "clean on–off" test instruments yield bimodal distributions. These skills are either possessed or not possessed by subjects.

The fact that scores were distributed bimodally in the discrimination study suggests that the ability to distinguish words from nonwords is a single skill rather than a composite of skills. What accounts for the possession of this capability by only a subportion of prereaders is puzzling. Unlike other bimodally distributed capabilities such as alphabet letter knowledge (Calfee *et al.,* 1972), word consciousness does not seem to be a skill that might receive instructional attention from literacy-minded parents. Age was not the critical factor separating the two groups. The correlation between chronological age and discrimination scores was .16, $p > .05$. As discussed previously, familiarity with printed language may have accounted for the success of some subjects (i.e., 5 out of 16 or 31% on the basis of spelling scores), but there was still a number of children who could play the *sense–silly* game yet could not read.

The possibility that prereaders can be distinguished as either possessing or lacking word consciousness is at variance with the view proposed by Ehri (1975, 1976) portraying prereaders as a unitary group typified by a lack of word consciousness. However, she did not examine the distributions of scores in her previous studies to confirm this hypothesis. To check on the possibility that prereaders might have been distributed bimodally in their ability to remember words, data from Ehri's (1976) word-learning study were exhumed and the number of learning trials for 70 prereaders were plotted. Results are presented in Fig. 2. Scores (horizontal axis) ranged from 2 to 22, the maximum number of trials given before learning was terminated. Consistent with the bimodal view, two distinct clusters of scores were identifiable, one peaking around seven trials

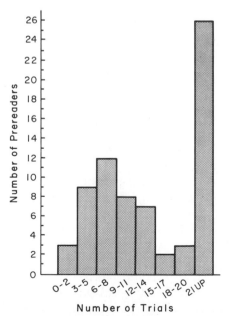

Fig. 2.   Total number of trials to criterion or termination required by prereaders to learn words.

and representing subjects who were able to learn all the words, the other sky-scraping at 22 trials and representing children who either had much difficulty or were unable to learn the words. Thus, in a somewhat different task requiring word memory rather than word discrimination, the same phenomenon was detected among prereaders. A suitable explanation for this awaits further investigation.

One other purpose of Ehri's (1977) discrimination study was to see whether some word classes, namely context-dependent words and monosyllabic words, would prove harder for the children to discriminate. The number of subjects who made errors on each word was counted and results are reported in Table I. (Responses of only those children performing above a chance level in recognizing the nonsense syllables were considered.) As expected, nouns and adjectives were very easy to identify. Also, present-tense verbs were detected more readily than most irregular past-tense forms. One reason for this may be that in contrast to present forms which may be uttered alone or may head imperative sentences, past-tense forms are almost always embedded in the middle of larger sentence contexts. Another possible reason is that kindergartners may be more familiar with overregularized versions of the irregular past verbs (e.g., *gived* versus *gave; runned* versus *ran; finded* versus *found; goed* versus *went*). Berko (1958) showed that overregularized forms are common in young children's speech.

Among the words most difficult to detect were some prepositions (*of, at*), possessive pronouns (*his, those*), a quantifier (*every*), and a verb form (*were*). The difficulty of these words may stem from their being strongly dependent upon sentence contexts for meaning. However, contextual dependency is not the whole story since a number of other similar words were successfully identified by most of the children: prepositions and conjunctions (*on, from, after, before, over, could, and, because*), pronouns (*she, what*), and a past-tense verb (*went*). One reason for performing this study was to resolve the puzzle over why prereaders had such trouble remembering words in Ehri's (1976) word-learning study. These results suggest that young children have difficulty recognizing some context-dependent units as real words when they are spoken in isolation and so this factor is important, but it is not the only source of difficulty making such words harder to remember.

From Table I, it is evident that syllabic structure of the words also failed to exert a consistent effect upon performance in the discrimination task. The number of errors with polysyllabic words ranged from 1 to 11, suggesting that it is not necessarily easier for youngsters to recognize more highly distinctive multisyllabic sounds as words. Apparently it depends upon the particular word.

One implication of the word-discrimination and word-learning findings for beginning reading instruction might be mentioned. The context-dependent words used in Ehri's studies were taken from the Dolch list of basic vocabulary terms. The fact that prereaders had difficulty recognizing or remembering these words

TABLE I

List of Form Classes, Words, and Number of Children Failing to Recognize Each[a]

Form class	Preparatory phase test	Discrimination test			Mean	Range
		A	B	C		
Nouns	box (3)	milk (1)	car (1)	fish (4)	2.25	(1–4)
Adjectives	fast (2)	small (2)	white (3)	hot (5)	3.00	(2–5)
Present verbs	come (1)	make (2)	have (4)	say (5)	3.50	(1–5)
Past verbs	gave (12)	went (4)	found (6)	ran (8)	7.50	(4–12)
Prepositions (1 syllable)	on (1)	from (1)	of (10)	at (15)	6.75	(1–15)
Prepositions (2 syllables)	after (1)	before (1)	over (3)	into (7)	3.00	(1–7)
Pronouns	she (1)	us (6)	his (12)	those (13)	8.00	(1–13)
Q-Pronouns	who (7)	what (2)	how (6)	when (7)	5.50	(2–7)
Functors	could (3)	and (4)	is (8)	were (11)	6.50	(3–11)
Miscellaneous (2 syllables)	very (6)	because (2)	again (2)	every (11)	5.25	(2–11)
Mean	3.7		5.5		5.1	

[a] Only the 22 children discriminating nonsense syllables above chance were included here. Numbers in parentheses indicate the number of subjects who made errors.

suggests that the flash card method may not be very effective in teaching basic sight vocabulary words to youngsters. If children do not recognize the syntactic or semantic identities of the isolated words they are shown, then very likely they will learn merely to "bark at the print" and this learning may not transfer to the task of reading meaningful text.

III. THEORETICAL INTERPRETATIONS OF THE RELATIONSHIP BETWEEN WORD CONSCIOUSNESS AND READING

From results of Ehri's studies, it is evident that a substantial relationship exists between word consciousness and knowledge of printed language. To explain the connection, there are at least three logical possibilities available, each corresponding to alternative causal relationships implied by a correlation (i.e., A causes B, or B causes A, or C causes both A and B). Various investigators have adopted one or another of these as the preferred explanation. Ehri (1976) has maintained that B causes A, that is, learning to read brings about enhanced lexical awareness. Bereiter and Englemann (1966) and Ryan (in press) have opted for the reverse of this, that superior lexical awareness is a prerequisite for learning to read. The third possibility, favored by Piagetians, is that the two are simply correlates and that the emergence of general cognitive capabilities underlies both reading acquisition and word consciousness. Although suggestive, the available evidence in support of any of these positions must be regarded as inconclusive since the studies are correlational rather than manipulative.

A. Cognitive Development

According to the Piagetian view, lexical awareness is an outgrowth of the development of more basic cognitive capacities such as the extension of the child's working memory space (Pascual-Leone, 1970), or the ability to decenter and attend to multiple aspects of a stimulus simultaneously (Inhelder and Piaget, 1964). Decentration emerging around age 7 has been cited by Elkind (1967) as a factor important for reading acquisition as well as for linguistic awareness.

The hypothesis that cognitive development underlies the emergence of word consciousness was tackled in a study by Holden (1972) and Holden and Mac-Ginitie (1973). They measured kindergarteners' and first-graders' ability to extract words included in spoken contexts and also their ability to seriate. The test of word awareness required children to listen to pairs of almost identical sentences and word lists and to pick out the one or two words added to the second sentence or list distinguishing it from the first (e.g., "Joe wore a hat. Joe wore a hat and coat."). The Piagetian task required subjects to insert nine additional sticks into an array of ten sticks already ordered from short to long. Successful performance on this task is regarded as indicating that a child can decenter and has reached the stage of concrete operational thinking. Results of the study indicated some relationship between linguistic awareness and Piagetian operational levels. The correlation between word awareness scores and seriation was .32, $p < .01$. However, Holden (1972) reported that while most of the children functioning at the concrete operational level performed well on her word analysis task, there were several linguistically advanced children who were still preoperational in their thinking. This suggests that superior lexical awareness is not necessarily contingent upon achievement of the concrete operational stage of thinking but may come earlier.

In their studies, Holden and MacGinitie also took a look at the relationship between word awareness and reading ability. Kindergarteners were given the Gates-MacGinitie Readiness Skills test which includes subtests measuring children's familiarity with printed language (i.e., visual discrimination among words, letter recognition and production, word recognition). These scores correlated .60 ($p < .01$) with word awareness scores, a value substantially higher than the correlation between seriation and word awareness. For first graders, reading test scores on the Gates–MacGinitie Reading Test correlated .38 ($p < .01$) with word scores. In addition, first graders outperformed kindergartners, with contrasting means of 48.5 versus 31.4 words correctly identified (maximum = 60). Furthermore, the standard deviation of first-graders' scores was half as large as that for kindergartners' scores (7.3 versus 14.1), indicating less variation in lexical awareness among those children who had undergone some reading instruction.

In a subsequent study, Holden (1975) compared kindergartners and first graders on a homophone word awareness test. Subjects were given sentence pairs where the additional words produced a change in the overall meaning (e.g., "John has two hats. John has too **many** hats."). Whereas kindergartners identified 43% of the word additions correctly, first graders identified 85% correctly. In sum, Holden's results lend less credence to the Piagetian cognitive developmental hypothesis than they lend to the hypothesis that word consciousness and experience with printed language are directly related.

Results of Ehri's (1976) word-learning study also pointed to reading rather than cognitive development as the important factor. Kindergarten readers 6 years of age learned the words much faster than 6-year-old prereaders and they performed as well as older first-grade readers. However, since readers and prereaders were matched not according to cognitive development but only by age, it might be argued that the readers were more mature cognitively than the prereaders since they were self-selected. Working against this possibility is the sizeable difference in performance distinguishing kindergarten readers from prereaders. Inspection of the learning trials required by those kindergartners who had high scores on measures of reading ability ($N = 9$) revealed a mean of 2.8 trials to criterion and scores ranging from 1 to 5 trials. In contrast, only 3 out of 70 prereaders (.4%) learned the words in fewer than 3 trials and 17% in fewer than 6 trials (see Fig. 2). It is unlikely that the sample of kindergarten readers was this far superior cognitively to the prereaders. This evidence is merely suggestive, however. Clearly, more direct research is needed before one concludes that cognitive development contributes little to the emergence of word consciousness.

B. Lower-Class Language Deficiency

In contrast to Piagetians, Bereiter and Englemann (1966) have regarded lexical awareness as causally rather than just coincidentally related to reading acquisition. They have proposed that inadequately developed knowledge about words as units of language distinguishes disadvantaged youngsters from middle-class youngsters, that this difference stems from differences in basic linguistic competence, and that lack of word knowledge contributes to the difficulty lower-class children have in learning to read.

On the basis of informal observations with lower-class black preschoolers exclusively (at least the report of their observations is casual), Bereiter and Englemann have concluded that the language of lower-class children is qualitatively different from that of middle-class children. Disadvantaged children are unable to segment sentences into word units in speech and their pronunciations of words, particularly highly frequent context-dependent words, are imprecise making these words hard to discriminate.

> The speech of the severely deprived children seems to consist not of distinct words, as does the speech of middle-class children of the same age, but rather of whole phrases or sentences that function like giant words. That is to say, these "giant word" units cannot be taken apart by the child and re-combined; . . . . Instead of saying "He's a big dog," the deprived child says "He bih daw." Instead of saying "I ain't got no juice," he says "Uai-ga-na-ju." Instead of saying "That is a red truck," he says "Da-re-truh." Once the listener has become accustomed to this style of speech, he may begin to hear it as if all the sounds were there, and may get the impression that he is hearing articles when in fact there is only a pause where the article should be. He may believe that the child is using words like "it," "is," "if," and "in" when in fact he is using the same sound for all of them—something on the order of "ih." (This becomes apparent if the child is asked to repeat the statement "It is in the box." After a few attempts in which he becomes confused as to the number of "ih's" to insert, the child is likely to be reduced to a stammer.)
>
> If the problem were merely one of faulty pronunciation, it would not be so serious. But it appears that the child's faulty pronunciation arises from his inability to deal with sentences *as sequences of meaningful parts.* (Carl Bereiter and Siegfried Englemann, "Teaching Disadvantaged Children in the Preschool," © 1966, pp. 34–35. Reprinted by permission of Prentice-Hall, Inc. Englewood Cliffs, New Jersey.

Bereiter and Englemann related their claim that lower-class children speak in "giant word phrases" to Bernstein's (1962) portrayal of lower-class speech as a restricted linguistic code. Bernstein described restricted forms as condensed and stereotyped, often involving nonspecific clichés, with meanings that are vague and implicit. This contrasts with an elaborated code characterizing middle-class speech which, Bernstein asserted, is individualized, differentiated, and precise. Bereiter and Englemann suggested that lack of linguistic awareness is a consequence of the acquisition of a restricted language code and that this lack causes trouble in learning to read. They attempted to repair the deficit early in the Distar beginning reading program by providing lessons to teach children how to segment speech into word units.

Bereiter and Englemann's view is reconstructed here because it entails some interesting hypotheses about lexical inadequacies in the speech of prereaders. However, Bereiter and Englemann's claims must be regarded as extremely tentative since their position rests on logical rather than empirical ground. In fact, their evidence is deficient or nonexistent. Most obviously, they fail to compare directly the speech of lower-class and middle-class children and merely assume that middle-class children can segment speech into words. As is evident in studies discussed previously, this assumption is false. Other aspects of their theory and solutions also remain untested. It is not at all clear that instruction in the oral mode can enable prereaders to become conscious of words or help them learn to read. Two other researchers have recognized and tackled some of these uncertainties.

Chappell (1968) sought evidence for the claim that middle-class youngsters differ from lower-class youngsters in word awareness. In a study patterned after Karpova's (1955) procedures with Russian children, she succeeded in detecting differences favoring middle-class children. However, she employed several syntactically complex sentences probably less familiar to lower-class children. Also, as noted by Hatch (1969), Karpova's tasks may not measure lexical awareness very adequately. Thus, Chappell's findings remain doubtful.

Thomson (1968), a student of Bereiter's, attempted to test three hypotheses derived from the Bereiter and Englemann position: (1) that middle-class youngsters possess superior lexical awareness; (2) that lower-class youngsters have particular difficulty segmenting word sequences taken from their own speech and presumably functioning as "giant word phrases"; (3) that preschoolers can be successfully trained to segment oral language into lexical units. Also Thomson was interested in comparing the ease of segmenting various types of grammatical and anomalous three-word sequences. The segmentation task he used required subjects to repeat each sequence and then to say it backwards. He recruited middle-class and lower-class children varying in age from 4:7 to 5:7, none of whom knew how to reverse the order of three-word sequences at the outset of the experiment. First, Thomson trained his subjects to invert oral sequences of words until they could perform perfectly on three noun–verb–noun strings (e.g., "Elephants eat leaves."). When subjects had achieved criterion, they were presented with the transfer task consisting of 24 grammatical and anomalous three-word sequences. Some of these had been obtained from children's speech samples and were thought to be "giant word phrases."

Contrary to his expectations, Thompson failed to observe any differences as a function of socio-economic status (SES) level. Calculation of the extent to which children preserved the original order of words in their attempts to reverse the sequences revealed low scores and no greater word amalgamation tendency among lower-class than among middle-class children. Furthermore, he found that advantaged as well as disadvantaged children had much trouble reversing the order of segments taken from actual speech. These results do not support Bereiter and Englemann's hypothesis that disadvantaged children learn different units of speech from middle-class youngsters at the same age (4–5 years old). Rather it appears that both groups are similar in their treatment of lexical units.

Thomson reported mixed success in training children to segment speech. On the transfer task children performed almost perfectly on the six grammatical strings which resembled those used in training, ones with nouns in first and final positions (i.e., *jar in water, cats climb trees, shoe and sock, chair on rug, dogs bite cats, Billy saw Mary*). In contrast, they did poorly on sequences that were taken from speech samples and contained several function words and few nouns (i.e., *big fat tree; a big one; in a hat; if it rains; gave it to; in three big*). Whereas the mean number of word pairs reversed correctly was 15.5 in the former case (maximum score = 18), the mean was 3.9 for speech sample sequences. Performance was somewhat better on anomalous sequences (i.e., *over the ran*), particularly when the sequence pronounced backwards made sense (i.e., *sky blue the*), with means of 5.8 and 7.6, respectively. However, it was still inferior to performance with the grammatical noun-dominated sequences. These results suggest that training in the auditory mode can enhance lexical analysis of noun-verb–noun sentences but that effects do not generalize to new types of lexical units or phrases containing more function words and fewer nouns.

Given the low scores on the speech samples, one might be tempted to infer that "giant word phrases" are indeed difficult for children to segment into component words. However, inspection of the subjects' errors revealed that this was not the case. Children were able to analyze the phrases into words. The source of their trouble was in sequencing the three words correctly, in reverse order. In their responses, the words were jumbled up in an order different from that in the stimulus. Given that phrases were successfully segmented albeit in the wrong order, one might argue that children did acquire the idea of lexical analysis from training with speech. However, there is an additional problem checking this inference. Almost all the words were monosyllabic. It may be that children distinguished words on the basis of syllabic divisions in sound, and correct word segmentation was accidental. In conclusion, Thomson's results are interesting but his word sequences and his reversal task may have been less than adequate for revealing whether preschoolers can acquire lexical awareness through practice in analyzing oral language.

C. Metalinguistic Awareness

Ryan (in press) has agreed with Bereiter and Englemann that children need to be aware of word units in order to learn to read. However, her position is quite different. Whereas Bereiter and Englemann regard word awareness as part of basic linguistic competence, Ryan distinguishes between implicit functional knowledge of language and metalinguistic awareness, and she places word consciousness in the latter category. According to Ryan, most youngsters between the ages of 4 and 6 have command of oral language in the sense that they can combine and recombine words to comprehend and produce speech quite effectively. However, what they lack is the ability to detach language from its meaning and to reflect upon or analyze its form. These latter capabilities, referred to as metalinguistic strategies, require flexibility and a capacity to decenter from the most salient attribute of a message. Ryan cites various lines of evidence suggesting that an active deliberate control over various forms of language develops from age 5 onward, and she proposes that certain levels of linguistic awareness may be necessary in the acquisition of literacy skills, writing as well as reading. Word consciousness is considered to be one of these linguistic analytic skills but there are many others. In fact the reading process itself is portrayed as a metalinguistic task. Ryan points out that, like other metalinguistic tasks, reading

> ... differs from primary speech in that the utterances are isolated from their natural contexts.... Not only are the background meaning cues missing, but the very motive for speech, the need to communicate, is absent.... For young children with little ability to apply language strategies where meaning is not naturally and obviously apparent, more explicit instructions and more meaningful reading tasks may be required in order to elicit the appropriate strategies. (p. 16)

Ryan does not attempt to explain the gradual emergence of metalinguistic awareness strategies other than to indicate that linguistic self-awareness and reflection may lag behind but inevitably follow acquisition of implicit linguistic knowledge. However, she does suggest that a general underlying cognitive capability—development of "executive functioning"—may be involved. This term refers to the ability to select, monitor, and revise stretegies in problem-solving tasks (Belmont and Butterfield, 1975).

Ryan, McNamara, and Kenny (1977) have offered some evidence for this view. They reasoned that if lexical awareness is a prerequisite for achieving reading proficiency, then children who are deficient in lexical analytic skills may have trouble learning to read. Several tasks were administered to first and second graders in one experiment and to third- and fourth-grade remedial readers in a second experiment. Results revealed strong intercorrelations among various measures of lexical awareness and reading ability. Reading level of the younger subjects was significantly correlated with (1) their ability to classify auditory sounds as words, nonwords, or two words, (2) their ability to identify the one or two words added to a second sentence distinguishing it from the first, and (3) their ability to indicate awareness of a second meaning for a word by embedding it in a sentence. The correlations were all above .57, $p < .01$. However, reading ability was not correlated with performance in an oral sentence-segmentation task requiring that spoken words be marked with taps. In the experiment with remedial readers, reading level was significantly correlated with the ability to classify auditory sounds as words, nonwords, or two words ($r = .69$, $p < .001$) but not with sentence segmentation. (The other lexical tasks were not given in this experiment.) Furthermore, poorer remedial readers had more trouble in a written sentence-segmentation task and a written cloze task, and scores in these tasks were highly correlated with the auditory word-classification task (r above .63). These results lend some credence to Ryan's thesis that children with deficient metalinguistic knowledge also are less advanced in their reading ability. However, one question can be raised. Inspection of the mean performances of more and less proficient readers on the lexical analytic tasks revealed relatively high levels of performance by both groups, and even though mean differences were statistically significant, they were quite small between the groups. Thus, it is uncertain whether the less capable readers' lexical skills can be regarded as really deficient. Though these results are suggestive, what is needed is more direct evidence in an experimental study to determine whether enhancing the metalinguistic skills of readers facilitates their progress in learning to read.

There are two other studies offering some evidence consistent with Ryan's view—Ehri's (1977) word–pseudoword study and her word-learning experiment. The bimodal distributions evident in Figs. 1 and 2 suggest that a number of children do possess some lexical awareness before they learn to read. This makes Ryan's position more tenable in the sense that if lexical awareness is indeed a prerequisite or a facilitator of reading acquisition, then one would expect to find this capability among at least some prereaders. However, it remains to be determined whether children who possess lexical-analytic strategies are any more adept at learning to read than children who do not, and, moreover, whether children who lack such skills find it impossible to learn to read.

One discrepancy between the Ryan *et al.* study and Ehri's word-consciousness (1975) study occurred. In contrast to Ehri's positive results, Ryan failed to detect a relationship between performance on a sentence-segmentation task and reading level. This difference in findings may be a consequence of the fact that Ehri compared beginning readers to prereaders whereas Ryan *et al.* compared better to poorer readers. It may be that once a child has learned the rudiments of reading, he has acquired sufficient awareness of words to be able to succeed in some types of lexical-analytic tasks. In Ehri's word-learning study, this was true. Beginning readers at kindergarten, primer, and first-grade levels did not differ, and all learned the words in very few trials. This suggests that some metalinguistic operations with words may be easier and may be acquired earlier than others.

D. Experience Matching Print and Speech

Whereas Ryan (in press) has regarded lexical analysis as one type of meta-linguistic strategy, Ehri (1976, 1978) has viewed lexical awareness as a knowledge-based rather than a strategy-based capability bearing no necessary relation-ship to other metalinguistic capabilities. Rather it is word-specific and in-volves the possession of explicit knowledge about words, particularly context-dependent words, as discrete units of language. Word consciousness is thought to emerge as a consequence of the child's experience with printed language and his attempts to match up print and speech. Because words are the units of print, the child begins noticing and isolating words in speech, perceiving their component sounds, and amalgamating these sounds to their printed letters. Also, he becomes aware of the syntactic and semantic functions of words and connects these with their orthographic and phonological identities. Such experiences may be essential for becoming conscious of context-dependent words.

Although little evidence is available for deciding among alternatives, Ehri (1976) has identified three ways that word consciousness might emerge in the beginning reader. One possibility is that, as a consequence of interacting with print, the beginner suddenly awakens to the fact that meaningful sentences are comprised of word units. Achieving word consciousness may be like turning on the lights in his lexicon, rendering his implicit knowledge of words suddenly explicit and available for use. Alternatively, it may be that the beginner achieves lexical awareness only gradually, word by word, as he decodes and stores the printed forms of the words in his memory. This is the word-convention view grounded on the notion that segmentation of speech can be conducted in a variety of ways and that print conventions of English specify only one of these as correct. A third possibility is that, as a consequence of learning how to spell words, the reader acquires an orthographic representational system useful for creating visual forms of word sounds which otherwise are transitory and ephem-eral (Ehri, in preparation). This capacity to concretize word sounds may be especially important in the case of function words that have particularly short and nondistinctive acoustic forms and which lack any semantic markers to tie the words in memory.

The evidence for Ehri's position that learning to read enhances lexical aware-ness comes from several correlational studies (discussed previously) indicating that beginning readers do uniformly well on word-analytic tasks and they do substantially better than prereaders who are much more heterogeneous and in some respects deficient in their lexical-analytic skills. However, this evidence is correlational and so falls short of revealing whether readers acquired their word consciousness as a result of learning to read. Furthermore, there is evidence that not all children attain word awareness in this way. As indicated by the bimodal distributions in Figs. 1 and 2, there exist some children who are fairly sophisticated about words before they learn to read. For Ehri's view, this means that experience with written language is not a necessary condition for acquiring lexical awareness but only a sufficient condition. Although it may enhance word consciousness, there are other sources of word awareness as well.

E. Concluding Comment

Although Ehri's and Ryan's positions have been depicted as mutually exclusive with respect to the question of whether lexical awareness functions as a cause or a consequence of learning to read, this distinction may prove more apparent than real. There are two reasons for this. First, word consciousness may be more complex and multifaceted a capability than is recognized. For example, it is not clear whether the various lexical-analytic skills—segmenting sentences into words, discriminating words from nonsense syllables, recognizing and remembering isolated words, detecting single word changes in pairs of sentences—all entail the same degree of sophistication about words. To the extent that different aspects of lexical awareness are involved, and to the extent that these emerge successively rather than simultaneously, it becomes difficult to tie the capability to any one task or point in time.

Second, although alternative causal relationships between lexical awareness and learning to read may be distinguishable logically, they may not be all that separable and mutually exclusive in reality. Rather lexical awareness may *interact* with the reading acquisition process, existing as both a consequence of what has occurred and as a cause facilitating further progress. For example, the beginning reader may learn first the printed forms of sounds he recognizes as real words. In this case, lexical awareness helps him learn to read. Once known, these familiar printed landmarks may, in turn, aid him in recognizing the syntactic-semantic functions of unfamiliar printed words so that he can mark these as separate words in his lexicon. In this case, decoding written language enhances lexical awareness. If this picture of the process is more accurate, then there exists truth in both positions. Rather than struggling to determine which comes first, it may be more fruitful to adopt an interactive view and to investigate how a child applies his knowledge of spoken words to the task of reading printed language, and how enhanced familiarity with written words changes his knowledge of speech enabling him to accommodate better to print.

IV. ACQUISITION OF PRINTED LANGUAGE CONCEPTS

A. Vocabulary

The intent of research on lexical awareness has been to see whether children distinguish and recognize words as units of language, not to see whether children know the definition of the lexical term "word." This distinction is subtle but real (although in practice the distinction may be obscured by inadequately designed tasks). Whereas the vocabulary researcher constructs his tasks so that successful performance is dependent primarily upon the child's correct interpretation of terms such as *word* and also other printed language terminology, the lexical awareness researcher takes pains in his tasks to make sure that the child can figure out what he is supposed to do even though he does not know what *words* are. In the latter case, verbal instructions directing attention to word units are usually supplemented by examples, modeling, or practice with corrective feedback.

Although distinguishable, these two aspects of word knowledge are very likely closely tied. That is, the processes involved in learning the jargon of printed language may very well supplement the process of learning to organize one's perceptions in terms of these concepts. Children's acquisition of the meanings of terms describing printed language and the activity of reading has received some attention from investigators. Results suggest that prereaders possess little understanding but that as reading instruction progresses, they gradually acquire these verbal concepts.

Reid (1966) interviewed 5-year-olds enrolled in their first year of school. She inquired about their meanings for terms such as *word, number, letter, sentence, page, story, reading, writing, drawing, sounding out,* and *spelling.* She found that their use of these words was vague and confused. Many children failed to distinguish pictures from written symbols, words from names, letters from numerals. Repeated interviews later in the year revealed that some of these confusions had begun to disappear. A problem with Reid's study is that she limited her interaction with children to the verbal mode, and so it is hard to tell whether her subjects simply mixed up the terms in speech or whether they actually confused the referents.

Downing (1970a) replicated Reid's interviews and in addition structured his tasks to include concrete aids. Downing's subjects ranged in age from 4:11 to 5:3. Their answers to verbal questions resembled those of Reid's children. However, when asked about the meanings of terms with a real book in hand, Downing's subjects produced technical terms more frequently and more accurately although some confusion was still apparent. Downing also gave his subjects a word- and sound-discrimination task. Single nonhuman noises, vowel phonemes, words, phrases, and sentences were presented, and the child's task was to judge ("yes" or "no") whether each was a word and also whether each was a sound. He found that none of the children was successful in either task. Some thought the distinctions referred to human utterances versus nonhuman noises, others to meaningful utterances versus meaningless verbalizations and noises. In another paper, Downing (1970b) described results of a follow-up interview with these kindergartners 7 months later. Even at this point, none of the children had narrowed the term *word* to denote only single words in the discrimination task. However, a few correctly regarded *sound* as referring only to single phonemes. To explain his findings, Downing suggested that children below age 7 are at the intuitive stage of thinking and so have trouble dealing with abstract concepts such as those describing printed language.

Francis (1973) interpreted her results as challenging Downing's Piagetian-based explanation. She compared the relative importance of abstract conceptual development and reading instruction in accounting for children's comprehension of printed language terms. She tested 5- to 7-year-olds at four 6-month intervals during the course of learning to read. Their reading program began with a sight-word approach, shifted to phonics, and stressed practice in writing as well as reading. Francis gave the children reading tests, the Stanford Binet vocabulary test (her measure of abstract conceptual development), and she used concrete examples of printed language to explore their understanding of terms such as *letter, word,* and *sentence*.

Results on the printed language test revealed that initially children confused these concepts but that their confusion diminished over the 2-year period. They learned the concept *letter* before *word* and *word* before *sentence*. Francis suggested that confusion among the terms *word, letter, number,* and *name* occur not because the words are abstract but primarily because the concept *word* is ill defined and frequently overlaps in its application with the other terms.

In order to determine whether comprehension of printed language terms is more strongly related to reading ability or to abstract conceptual ability, Francis examined the rank–order correlation coefficients between measures of these abilities taken at age 7. She obtained the highest correlation between reading and printed language ($r = .41, p < .001$). When effects of abstract vocabulary level were partialed out statistically, a substantial relationship was still evident (partial Kendall $r = .34$). From this, Francis concludes that the ability to deal with abstract concepts is not as important a factor in the child's acquisition of printed language terminology as success in learning to read.

That children had derived their knowledge of printed language concepts from the reading–writing process was apparent in their answers to questions about use (i.e., "What do we use letters, words, sentences for?"). Francis reported that all children referred to spelling, reading, and writing in their replies, and few if any mentioned the use of words or sentences in spoken language. When the topic of words in speech was raised during informal conversations, some children claimed they "thought a pause occurred between all spoken words because there were spaces between words in writing" (p. 20). This observation suggests that printed language may provide children with the schema for conceptualizing and analyzing the structure of speech after they have learned how print works. Thus, Francis takes a position similar to Ehri's in suggesting that it is as a result of reading instruction that young children develop a consciously analytic approach to speech and acquire the notion that language can be divided into word and sound units.

B. Printed Word Forms and Boundaries

Children's awareness of structural features of written language, specifically their notions about what words look like and how they are separated in print, has also received attention from investigators. In his follow-up interview conducted 4 months after the first interview, Downing (1970b) questioned children about the spaces between words on a printed page. He found that few children were able to give clear explanations (which was not surprising since the concept of *word* had not yet been mastered). Most children merely indicated that without the spaces they would get "mixed up." When asked whether various printed units were words or not, children often judged in terms of length and excluded small words such as *a* and *in*.

Meltzer and Herse (1969) reported similar findings. They selected children who had been in first grade for 2½ months and examined how they identified the boundaries of printed words. These children had been reading in primers emphasizing vocabulary and sentence control rather than letter-sound correspondences. According to Meltzer and Herse, the word boundary convention had not been mentioned in the primers, and so children had been left to discover it for themselves. Each child was given two sentences printed on long strips of paper (17 by 3 inches) with oversized letters and "half again as much space between letters and words as in standard print," and was told to count and point to each word and then either to draw a circle around each word or to cut successive words off with scissors. Meltzer and Herse report the following sorts of errors which they order as possible stages in the emergence of the word boundary concept: (1) misinterpreting *word* to mean *letter* and segmenting each letter; (2) grouping multiple letters but disregarding boundary spaces as the dividing points; (3) using boundary spaces for divisions except for especially long words which were divided or short words which were combined; (4) using boundaries and also tall letters occurring in the middle of long words as dividing points. Also a relationship between primer reading level and type of error was detected, with better readers displaying fewer of the earlier error types. Meltzer and Herse traced these strategies to the structure of the children's preprimers, containing words five letters or less in length and an abundance of words beginning or ending with tall letters, including capitals.

Although these findings may appear to expose children's criteria for distinguishing printed words, there are some problems with the study. Meltzer and Herse ignored the influence of word-recognition ability, the most important basis for separating out words in print. In their study, it is not clear whether any, some, or all of the children could read the words in the sentences. If the better readers could recognize some words while the poorer readers could not, then performance differences in the task were actually reflecting different word-recognition abilities rather than different stages in the development of word-boundary concepts. Stages 1 and 2 where word boundaries were totally ignored may characterize children unable to recognize any of the printed words whereas Stages 3 and 4 may represent children recognizing some words but making division errors.

A similar investigation of prereaders' success in matching print and speech at the word level was undertaken by Holden and MacGinitie (1972). Several steps were involved in assessing whether a child could identify the visual representation of each utterance. First, he was required to segment the sentence orally by pointing to a poker chip as he pronounced each unit, then he counted the number of chips, then he was shown the correct printed form appearing with three distractors on a card and was told to point to the correct line. Some of the subjects were shown sequences of printed nonsense letter clusters, some actual sentences. Prior to the task, children were told about the convention of using empty spaces to mark word boundaries in print. In the final matching task, Holden and MacGinitie scored the number of responses in which printed segments were congruent with the child's oral segmentations (number of poker chips) and also the number of responses which conformed to printing conventions. They found that some subjects were able to respond congruently, and a few were able to respond conventionally on a majority of the sentences, although no child chose conventional representations consistently who did not also segment the sentences correctly in the oral mode. However, most of their subjects responded inconsistently or failed.

What to make of Holden and MacGinitie's results is not obvious. Like the study by Meltzer and Herse, this study slighted the importance of word recognition and the possibility that whether or not a child notices word-boundary markers and whether or not he can coordinate written and spoken language is very likely regulated by his ability to recognize the printed words comprising the sentences. Holden and MacGinitie provided some indirect evidence for this in reporting that their nonsense print confused those children who were familiar with sound–letter correspondences and who attempted to match print and speech on this basis. It is not clear why researchers would expect children who cannot read printed words and who have no decoding skills to notice or make use of word boundaries. And it appears trivial to investigate the word boundary knowledge of children who have these skills unless one is studying their reading or word-recognition abilities. Metalinguistic awareness normally **follows** acquisition of the basic linguistic skill. One does not expect a child to make grammatical judgments about totally unfamiliar sentence structures. Likewise, inquiring whether prereaders know about word boundaries makes little sense when they lack much experience with printed words.

A study by Mickish (1974) revealed that perception of word boundaries does develop slowly and is not fully complete even in children who have had a year of reading instruction. She tested 117 first graders at various levels of reading proficiency. After receiving preparatory instructions, children were shown one sentence comprised of familiar printed words with no spaces between them and were told to place marks between the six words. The sentence was read and repeated orally to them as they responded. The percentages of children successful at each reading level were: readiness (0%), preprimer (18%), primer (57%), and first-grade level (81%). Although results are impressive and surprising, the study is perhaps less than adequate procedurally. Children should have been provided with more than one sentence to mark, and the desired behavior should have been modeled to ensure that children understood what they were to do. Also, the claim that words were familiar and children could recognize their printed forms in isolation should have been verified. Despite its shortcomings the study does suggest that children do not acquire metalinguistic awareness of word boundaries until after they have achieved some reading proficiency. Hence, it is a waste of time to study these capabilities in prereaders.

C. Synthesis of Printed Word Symbols

One other line of studies, this line exploring children's ability to organize printed word forms into syntactic units has been conducted to determine whether young children might find this synthetic operation with written language particularly troublesome. Farnham-Diggory (1967) studied youngsters' ability to integrate sequences of printed symbols into meaningful sentences, an operation regarded as central in beginning reading. She tested normal children ranging in age from 3:4 to 7:3 and also a brain-damaged group. To avoid perceptual decoding problems as a factor limiting performance, she used simple line drawings (logographs) rather than alphabet letters to symbolize the following words: jump, walk, block, around, over, clap, hands, teacher. First she verified that children comprehended word meanings by having them act out a spoken command containing each of the words (i.e., "Show me how you can **jump.**"). Then these words were transferred to visual symbols printed on cards. Finally, eight two-word and three-word "sentences" were constructed for the child "by overlapping the logograph cards so that a connection between the symbols was suggested." For example, three cards displaying the symbols for *jump, around,* and *teacher* were placed together. The experimenter said "Now read this," prompted the child with the words if he had trouble, and told him to "do it."

The important finding was that despite being able to read the sequence of logographs, normal children below the age of approximately 6:6 and also brain-damaged youngsters as old as 13 demonstrated disjoint concepts rather than synthesized wholes. For example, in response to "Jump around teacher," they would jump up, then run around an object, then point to the teacher rather than simply hop around the teacher. On the basis of these results, Farnham-Diggory postulates a stage of neurological readiness which must be reached before children are able to integrate symbols into higher-order ideas.

In a follow-up study, Denner (1970) discovered that problem readers (first, third, fourth, and fifth graders) performed like Farnham-Diggory's younger subjects whereas average first-grade readers produced integrated meanings. Also, Farnham-Diggory and Berman (1968) examined the relationship between concrete operational thinking and logographic synthesis ability, and they found that while conservers performed almost perfectly, nonconservers responded to the separate words. From these results, it was concluded that poor readers, prereaders (below 6:6), nonconservers, and brain-damaged children, lack the requisite maturation and/or experience to be able to create integrated meanings out of the symbols.

However, some alternative explanations were examined by Hall, Salvi, Seggev, and Caldwell (1970). They pointed out that in the studies discussed in the preceding paragraphs, initial training on the separate pictographs and logographs gave the children a set for responding to the words individually rather than as whole sentences, and nothing was done subsequently to change this set. Also, some of the sentences may have eluded detection as wholes since they were ambiguous (and also since they lacked function words to signal syntactic units and relations). Third, the critical distinction between subjects succeeding and failing in the Farnham-Diggory and Berman (1968) study may not have been their stage of cognitive development but rather their training in reading, since nonconservers were more than a year younger than conservers.

In the Hall *et al.* study, 3- and 4-year-olds were trained to synthesize logographs, and their performance was compared to that of a control group. Training preceded testing by at least 2 days. Results revealed that trained subjects, despite being much younger than 6:6, synthesized most of the sentences while control subjects performed poorly. In a second experiment, Hall *et al.* replicated Farnham-Diggory's procedures with first-grade conservers and nonconservers who were equivalent in age and reading experience and found no differences in performances, with both groups successful. These findings refute the neurological readiness hypothesis and they suggest that reading ability rather than cognitive development underlies successful performance in the absence of clear instructions. From these results, it is concluded that since even 4-year-olds can construct an integrated meaning from a sequence of printed symbols provided they understand what to do, this operation with printed language is probably not a major source of difficulty in learning to read.

Hall *et al.* (1970) offered an important footnote for anyone studying individual differences in the acquisition of cognitive capabilities. They pointed out that when the purpose of a task is to distinguish stages of development or to identify capacity limitations or to infer lack of competence, the researcher

> ... must investigate and rule out alternative explanations. A more plausible solution to employ when a task proves too difficult for a group of subjects is to continue searching for other possible training conditions rather than using labels (such as maturation) as explanations. One strategy for looking at these other possibilities is to employ a detailed analysis of the criterion task. (p. 427)

This was the strategy used by Hall *et al.* to discover the flaws in the symbol synthesis task. Since conclusions involving capacity limitations are reached in many of the studies reviewed in this chapter, this constitutes an important strategy to apply in the evaluation of studies already completed, and an important precaution to keep in mind in the conduct of future studies.

V. SOUND CONSCIOUSNESS AND ITS CORRELATES

Despite the fact that they can pronounce words distinctly, at least well enough to be understood, young children have some difficulty detecting the presence of sound segments in spoken words, particularly phonemic units. Evidence from various studies suggests that the extent of their difficulty depends upon the complexity of the sound–analytic task they are given and the amount of training or practice provided. Once children learn how to read, however, many of these tasks become "duck soup" (Calfee, 1975). It remains unclear, though, whether sound consciousness is needed in order to begin learning to read and, if so, how it might be taught to prereaders.

One of the earlier studies exploring children's sound-analytic difficulties was conducted by Bruce (1964). Youngsters ranging in age from 5:1 to 7:6 were given 30 familiar words to analyze. The task was to report what word remained when a particular sound (either a first, middle, or final sound) was removed from the test word (e.g., pin-K, car-D, H-ill, mon-K-ey, ne-S-t; capital letter denotes the sound to be removed). Subjects were taken through several examples first to illustrate correct word analysis. Bruce found that children below a mental age of 7 were unable to perform the task although errors of children above age 6 indicated that they were attending to phonological features of test words. Above the age of 7, greater success was evident among children from schools emphasizing a phonics approach to reading, although the ability to spell was not predictive of successful sound analysis. Not surprisingly, middle sounds were harder to extirpate than first or final sounds. Bruce concluded that "a certain level of basic mental ability is necessary before the child can analyze words in this way" and that teaching experience can influence analytic skill once the basic mental age is attained. However, an alternative interpretation for Bruce's data is that ability to read is the factor underlying performance differences between 6- and 7-year-olds. It is hard to imagine how a child could make sense of instructions to remove sounds from words unless he had some means of representing and thinking about sounds as separate entities. A beginning reader's knowledge of alphabet letters as symbols for sounds might help him separate and hold the sound units in mind so he could analyze them.

Some confirmation for this interpretation was offered by Rosner and Simon (1971). They employed an auditory analysis test (AAT) very similar to Bruce's test, and they gave it to children in kindergarten through sixth grade at the end of the school year. The AAT consisted of 40 English words varying in length (one to four syllables). The child's task was to pronounce each word and then to repeat it with a specified sound omitted (i.e., syllable or consonant in initial, medial, or final position). The greatest gap in performance occurred between kindergarten and first grades, with mean scores of 3.5 versus 17.6 words correct, respectively. This indicates that reading instruction may very well be the important factor enabling children to conduct this sort of phonological analysis of words. However, performance continued to improve throughout the grades, with the second largest jump occurring between second and third grade (means of 19.9 versus 25.1 words correctly analyzed). This suggests that substantial reading proficiency may in fact be required to achieve complete success on sound extraction tasks. Clearly this is a capability not within the grasp of prereaders, at least not without some specific training. In a subsequent study, Rosner (1974) reported an attempt to teach 4- and 5-year-olds auditory-analytic skills. Although children did improve after a year's worth of instruction, they apparently did not achieve levels of mastery beyond the removal of first syllables or first sounds of words.

McNeil and Stone (1965) designed a phonological-analytic task which made fewer cognitive demands on the young child than the AAT. Theirs was a training study to determine whether phonetic analysis of words might be particularly difficult because of the holistic nature of words in the child's experience. They trained kindergarten prereaders (age 6 and below) to identify the presence of /s/ or /m/ sounds in either real words or nonsense syllables. For example, "Do you hear /s/ or /m/ in 'Came'?" Introductory examples were used to clarify the task, and responses were corrected following each test item (24 stimuli). The posttest consisted of four words and four nonsense syllables not presented during training. McNeil and Stone found that subjects analyzing nonsense terms produced more correct responses during training as well as on the posttest than subjects analyzing real words. In fact, the latter group performed only slightly above a chance level. This suggests that prereaders' difficulties in some phonological-analysis tasks may stem from the fact that they are required to break apart meaningful words whose semantic values may be distracting.

Kamil and Rudegeair (1972) uncovered another task-based factor limiting detection of the full extent of a child's competence at phonological analysis. They presented repeated contrast pairs distinguished by two consonants (e.g., /bob/ versus /dod/) and minimal contrast pairs differing only in the initial or final consonant (e.g., /bob/ versus /dob/; /bob/ versus /bod/) to kindergartners and first graders (mean ages 5:6 and 6:6, respectively). Children listened to one sound from a speaker on the left, the other sound from a speaker on the right, then they were asked "Who said X?" with the question coming from both speakers. Subjects were tested 6 times, 1 session per day, 5 minutes per session. Performance on contrast pairs differing in two consonants was superior to performance on minimal pairs. A more important observation was that performance on Day 1 was significantly poorer than performance on succeeding days. The error rate for kindergartners on the first day was 27.8% but it dropped to 15.7% on Day 2. The drop for first graders was from 18.6% to 8.5%. These results suggest that without repeated testing to allow youngsters to adapt to unfamiliar tasks, an examiner can be misled and may underestimate the extent of a child's competence in phonemic discrimination. However, although error rates were higher on Day 1, even kindergartners performed above chance. Thus, having only Day 1 scores would not cause one to conclude erroneously that subjects totally lacked the capability.

Calfee et al., (1972) administered several types of acoustic-phonetic tasks to kindergartners of ages 4:9 to 6:3. On a task resembling that used by Kamil and Rudegeair, they found that despite pretraining, children were uniformly unsuccessful in making phonetic judgments about word pairs. The task involved saying "yes" or "no" to indicate whether two CVC (consonant vowel consonant) words had the same or different initial sounds, or the same or different final rhyming segments. Why Kamil and Rudegeair's subjects performed so much better with essentially the same type of sound-matching discrimination task, even on Day 1, is unclear and probably has to do with task details. For example, pointing to a particular speaker may be less ambiguous a response than saying "yes" or "no." Also, use of nonsense sounds may have been less distracting than use of words, as McNeil and Stone found.

In the other tasks given by Calfee et al. (1972), subjects were more successful. About half of the sample was able to produce rhymes for words. The remaining subjects failed, yielding a bimodal distribution of scores. Also, some children were able to learn phonological segments of words in a paired associate learning task. The stimuli were familiar CVC words and the responses were final–VC segments (e.g., feel–eel, soap–oap). Furthermore, subjects were able to transfer the principle to different but related words. About 60% of the responses in the learning and transfer tasks were either correct or phonological errors indicating that the children were sensitive to the phonological character of the word pairs. A bimodal distribution of scores was also apparent here indicating that children either understood the relationship or missed the idea completely. Performances on the rhyming and the learning tasks were positively correlated, and in addition success on each was associated with superior alphabet letter knowledge. These results indicate that some kindergartners can analyze words phonetically given the right task, and that letter knowledge may play some role in this capability, although Calfee *et al.* (1972) are skeptical about the latter possibility.

In order to see whether performance in the *feel-eel* paired-associate learning task could be boosted, Calfee (1975) analyzed carefully the demands made in this task and designed some modifications to eliminate problems. The most significant problem turned out to be response availability. That is, prior to the time the child discovered the segmentation concept and could use the stimulus word to derive the response, he had trouble remembering the set of responses. By providing the child with a set of cards depicting acts or objects associated with the response words (i.e., *eyes, eat, ache*) and by teaching these responses first, the success rate during training on words such as *spies, heat, make* was increased to 90%. Also, generalization of the segmentation skill was substantial to both new stimulus words and new response words, about 70%, although performance declined somewhat when the task was conducted orally with no cards to prompt responses. Calfee further reports that kindergarten scores on these measures of phonemic skills predicted reading achievement at the end of first grade. This was particularly true for rhyming "errors" during training and phonemic segmentation transfer scores. The relevance of these capabilities for learning to read is clearly indicated.

Calfee added a footnote resembling the one by Hall *et al.* (1970), cited earlier, in which he underscored the importance of designing tasks which are fully adequate for revealing children's competencies:

> The point . . . is *not* to suggest that children can learn skills that they do not have to begin with. That would be worth little note. Rather, it is that under suitable training conditions, performance may change quickly and abruptly, as if the training were operating as an extended set of instructions. The child then demonstrates substantial competence in what earlier appeared to be a non-existent skill. (p. 30)

A. Phonemic and Syllabic Segmentation

Although the investigators mentioned in the preceding section have adopted various types of speech-analytic tasks in an effort to study capabilities related to beginning reading, none has employed a segmentation task to determine directly whether the child is able to perceive the sequence of units in speech which he must learn to match up to letter symbols in print. Liberman and Shankweiler (1977) have argued that even though a young child can discriminate minimal contrast pairs or isolate single sounds in words, he still may not be able to analyze successive sounds in words. Liberman, Shankweiler, Fischer, and Carter (1974) have explained why the sound-segmentation task presents special difficulties for children. Research on the nature of the acoustic signal has revealed that there are no acoustic boundaries separating phonemes in speech (Liberman, Cooper, Shankweiler, and Studdert-Kennedy, 1967). Rather phonemes overlap and are often coarticulated. Although a word such as *bat* may have three phonetic segments, it has only one acoustic segment which is approximately the size of a syllable. Liberman *et al.* (1974) state,

> In "bat," for example, the initial and final consonants are, in the conversion to sound, folded into the medial vowel, with the result that information about successive segments is transmitted more or less simultaneously on the same parts of the sound. . . . There is, then, no acoustic criterion by which one can segment the sound into its constituent phonemes. (pp. 203–204)

One who thinks he hears the separate phonemes may actually be imposing his knowledge of the alphabetic structure of printed language on speech. Or he may be basing his segmentations on articulatory gestures rather than acoustic cues.

The difficulty of conceiving of spoken language in terms of phoneme segments is also suggested by the fact that the alphabetic system of writing has been invented only once, relatively recently. In contrast, syllabaries and logographic systems have existed for thousands of years and have been independently invented several times (Gelb, 1963). Unlike phonemes, syllabic units are clearly marked in speech. Each contains a vocalic nucleus which functions as a peak of acoustic energy, and these peaks are audible cues corresponding roughly to the center of syllables. Although these acoustic cues do not enable the listener to distinguish boundaries of syllables, they do permit detection of the number of syllables present in speech and hence supply a basis for segmentation at the syllabic level.

In terms of reading acquisition, these facts suggest that the decoding-blending process routinely taught to beginning readers in phonics programs may be difficult if not impossible to perform. In learning to sound out printed letter sequences, the child is instructed to produce a sound for each letter and then to articulate the sounds in rapid succession. However, it is impossible to utter single phonemes without embedding them in syllables containing other phonemes. (There are a few exceptions such as the continuants /m/ and /s/.) If the child does as he is told, his production will necessarily bear little resemblance to the word he is sounding out. Blending the separate sounds of *bat* will yield the three-syllable nonsense form *buhatuh* rather than a one-syllable form. In order for this approach to succeed, the child needs to learn how to **abstract** the critical part from each syllabic segment, that part associated with the printed letter, and to blend just these abstracted "sounds" into one, not three syllables. This appears to be a fairly complex operation, particularly for the learner who does not yet understand the system. The difficulty stems mainly from the fact that pronunciation cannot proceed letter by letter but must weave together strands larger than a letter, sometimes extending across syllables, before the correct sound can be produced.

Liberman *et al.* (1974) have not attempted to explain how the child becomes able to segment the sound structure of spoken words. Perhaps it comes as a consequence of intensive instruction in reading and writing, perhaps from cognitive maturation. However, they have regarded as incontestable the point that if the beginner is to take advantage of the alphabetic system in learning to read, he must become aware of the phonemic segments in words so that these can be matched up to their corresponding letters in printed words.

In an experiment with preschoolers, kindergartners, and first graders, Liberman *et al.* (1974) demonstrated the greater difficulty of phonemic than syllabic segmentation of speech. Children were trained and tested to criterion in a tapping task. Each child listened to and repeated each word or sound, and then tapped out the number of segments (from one to three) with a stick on the table. During training, the child observed the correct segmentation of four sets of stimuli. He attempted to segment each himself both with and without a prior demonstration. A test trial followed in which 42 items (one to three segments long) were presented without demonstration. Incorrect segmentations were corrected by the experimenter. Testing was terminated early if the child tapped correctly on six consecutive items. Half of the subjects were given one-, two- and three-syllable words (e.g., *dog, yellow, popsicle*) to divide into syllables. Half were given one-phoneme nonsense sounds (e.g., /o/ as in boat) and two- and three-phoneme words (e.g., *he, toy*) to analyze into phonemes. Results revealed that at all grade levels phonemes were harder to identify than syllables. Furthermore, children in the lower grade levels had more trouble than older groups. In the phoneme segmentation task, none of the preschoolers and only 17% of the kindergartners reached criterion, whereas 70% of the first graders were successful. By contrast, in the syllabic task, nearly half of the preschoolers (46%) and kindergartners (48%) and most of the first graders (90%) reached criterion.

In order to examine the relationship between phonemic analysis and reading ability, Liberman (1973) administered a word-recognition test (Wide Range Achievement Test, WRAT) to the group of beginning second graders who had been given the phoneme segmentation task 3 months earlier as first graders. She found that among the poorer readers (i.e., the lower third of the sample divided according to WRAT scores), half had not reached criterion in the segmentation task. In contrast, none of the good readers (i.e., upper third) had failed the segmentation task. In a subsequent paper, Liberman and Shankweiler (1977) cite additional confirmation for the relationship between phoneme segmentation and early reading acquisition. Helfgott (1976) examined a number of skills in kindergartners and found that the best predictor of reading achievement measured (by

WRAT) the following year was the ability to segment spoken CVC words into their three constituent phonemes, with a correlation of $r = .75$. Studies by Zifcak (1976) and Treiman (1976) employing different procedures and populations of children obtained essentially the same highly significant relationship. Liberman (1973) concluded that "lack of awareness of phonemic segmentation may be one serious roadblock to reading acquisition."

Another study comparing phonemic and syllabic segmentation was conducted by Fox and Routh (1975) who employed a task less dependent upon memory than the tapping task employed by Liberman. The child was required to say "just a little bit" of a word or syllable spoken by the examiner (see Section II on Word Consciousness in this chapter for a more complete description of the procedure). Although they did not report how it was determined that a child had isolated a phoneme successfully, their results concurred with Liberman *et al.*'s (1974) findings in suggesting that syllabic segmentation is easier than phonemic segmentation. Whereas even 4-year-olds could identify syllable segments, not until age 6 did the ability to extract phonemes emerge. Furthermore, a substantial correlation between phonemic analysis scores and reading achievement ($r = .50$, $p < .01$) was obtained.

From the preceding studies, it is apparent that phonological segmentation and reading ability are closely related. However, the evidence presented has been primarily correlational. That is, individual variations in both capabilities have been produced by "nature." As a result, it is not clear whether one causes the other, and if so, which causes which. There are two studies which involve attempts to go beyond this and to manipulate at least one variable experimentally. The first was performed by Fox and Routh (1976) who explored the relationship between phonemic segmentation ability and success in a sequence of tasks analogous to decoding and word recognition operations. Four-year-old children (mean IQ = 112) from professional families were classified as segmenters or nonsegmenters according to whether they scored above or below the median on Fox and Routh's test of phonemic segmentation. These children underwent a series of experiences: (1) they were taught to discriminate Gibson letterlike symbols; (2) they were trained to point to letters in order from left to right; (3) half of the children were presented with pairs of separate sounds and were trained to blend the sounds to produce a word—the other half received no blending training; (4) all children were given a maximum of 20 trials to learn associations between the five letterlike forms and five spoken sounds; (5) finally, they were taught to recognize two lists of printed words (me, see, way; we, say, may) comprised of the letter–sound relationships taught previously. Learning was continued to a criterion of two consecutive errorless trials or 20 trials. Results revealed that whereas segmenters were able to learn the word lists (Task 5, $\bar{X} = 12.9$ trials) none of the nonsegmenters reached criterion in 20 trials. Furthermore, blending training (Task 3) facilitated word learning among segmenters ($\bar{X} = 10.3$ trials with blending versus 15.6 trials without blending) but not among nonsegmenters. This suggests that children who can recognize phonemic segments in speech may very well have an easier time making sense of and mastering component skills in beginning reading.

Although results are interesting, there are some problems with the Fox and Routh (1976) study limiting conclusions. First, it is not clear to what extent the segmenters had already learned the rudiments of reading and the alphabetic principle underlying printed language. Upper-middle-class 4-year-olds were sampled, and segmentation ability was employed to select subjects. Since segmentation is highly correlated with reading skill (as previously mentioned), and since some 4-year-olds do learn to read (Durkin, 1966), this is not an unlikely possibility. It may be that segmenters could keep up with the sequence of tasks because they were already familiar with these operations. One other problem with the study is that it is not clear whether inadequate phonemic segmentation skills rather than some other difficulty accounted for poorer performance on Task 5. Subjects were trained on three to four tasks prior to the word-training task. Since mastery was not required in these other tasks, and since the skills taught were prerequisites for the final task, failure on any one might account for troubles on the word task. Since performances on these other tasks were not reported, one cannot be sure what the source of nonsegmenters' difficulty was on the word-learning task. In conclusion, it may be that children need to be able to segment phonemically in order to learn to read. However, this study falls short of demonstrating this relationship.

Whereas Fox and Routh (1976) and Liberman and Shankweiler (1977) viewed segmentation ability as a prerequisite for learning to read, there is the alternative possibility that children improve dramatically in phonemic analysis as a consequence of learning to read. Goldstein (1976) examined both of these possibilities. He pretested 4-year-olds, selected only prereaders and divided them into experimental and control groups ($N = 23$), gave the experimental subjects 13 weeks of reading instruction using a special method proven effective with mentally retarded children (the "Ball–Stick–Bird" system by Fuller, 1974), and then administered the posttests. The pre- and posttests included measures of children's ability to synthesize separate syllables and phonemes into recognizable words and to analyze words into component phonemes and syllables. Intercorrelations among these tests were very high suggesting that a common factor accounted for performance, namely, sensitivity to the sound properties of spoken words. Goldstein found that the reading training was effective and that among children receiving instruction, pretest scores on the word analysis–synthesis tests were good predictors of reading achievement independent of IQ ($r = .51$, $p < .05$, on a word recognition test; $r = .69$, $p < .05$, on a story reading test). Furthermore, among experimental subjects, there was a significant negative correlation between pretest word analysis–synthesis scores and improvement of these skills on the posttest ($r = -.92$, $p < .001$). Although the same relationship was evident among control subjects ($r = -.56$), the correlation was not statistically different from zero, and was significantly smaller than the experimental group correlation ($p < .05$). Also, among experimental subjects, there was a substantial drop in the variation of analytic–synthetic scores from the pretest to the posttest (i.e., the standard deviation declined from 11.7 to 5.4 for the experimental group, from 13.7 to 11.4 for controls). These results suggest that phonological sensitivity is both a contributor to and a consequence of learning to read. That is, possession of these skills helps children learn to read, but also learning to read improves these skills. In terms of criteria identified in the preceding discussion, phonological sensitivity would appear to be a facilitator of reading acquisition rather than a prequisite or merely a consequence.

Goldstein's proposal that phonemic sensitivity operates as both a cause and a consequence is particularly noteworthy. It constitutes an interactive view of the relationship between a linguistic capability and learning to read. This sort of interactive view was also proposed earlier in this chapter as a means of portraying the relationship between word consciousness and learning to read. Such a view is perhaps less common than the view that, if a prereading capability is causally related to reading acquisition, then it must be a prerequisite. In order to qualify as a prerequisite, however, it is necessary to demonstrate that the capability must be fully acquired before instruction in reading can commence successfully. This was apparently not the case in Goldstein's study. Rather, children insensitive to sounds at the outset nevertheless made progress in learning to read. One reason why investigators may be quick to confer prerequisite status on capabilities is that among instructional theorists, it is currently fashionable to regard component skills as prerequisites (Gagné, 1970; Otto and Chester, 1976). The approach recommended is to conduct a task analysis of a particular capability, identify component subskills, order these hierarchically, and regard those lower down in the hierarchy as prerequisites to be mastered before higher subskills are learned. However, the term ''prerequisite'' may be applied all too casually without sufficient evidence to distinguish it from facilitator skills.

Although Goldstein's findings suggest that sensitivity to word sounds may be a facilitator of reading acquisition, his results are not conclusive. Neither he nor Fox and Routh manipulated this variable experimentally. Rather than creating individual or group differences in their studies, they left the variations to ''nature.'' Because of this, the relationships observed remain essentially correlational. In order to test experimentally the hypothesis that a skill such as phonemic segmentation is a prerequisite for learning to read, one needs to select prereaders who are not able to segment, assign them randomly to experimental and control groups, teach the experimental group to segment, then provide reading instruction to both groups and compare their progress. If the experimental group advances while the control group does not, then the claim for prerequisite status is confirmed.

This experimental design would also be appropriate for identifying facilitator skills. Facilitator status would be indicated if the experimental subjects achieved quicker success and moved along more rapidly in learning to read but the controls also made progress. In addition, if the target skill is central to the reading acquisition process, then the controls should be observed to acquire the skill without being explicitly taught. It is important to note that in such a study, effects of the experimental treatment may last only temporarily. Because learning to read involves acquisition of many capabilities besides those under the influence of the target skill, sooner or later, the untutored controls will "catch up" to those who possessed the skill beforehand. At this point, earlier skill differences among learners will no longer correlate with reading achievement. This fact is important for studies evaluating the benefits of advance training in facilitator skills. Since it is not clear how long the effects of training will last, reading progress must be monitored rather than simply measured once at the end of the year.

One other part of Goldstein's (1976) study merits attention in terms of its implications for reading instruction. He reported that skill improvement among his trained subjects was uneven, that when change scores on the analytic and synthetic syllable and phoneme tests were analyzed separately, all but the phonemic segmentation scores improved among experimental subjects. One reason why phonemic analysis might not have been influenced by reading instruction, he speculates, is that this capability was not important in the Ball–Stick–Bird system. According to Goldstein's task analysis, the ability to synthesize phoneme segments played the central role. This raises the possibility that whether phonemic segmentation or phonemic synthesis or any other linguistic capability contributes to the reading acquisition process may depend on the skill requirements of the particular instructional program employed. Venezky (1976) has advocated this point of view in his discussion of prereading capabilities. He separated prereading skills into two groups according to the locus of their impact on initial reading—whether they are important for sight word recognition or for acquisition of decoding skills. Three skills are thought to be important for sight word recognition: attending to letter orientation; attending to letter order; attending to word detail. Four capabilities are regarded as prerequisites for acquisition of decoding skills: differentiating letters; associating sounds with letters; blending sounds to produce words; identifying and matching sounds within words. To what extent the linguistic capabilities considered in this chapter are more central to some aspects or methods of learning to read than to others remains to be investigated.

From the preceding discussion, one might gather that prereading instruction is a matter of selecting and teaching those skills which are found to contribute to the reading acquisition process. This is the approach advocated by Venezky (1976) among others. However, Goldstein (1976) mentioned another approach. Rather than developing subskills separately, one might employ simplified reading systems which are compatible with prereaders' existing skills and which engage them in the reading process. Two possibilities are the syllabary program designed by Gleitman and Rozin (1973), and invented spelling activities discussed by Chomsky (1977) and Read (1971, 1973). These are described in greater detail further on in this chapter. Goldstein mentioned a third, Fuller's (1974) Ball–Stick–Bird system. Goldstein favors the simplified system approach as a means of preparing prereaders for beginning reading because such systems inform children how the various component skills are to be employed in the reading task. These children are thus better equipped to transfer their skills and knowledge to formal reading instruction than are children who have simply practiced components in isolation.

Before concluding this section, there is one other sound-analytic study to be mentioned. The work of Liberman *et al.* (1974) and Fox and Routh (1975) already discussed indicated that the task of segmenting words into syllables is fairly easy for young children. Rozin, Bressman, and Taft (1974) offered some evidence contrary to this, although the task they used was not a segmentation task but rather required the child to match spoken and printed words on the basis of sound and letter length. Urban and suburban kindergartners and also older urban children were tested. Each was shown two words or nonsense sounds printed on a card, the words/sounds were pronounced, and the child was told to point to one of them. For example, the experimenter said, "One of these words says *mow*. Say *mow*. The other word says *motorcycle*. Say *motorcycle*. Now point to the word that says *motorcycle*." Preliminary instructions were given, but the child's responses were not corrected. The long word was the target half of the time, the short word the other half. In another test, the printed words were shown and then hidden in boxes differing in length. This was done to eliminate the distracting influence of the letters among subjects who concentrated on decoding them. Also, a short training program was employed to clarify instructions for subjects having trouble with the task. Results revealed that whereas 43% of the suburban kindergarteners were able to recognize most of the sounds correctly and explain their responses, only 8%–11% of the urban kindergartners could do this. Mean scores of the latter subjects were at a chance level. Even with training, scores of the urban kindergartners improved very little. Among urban first and second graders, there was still a number of children unsuccessful despite having completed (without success) at least a year of reading instruction with a phonics-oriented method. Rozin *et al.* concluded that, for some unknown reason, inner city children have great difficulty grasping the nature of the writing system and learning the basic sound-tracking principle of written language.

B. Acquisition of Sound Consciousness

The research on prereaders' ability to conduct phonological analyses of the speech stream suggests that the capability is not easily displayed, particularly at the phonemic level, and that mastery may require substantial instruction or practice. Because of the possibility that sound-analytic capabilities stand as prerequisites or facilitators of reading acquisition, various ways of teaching these skills have been devised. There are three fairly diverse approaches which are tailored to handle some of the difficulties previously described, although observations and claims by proponents are preliminary and in need of further empirical verification.

1. Syllabary

Gleitman and Rozin (1973) have attempted to simplify the mapping of speech in written language. They employed printed syllable units rather than phoneme units so that correspondences between the visual code and the sound stream were more transparent. They based their proposal on the premise that the various psychoacoustic tasks given all at once in alphabetic systems prove very confusing to the beginning reader. He is expected to track the sound stream in terms of phonemic segments but many of these segments are impossible to isolate as separate sounds. He is expected to distinguish between letter names and letter sounds and to perceive the relevant phoneme clue in only one part of the sound he produces (i.e., letter *B*, sound *buh*, critical part /b/). He is expected to blend the critical parts of these letter sounds to form recognizable words and then to think about their meanings. This is clearly expecting too much of the beginner. What Gleitman and Rozin proposed was to simplify these tasks so that the principles of sound tracking, segmentation, and blending would be easier to acquire. Since the syllable as a unit of sound is more accessible for reflection than the phoneme, they proposed that children be taught to segment the sound stream into syllables and to read printed syllable symbols before they tackled the problem of phonemic segmentation with alphabet letters. Gleitman and Rozin were particularly interested in making the analysis of sound accessible to inner city youngsters who have problems learning to read presumably because of the special difficulty posed by this psychoacoustic analytic process (Rozin, *et al.*, 1974).

Gleitman and Rozin outlined the components of their program as follows. An example of their materials, entitled "Candy for Andy," is presented in Fig. 3.

1. The child is first shown that the relation between sound and meaning can be represented visually; this is accomplished with sequences of pictographs.
2. A syllabic segmentation of normal English orthography is then introduced, using both the monosyllabic pictographs of (1) and some further syllables written as arrays of English letters.
3. Employing a rebus approach, we next show the child that these syllabic units can be combined on the basis of their sound values to yield further meaningful words, thus

Fig. 3.   Sample of syllabary employed by Gleitman and Rozin (1973, p. 467).

emphasizing that the orthography tracks the sound system.
4. Very much later, we will try to show the learner that the abstract unit represented by the
   alphabetic sign is an efficient mnemonic for the inconveniently large set of syllables.
   Traditional phonics or linguistic methods will putatively be more useful at this stage, when
   the insights of the first three steps have been acquired. (p. 464–465)

Gleitman and Rozin reported the results of a preliminary study exploring the feasibility of a syllabary approach with kindergartners, some of whom had already failed to learn the principles with phonemes and letters. They found that components were mastered very easily. Syllables in spoken words were recognized, children learned to name and combine separate symbols, half pictographic, half word spellings, and they could transfer their learning to new blends of symbols never seen or read before. Gleitman and Rozin suggested three possible applications of their approach:

> The syllabary may serve as an introduction to an explicit phonemic program, or it may
> serve as a substitute for such a program in case phonemic concepts can be induced spontane-
> ously from the syllabic basis, or, finally, the syllabary may serve as a remedial approach in
> case some learners cannot grasp the phonemic principle. (p. 474)

However, no evidence has as yet been provided to verify that syllabary instruction facilitates acquisition of phonemic segmentation skills. In a study to investigate whether a base syllabic curriculum might improve urban children's success in learning to read, Gleitman (1974) reported essentially negative results. Thus, the value of a syllabary in accomplishing the claims of its creators remains uncertain.

2. Materializing Sounds

A very different approach has been proposed by Elkonin (1973), a Russian psychologist, who agrees that phonological analysis is the major hurdle in learning to read. However, rather than simplifying the spoken unit of analysis from phonemes to syllables, he proposed that the notational system for representing sequences of phonemes in words be simplified. Elkonin's position is that beginning readers must become aware of **sequences** of sounds in words and this must be mastered before they learn how alphabetic characters function as models of these sequences. Evidence indicates that children may be able to hear individual sounds in words but they are not necessarily able to analyze successive sounds. Because it is difficult to utter acoustic segments which correspond exactly to the separate phonemes, these spoken units must be represented concretely to help the child focus on and objectify the sounds as they are sequenced. Elkonin proposed a series of instructional stages by which children learn to analyze sound sequences. At the first stage, unmarked counters rather than alphabet letters are employed as materialized speech forms. This eliminates confusion resulting from similarities and differences between and among sounds, letters, and letter names. An example of Elkonin's Stage 1 materials is presented in Fig. 4. The child is shown a picture to remind him of the word (e.g., *balloon*) and below it a horizontal rectangle divided into squares to indicate how many sound segments the word contains. (Note: The diagrams in Fig. 4 correspond to Russian rather than English words.) He is trained to "pronounce every sound in succession in a drawl" and to place a cardboard counter in a square of the diagram for each sound. "For example, 'mama' must be pronounced in succession like this: 'm-m-mama' ma-a-a-ma' mam-a-a-a.'" A counter is placed in the diagram as each sound is stressed in its context. When finished, the child names the sounds corresponding to the counters. At the second stage, the analysis is performed orally without counters, at the third stage, mentally with no oral analysis. According to Elkonin, this serves to implant the abstract idea that words are structured in terms of successive sounds. Initially, the temporal succession of the sounds is materialized in the form of spatial successions with the diagram and counters. With training and practice, this representation becomes internalized and the child becomes able to perform the analysis in his head.

Elkonin (1971, 1973) reported a series of experiments with 6-year-old prereaders who at the outset were unable to analyze sounds in words. Groups were given five to seven training sessions of various types, each group with an equivalent number of words. Results confirmed Elkonin's hypothesis that materialization of the sound-analytic task would enable children to master the procedure of analyzing words into component sounds. Children who were trained to segment words first with pictures, diagrams, and counters, and then with counters alone,

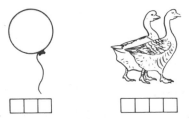

Fig. 4.   Apparatus for materializing the sound structure of words. From Elkonin (1973).

were able to analyze 82% of the words correctly on a transfer task requiring oral segmentation of words without counters. In contrast, children given training with counters but no pictures or diagrams analyzed only 31% of the words correctly, and children trained to segment by uttering sounds aloud without any materialization completely failed the transfer task. Analysis of errors of the third "no materialization" group revealed that the greatest difficulty was in overcoming the more natural articulatory division of words into syllables so that vowels and consonants could be separated. The second group given counters but no other prompts differed most from the successful group in their ability to segment polysyllabic words. Elkonin attributed the partial success of the second group to the effect of the counters in helping them discriminate the separate sounds. He attributed the complete success of the "full materialization" group to the presence of a diagram which helped them distinguish the order of successive sounds and recognize the full sound structure of the words. However, the diagram also served to guide subjects' analyses and provide immediate printed feedback. Responses of the other groups during training were less adequately prompted and corrected. These results indicate that children can be taught to analyze speech into phonemic segments with the help of concrete markers and diagrams before they are introduced to alphabet letters and actual printed language.

Elkonin (1973) suggested some additional steps in preparing the child for printed language. Once he can analyze sounds without the aid of diagrams and counters, these are reintroduced, attention is drawn to the distinction between vowels and consonants, and the child is given counters in two colors to fill in the diagrams. Next a third color is added and the distinction between hard and soft consonants is learned. Also, phonemic categories are named. When this analysis can be performed without counters and diagrams, the child is ready for printed characters marking vowel phonemes. In this fashion, printed language is introduced gradually step by step. Although Elkonin presented no data, his claim is that such experiences will facilitate the process of learning to read.

Liberman and Shankweiler (1977) have regarded Elkonin's approach as a most promising means of teaching phonemic segmentation skills. In fact, they have carefully spelled out its "pedagogical virtues." Regarding Stage 1 procedures, they have commented:

> First, the line drawing keeps the whole word in front of the child throughout the process of analysis so that he does not have to rely on auditory memory to retain the word being studied. Second, the diagram provides the child with a linear visual-spatial structure to which he can relate the auditory-temporal sequence of the spoken word, thus reinforcing the key idea of the successive segmentation of the phonemic components of the word. Third, the sections of the diagram call the child's attention to the actual number of segments in the word, so that he does not resort to uninformed guessing. Fourth, the combination of drawing, diagram, and counters provide concrete materials which help to objectify the abstract ideas being represented. Fifth, the procedure affords the child an active part to play throughout. Finally, the color

coding of the counters leads the child to appreciate the difference between vowels and consonants early in his schooling. (p. 25)

Liberman and Shankweiler made some additional recommendations regarding the phonemic structure of the words given to the child to segment at Stage 1. Analysis should begin with words containing continuant consonant phonemes (e.g., /s/, /n/, /m/) so that the child can utter each of the phoneme segments separately without attaching extraneous vowels to the consonant sounds (i.e., *uh* sound in /b/ uttered *buh*). Also, since evidence suggests that VC syllables are easier to analyze than CV syllables which in turn are easier than CVC syllables, Liberman and Shankweiler recommended that this order be employed to select and present words at Stage 1.

3. Invented Spelling

In contrast to the foregoing approaches, the third means of introducing pre-readers to printed language has been proposed not as an instructional system to be taught but rather as an activity youngsters can practice and enjoy for its own sake. It is the activity of creating spellings for words and sentences. Proponents assert that, as a consequence of continued efforts to perform more effectively, prereaders gradually acquire phonemic segmentation skills, letter-sound knowledge, and a strong interest in learning to read. Findings reported by Read (1971, 1973), Chomsky (1971, 1977), Paul (1976), and Conway (1976) are rich in suggesting how the ability to invent spellings evolves and how it might be linked and contribute to the process of learning to read. However, systematic evidence for this approach has not yet been gathered, and there are some inadequacies with the data stemming from the fact that it was collected more or less informally. Criteria for the inclusion or exclusion of subjects are not mentioned and hence the characteristics of children able and unable to invent spellings remain unknown. In most cases, the reading ability of subjects has not been determined to clarify whether they are readers or prereaders. Nevertheless, observations and hypotheses from these reports are valuable in suggesting how invented spelling activities might prepare children for reading instruction.

In contrast to Elkonin, Liberman, and Shankweiler who recommended delaying the introduction of alphabet letters to spell words until the child can segment speech phonemically, Read and Chomsky have suggested spelling as a beginning point. They have argued that even 4-year-olds have some knowledge of letter names and sounds and that they can use this knowledge effectively to invent their own spellings for words and messages. For children who cannot print the alphabet, moveable letter cutouts or blocks are provided. In selecting letters to represent sounds detected in spoken utterances, the children proceed systematically although their spellings deviate from conventional orthography. Although deviant, the spellings are surprisingly uniform across children. Chomsky (1971) cited the following inventions as typical: BOT ('boat'), GRL ('girl'), MN ('man'), CHRAN ('train'), YL ('while'). In deciding which letters to choose, the inventor pays attention not just to phonemes or acoustic segments but also to articulatory features. That is, he monitors what his mouth is doing during word and letter name pronunciations, and he abstracts from these dimensions in choosing his letters. Children may spend considerable time alternating and comparing letter-name and word sound pronunciations until they achieve a fairly close match, particularly for vowels. In choosing letters, novices may incorrectly regard the initial sound of letter names as the relevant part. Conway (1976) described one child spelling *day* who recorded the letters, DA. Then, detecting an additional sound at the end, he searched for a third letter. This entailed repeating the word together with several letter names and attending closely to the position of his tongue and mouth. He finally settled on the letter N, and *day* was spelled DAN, apparently because of the match detected between the initial sound in *en* and the final sound in *day*.

Chomsky has supplied other examples of unusual inventions reflecting this sort of careful analysis. Children commonly spell *track* and *chicken* very similarly, as HCRAK and HCICN, because they detect affrication at the beginning of both words and they select the letter H because the latter part of the name of this letter (aich) has this same sound. It is important to note how much abstraction from sound is performed by these children. Sound segments may share one phonetic feature but differ in another respect, and children consistently respond in terms of the shared feature, abstracting from the difference. In the foregoing example, they choose HC to represent initial sounds in *chicken* and *traffic* despite a difference in place of articulation. These capabilities are noteworthy in light of other research previously cited suggesting that acoustic-phonetic analysis is very tough for prereaders.

Relevant to the preceding discussion of word consciousness, Chomsky (1974) reported one particularly interesting characteristic in the inventions of younger children attempting to write out full messages: a failure to leave empty spaces between the words in their sentences. To the extent that prereaders lack word consciousness and are unfamiliar with this convention of printed language, their omission is not surprising. This is consistent with Ehri's (1976) contention that children do not become aware of word boundaries until they learn to read.

On the basis of her observations of kindergartners at different levels of reading readiness, Paul (1976) proposed that the emergence of invented spelling ability can be divided into four stages. At the first stage, spellers recognize and represent words in terms of their initial sounds only (e.g., F for *Friday*). At the second stage, both initial and final sounds are noticed and recorded (e.g., RT for *rabbit*). Also, vowels that "say their own names" may be represented (e.g., TE for *tea*). Third-stage children begin to separate short vowel sounds from conso-nants. Also, they represent medial sounds in print (e.g., FES for *fish*). Although

Read (1971) described an underlying system for their vowel choices, Paul (1976) reported being unable to discover any consistency in the sound–letter relationships displayed by her children. Rather they chose a variety of vocalic letters to stand as markers for vowel sounds. The fourth stage is exhibited mostly by children who have some reading ability. Their spellings bear a closer resemblance to conventional forms, and sight vocabulary words are printed correctly.

Comparison of the assertions of Chomsky (1977) and Paul (1976) regarding the development of invented spelling reveals a difference in their formulations. Chomsky suggested that certain prerequisite capabilities are needed in order to invent spellings, and she listed several requirements. The child must know alphabet letters. He must be able to segment phonemically. And he must be aware that letters can be used in sequence to represent sounds in the same sequence. In contrast, Paul's description of stages implied that these capabilities may emerge at one or another point as the child's inventive spelling ability develops. The following illustrates how Chomsky's prerequisites might be acquired at the various stages. Knowing only some alphabet letters, beginning spellers at Stage 1 might be prompted to learn the shapes and names of unfamiliar letters in order to expand their spelling capabilities. Lacking full sensitivity to phoneme segments, Stage 2 spellers might begin to recognize illusive phonemes within words after they have practiced detecting the more salient boundary phonemes and recording these letters. The letter sequencing principle might be acquired at Stage 3 as the child practices writing out words spelled with three letters. Conway (1976) observed spellers who successfully detected all three sound segments in words but printed the letters to reflect their order of detection—first, final, medial—rather than the temporal position of the sounds in the word. With practice or instruction, the sequencing principle might be easily picked up at Stage 3.

There is a problem with the stage view, however. The implication that children pass through all of the stages appears to be untrue. For example, Conway tested her kindergartners only once, and they were not practiced spellers, yet they performed at different stages revealing varying degrees of competence in accordance with their knowledge about speech and print. It may be that Paul's stages are better regarded as levels of sophistication in creating spellings, and it may be that the capabilities identified by Chomsky as prerequisites are among those which underlie and determine whether a child will be able to create spellings at Levels 1, 2, or 3. Additional theory and research on the relationship between children's developing spelling capabilities, their speech-analytic skills, and their knowledge of conventional letter-sound relationships and word spellings are needed to resolve some of these uncertainties.

Inventive spelling has been proposed as an activity to be employed in the kindergarten classroom. There are several features which make it attractive. This activity is fairly easily undertaken by prereaders. It holds intrinsic appeal. It enables children to utilize and possibly expand their knowledge about print and speech. And it introduces children to components of the reading process. The one reservation expressed by teachers and parents is that children may not learn how to produce conventional spellings for words. However, Chomsky's and Read's data suggest that this does not happen. Although early invented spellings may deviate substantially from standard orthography, deviancy declines as the child's experiences with printed language grow. Chomsky reported that once children began inventing spellings, they became very curious about printed language and began to notice and ask about all the words they saw. Also they employed their letter-sound knowledge to try to decode conventional words. Paul (1976) reported that when her students learned the standard spelling for a word they often spontaneously substituted it for their own invention.

Observations suggest that as the child's encounters with standard print mount, not simply his treatment of individual words but, what is more important, his spelling *system* shifts in order to accommodate to standard forms. One dimension of this shift is from phonetic to morphemic spellings for inflections (e.g., past tense sound /t/ spelled first as WALKT shifts to the letter D and becomes WALKD) (Read, 1971). Another principle acquired is the idea that there are silent letters in words. However, this principle may be applied in unexpected ways. Chomsky (1977) reported that her own child, an inventive speller, saw the word *Joan,* sounded it out as *Jane,* and then explained his mistake, "Oh. I see. The A is silent. I thought the O was silent."

It is interesting that both Read and Chomsky noted that children are not confused by discrepancies between how they spell and what they read. In fact, spellers often decode standard orthography more accurately than their own spellings, and they may invent several alternative spellings for the same word at one time or another. Inventors may even be unable to read back at a later time messages they have written. Chomsky (1977) gave an example of a child who spelled the word *pencils* as PASLS, then later read the printed word PENCILS correctly and also the form PASLS correctly as [paez-lz]. One reason previous productions are forgotten is that the speller's attention is focused upon creating an accurate phonetic transcription of sounds, not upon looking at and reading what they have written. Paul (1976) observed that the act of figuring out a word is far more intriguing than the final product which often goes unnoticed.

Chomsky (1977) indicated that she is firmly convinced that children who are introduced to the printed word through writing will have a much easier time learning to read. In fact, she claims that they may be able to teach themselves! One possible advantage of a child's being introduced to print in this way is that he may acquire knowledge of a very flexible sound-letter system having the potential for generating and justifying many alternative spellings. This may prove particularly valuable in learning to read English, a language that requires the beginner to store and remember conventional spellings which are systematic but highly variant (Venezky, 1970).

From a developmental perspective, the process of inventing spellings is especially appealing as an introduction to reading because of its natural evolutionary
course, a course consistent with Piaget's theoretical notions about the development of intellect in general (Rohwer, Ammon, and Cramer, 1974). The child
enters the process by using what he already knows: names and shapes of alphabet
letters. Instruction is required merely to get the analytic process underway, not to
teach the child anything really new. He applies what he knows to achieve a useful
valued end, i.e., written messages. No tasks requiring acquisition of interim
responses or routines later to be phased out are involved. Existing cognitive
structures in the form of spelling principles guide the child's productions. Processes cf assimilation and accommodation govern the fate of these principles as
they are modified and elaborated. As the child applies his rules successfully to
the spelling of new words, the principles receive confirmation. Encounters with
standard print introduce modifications into the system, and gradually the principles change to accommodate to conventional orthographic regularities. The child
learns to trust his own linguistic perceptions, and he judges his spellings primarily in terms of their consistency with his system and only secondarily as right or
wrong on the basis of conventional criteria external to the system.

Read (1971) in discussing the educational implications of his research on
inventive spellings, conveyed a similar view of the relationship between the
child's knowledge of language and the spelling–reading task,

> We can no longer assume that a child must approach reading and writing as an untrained
> animal approaches a maze—with no discernible prior conception of its structure.... Evi-
> dently, a child may come to school with a knowledge of some phonological categories and
> relations; without conscious awareness, he may seek to relate English spelling to these in
> some generally systematic way.... In the classroom, an informed teacher should expect that
> seemingly bizarre spellings may represent a system of abstract phonological relations of
> which adults are quite unaware.... Such a child needs to be told, in effect, that his phonolog-
> ical judgments are not wrong (though they may seem so to most adults), and that it is
> reasonable, indeed necessary, to categorize abstractly what he hears. (p. 32–33)

Read argued that reading instruction needs to build on the child's insights, not
ignore or reject them. What is essential is that, when the child interacts with
printed language, he employs his systematic knowledge of letter names and
sounds, regardless of his level of sophistication, and that his system be given
time to accommodate to conventional orthography, so that his knowledge will
continue to develop as a system rather than as arbitrary or rotely memorized
associations. Read has suggested that not only before but also during beginning
reading instruction, the child be encouraged to create spellings in accordance
with his expectations about how print and speech are systematically related.
Otherwise this systematic knowledge may not unfold.

4. Concluding Comment

Read's proposals as well as those of Chomsky, Elkonin, Liberman and Shankweiler, and Gleitman and Rozin, offer interesting possibilities regarding the introduction of printed language to preschoolers and kindergartners. Whether an approach where children are taught to read or write in simplified form or whether the prereading subskills approach will prove more adequate as a means of preparing students for beginning reading is a matter awaiting further investigation.

REFERENCES

Bellmont, E., and Butterfield, J. Assessing and improving the cognitive function of mentally retarded people. In J. Bailer and M. Sternlich (Eds.), *Psychological issues in mental retardation.* Chicago: Aldine, 1975.

Bereiter, C., and Engelmann, S. *Teaching disadvantaged children in the preschool.* Englewood Cliffs, N.J.: Prentice–Hall, 1966.

Berko, J. The child's learning of English morphology. *Word,* 1958, **14,** 150–177.

Bernstein, B. Linguistic codes, hesitation phenomena, and intelligence. *Language and Speech,* 1962, **5,** 31–46.

Bruce, D. J. An analysis of word sounds by young children. *British Journal of Educational Psychology,* 1964, **34,** 158–170.

Calfee, R. C. *Assessment of independent reading skills: Basic research and practical applications.* Unpublished manuscript, Stanford University, 1975.

Calfee, R., Chapman, R., and Venezky, R. How a child needs to think to learn to read. In I. L. Gregg (Ed.), *Cognition in learning and memory.* New York: Wiley, 1972.

Calfee, R. C., Fisk, L. W., and Piontkowski, D. *"On-off" tests of cognitive skills in reading acquisition.* Paper presented at Claremont Reading Conference, 1975.

Carroll, J. B. *Comprehension by 3rd, 6th and 9th graders of words having multiple grammatical functions.* Research Bulletin, Educational Testing Service, Princeton, N.J., 1971.

Chappell, P. F. *Early development of awareness of lexical units and their syntactic relations.* Paper read at American Educational Research Association Annual Meeting, Chicago, Ill., 1968.

Chomsky, C. Write first, read later. *Childhood Education,* 1971, **47,** 296–299.

Chomsky, C. Write now, read later: Young children's invented spelling systems. Presentation at the Institute in Reading and Child Development, University of Delaware, June, 1974.

Chomsky, C. Approaching reading through invented spelling. In L. B. Resnick and P. A. Weaver (Eds.), *Theory and practice of early reading.* Hillsdale, N.J.: Lawrence Erlbaum Association, 1977.

Conway, J. *On the road to reading.* Unpublished manuscript, University of California, Davis, 1976.

Denner, B. Representational and syntactic competence of problem readers. *Child Development,* 1970, **41,** 881–887.

Downing, J. Children's concepts of language in learning to read. *Educational Research,* 1970, **12,** 106–112. (a)

Downing, J. The development of linguistic concepts in children's thinking. *Research in the Teaching of English,* 1970, **4,** 5–19. (b)

Downing, J., and Oliver, P. The child's conception of 'a word.' *Reading Research Quarterly,* 1973–1974, **9,** 568–582.

Durkin, D. *Children who read early.* New York: Teachers College Press, 1966.

Ehri, L. C. Word consciousness in readers and prereaders. *Journal of Educational Psychology*, 1975, **67**, 204–212.

Ehri, L. C. Word learning in beginning readers and prereaders: Effects of form class and defining contexts. *Journal of Educational Psychology*, 1976, **68**, 832–842.

Ehri, L. C. *Can readers distinguish single spoken words from pseudowords?* Unpublished manuscript, University of California, Davis, 1977.

Ehri, L. C. Beginning reading from a psycholinguistic perspective: Amalgamation of word identities. In F. B. Murray (Ed.), *The Development of the reading process*. International Reading Association Monograph (No. 3). Newark, Del.: International Reading Association, 1978.

Ehri, L. C. Reading and spelling in beginners: The development of orthographic images as word symbols in lexical memory. In U. Frith (Ed.), *Cognitive processes in spelling*. London, England: Academic Press, in preparation.

Elkind, D. Piaget's theory of perceptual development: Its application to reading and special education. *Journal of Special Education*, 1967, **1**, 357–361.

Elkonin, D. B. Development of speech. In A. V. Zaporozhets and D. B. Elkonin (Eds.), *The psychology of preschool children*. Cambridge, Mass.: The MIT Press, 1971.

Elkonin, D. B. USSR. In J. Downing (Ed.), *Comparative reading: Cross-national studies of behavior and processes in reading and writing*. New York: MacMillan Company, 1973.

Farnham-Diggory, S. Symbol and synthesis in experimental "reading." *Child Development*, 1967, **38**, 221–231.

Farnham-Diggory, S., and Berman, M. Verbal compensation, cognitive synthesis and conservation. *Merrill–Palmer Quarterly of Behavior and Development*, 1968, **14**, 215–228.

Fox, B., and Routh, D. K. Analyzing spoken language into words, syllables, and phonemes: A developmental study. *Journal of Psycholinguistic Research*, 1975, **4**, 331–342.

Fox, B., and Routh, D. K. Phonemic analysis and synthesis as word-attack skills. *Journal of Educational Psychology*, 1976, **68**, 70–74.

Francis, H. Children's experience of reading and notions of units in language. *British Journal of Educational Psychology*, 1973, **43**, 17–23.

Fuller, R. Breaking down the IQ walls: Severely retarded people can learn to read. *Psychology Today*, October, 1974, 97–102.

Gagné, R. M. *The conditions of learning*. New York: Holt, Rinehart & Winston, 1970.

Gelb, I. J. *A study of writing*. Chicago: University of Chicago Press, 1963.

Gleitman, L. R. Teaching reading by use of a syllabary. Presentation at the Institute in Reading and Child Development, University of Delaware, June, 1974.

Gleitman, L. R., and Rozin, P. Teaching reading by use of a syllabary. *Reading Research Quarterly*, 1973, **8**, 447–483.

Goldstein, D. M. Cognitive-linguistic functioning and learning to read in preschoolers. *Journal of Educational Psychology*, 1976, **68**, 680–688.

Goodman, K. S. The 13th easy way to make learning to read difficult: A reaction to Gleitman and Rozin. *Reading Research Quarterly*, 1973, **8**, 484–501.

Hall, V. C., Salvi, R., Seggev, L., and Caldwell, E. Cognitive synthesis, conservation, and task analysis. *Developmental Psychology*, 1970, **2**, 423–428.

Hatch, E. *The preschool child's concept of words as lexical units*. Working paper, SWRL Educational Research and Development, 1969.

Helfgott, J. Phonemic segmentation and blending skills of kindergarten children: Implications for beginning reading acquisition. *Contemporary Educational Psychology*, 1976, **1**, 157–169.

Holden, M. J. Metalinguistic performance and cognitive development in children from 5 to 7. *Dissertation Abstracts International*, 1972 (Dec.), **33** (6-B), 2791–2792.

Holden, M. H. *Word awareness, reading, and development*. Paper presented at National Reading Conference, St. Petersburg, Florida, December, 1975.

Holden, M. H., and MacGinitie, W. H. Children's conceptions of word boundaries in speech and print. *Journal of Educational Psychology,* 1972, **63**, 551-557.

Holden, M. H., and MacGinitie, W. H. *Metalinguistic ability and cognitive performance in children from five to seven.* New York, N.Y.: Teachers College, Columbia University, 1973. (ERIC Document Reproduction Service No. ED 078-436.)

Huttenlocher, J. Children's language: Word-phrase relationship. *Science,* 1964, **143**, 264-265.

Inhelder, B., and Piaget, J. *The Early growth of logic in the child.* New York: Humanities Press, 1964.

Kamil, M. L., and Rudegeair, R. E. Methodological improvements in the assessment of phonological discrimination in children. *Child Development,* 1972, **43**, 1087-1089.

Karpova, S. N. Osonznanie slovesnogo sostava rechi rebenkom doshkol'nogo vozrasta. *Voprosy Psikhologii,* 1955, **4**, 43-55. (For an abstract in English, see D. I. Slobin, Abstract of Soviet studies of child language. In F. Smith and G. A. Miller (Eds.), *The genesis of language.* Cambridge, Mass.: MIT Press, 1966.)

Liberman, A. M., Cooper, F. S., Shankweiler, D., and Studdert-Kennedy, M. Perception of the speech code. *Psychological Review,* 1967, **74**, 431-461.

Liberman, I. Y. Segmentation of the spoken word and reading acquisition. *Bulletin of the Orton Society,* 1973, **23**, 65-77.

Liberman, I. Y., and Shankweiler, D. Speech, the alphabet and teaching to read. In L. B. Resnick and P. A. Weaver (Eds.), *Theory and practice of early reading.* Hillsdale, N.J.: Lawrence Erlbaum Association, 1977.

Liberman, I. Y., Shankweiler, D., Fischer, F. W., and Carter, B. Explicit phoneme and syllable segmentation in the young child. *Journal of Experimental Child Psychology,* 1974, **18**, 201-212.

McNeill, J. D., and Stone, J. Note on teaching children to hear separate sounds in spoken words. *Journal of Educational Psychology,* 1965, **56**, 13-15.

Meltzer, N. S., and Herse, R. The boundaries of written words as seen by first graders. *Journal of Reading Behavior,* 1969, **1**, 3-14.

Mickish, V. Children's perception of written word boundaries. *Journal of Reading Behavior,* 1974, **6**, 19-22.

Otto, W., and Chester, R. D. *Objective-based reading.* Reading, Mass.: Addison-Wesley, Co., 1976.

Pascual-Leone, J. A mathematical model for the transition rule in Piaget's developmental stages. *Acta Psychologica,* 1970, **32**, 301-345.

Paul, R. Invented spelling in kindergarten. *Young Children,* 1976, **31**, 195-200.

Read, C. Pre-school children's knowledge of English phonology. *Harvard Educational Review,* 1971, **41**, 1-34. Copyright © 1971 by President and Fellows of Harvard College.

Read, C. Children's judgments of phonetic similarities in relation to English spelling. *Language Learning,* 1973, **23**, 17-38.

Reid, J. F. Learning to think about reading. *Educational Research,* 1966, **9**, 56-62.

Rohwer, W. D., Jr., Ammon, P. R., and Cramer, P. *Understanding intellectual development.* Hinsdale, Ill.: Dryden Press, 1974.

Rosner, J. Auditory analysis training with prereaders. *Reading Teacher,* 1974, **27**, 379-384.

Rosner, J., and Simon, D. P. The auditory analysis test: An initial report. *Journal of Learning Disabilities,* 1971, **4**, 384-392.

Rozin, P., Bressman, B., and Taft, M. Do children understand the basic relationship between speech and writing? The Mow-motorcycle test. *Journal of Reading Behavior,* 1974, **6**, 327-334.

Ryan, E. B. Metalinguistic development and reading. In F. B. Murray (Ed.), *The development of the reading process.* Newark, Del.: International Reading Association, in press.

Ryan, E. B., McNamara, S. R., and Kenney, M. *Lexical awareness and reading performance among beginning readers. Journal of Reading Behavior,* 1977, **9**, 399–400.

Thomson, J. W. *The implicit unit of linguistic analysis used by advantaged and disadvantaged children.* Unpublished doctoral dissertation, University of Illinois, 1968.

Treiman, R. A. *Children's ability to segment speech into syllables and phonemes as related to their reading ability.* Unpublished manuscript, Department of Psychology, Yale University, 1976.

Venezky, R. *The structure of English orthography.* The Hague: Mouton, 1970.

Venezky, R. L. Prerequisites for learning to read. In J. R. Levin and V. L. Allen (Eds.), *Cognitive learning in children: Theories and strategies.* Madison, Wisc.: University of Wisconsin, 1976.

Zifcak, M. *Phonological awareness and reading acquisition in first grade children.* Unpublished doctoral dissertation, University of Connecticut 1976.

READING THAT COMES NATURALLY: THE EARLY READER

JANE W. TORREY

Department of Psychology
Connecticut College
New London, Connecticut

We often talk as though teaching were almost the same process as learning, that is, we assume that by whatever method we choose to teach reading, by that method the pupil learns. If we teach phonics, we think children must learn to "decode" letters into sounds. If we teach by the "look-and-say" method, we think they must be unable to "sound out" words. Yet every teacher knows that not every pupil learns everything that is taught and some learn things that are not taught. If we want to understand the process by which children learn to read, as opposed to the method by which they are taught, we must observe the learners themselves, how they try to do it, and what they actually learn to do. Unfortunately, it is difficult to make these observations in an unbiased way in the schoolroom where all procedures are controlled. The teacher sets each individual task. The text offers a selection of material based upon some theory of teaching reading. Testing evaluates skills which may or may not be relevant to the particular child's process of learning to read. Whatever theory of reading instruction guides the lessons, that theory is likely to dictate or at least strongly influence both the learning strategy of the pupils and the pattern of their early achievement. If we are to observe how reading comes about naturally, we need to find children who learn by themselves without having any standard instructional process imposed upon them. Unfortunately, reading usually does not happen when there is no teaching. Most humans who are not taught to ready simply do not learn. Schools can generally count on finding that very few of their first-graders already know much about reading. Happily for our purposes, however, there are a few exceptions, the so-called **early readers.** The self-taught have to be early readers because in order to learn by themselves in a society where education is compulsory, they have to start before they are put into school. Their first reading begins before the appointed age when the particular educational system deems the average child to be "ready" for reading.

One purpose of examining early readers in a collection on reading instruction is to be able to observe the nearest thing we can get to the "natural" process of learning to read. Early readers, at least most of them, do have help of some kind, but since they are not in a situation where learning to read is regarded as important, their efforts are purely voluntary. Because their learning activities are optional, they are more under their own control. Materials that do not interest them can be laid aside. Subgoals that seem irrelevant to them can be ignored, as can their failure in any particular "task." People will only be interested in what they do learn, and all their accomplishments will be credited to them, never taken for granted. Most important, their own purposes and only their own purposes will be served. Early readers are strongly motivated for whatever they learn almost by definition, because if they were not so motivated there would be nothing to make them learn, and nobody would notice the lack.

An examination of the available research on early readers together with some hypotheses about the nature of reading will serve as a basis for making inferences on the nature of their learning processes. Implications for research and teaching include some paths that have already been explored as well as some that remain to be tried. It is hoped that the early readers will provide some pointers for their more average fellows.

I. STUDIES OF EARLY READING

Dolores Durkin (1966) has explored the histories and abilities of two large samples of early readers in California and New York. Her findings constitute the great bulk of our evidence on the subject. Durkin's California study began with 5103 children entering first grade in Oakland one year, substantially all in the system. In the first 2 weeks of school they were tested, and 49, or about 1%, were able to meet the criterion of identifying 18 words from a list of 37. These children were tested to determine any special abilities, their home backgrounds were investigated for clues as to how and why they could read, and their careers in school were followed for several years to determine the implications of early reading for later education. Durkin continued her work with a sample selected from 40 New York City schools. This time it was necessary to select schools, but an attempt was made to include all socioeconomic levels. About the same number of first graders were tested as in Oakland. This time 156 qualified as early readers by the same criterion. A control group was also formed of 30 nonearly readers matched for intelligence and first-grade teacher with 30 of the early readers.

Other studies of early readers have been on a smaller scale. Evans and Smith (unpublished) examined certain characteristics of 19 children in Columbia, South Carolina, who read at or above the second-grade level before they were 6. King and Friesen (1972) selected 31 children from kindergarten in Calgary, Alberta, by having teachers nominate possible early readers (out of a total of 4282 in the kindergartens) and then administered a standardized reading test at the first-grade level. Plessas and Oakes (1964) located early readers from the San Juan Unified School District near Sacramento, California, by administering the California Reading Test to 40 children nominated by their first-grade teachers. Those with scores of 2.0 were investigated further to discover what their prereading experiences had been. Briggs and Elkind have done two studies. In the first study (1973) a sample of 16 early readers and matched nonearly readers were collected by means of advertising in Rochester, New York. Briggs and Elkind compared the groups' performances on Piagetian tasks. In the second study (unpublished) 38 early readers were located by means of Durkin's 37-word screening test in the population of about 2700 children entering kindergarten in two school districts, one urban and one suburban. A control sample was matched for IQ, age, sex, classroom, and scores on the Peabody Picture Vocabulary Test. Morrison, Harris, and Auerbach (1971) selected in New York City 58 black disadvantaged children, 4% of those tested, who could read one or more words when they entered first grade. They were compared with matched and unmatched nonreaders. McCracken (1966) reported measures of eight kindergarten and first-grade children in Fulton, New York, who were found by their teachers to be reading in the first weeks of the school year. In addition to these formal studies, we have the report of Mayne (1963), who described two early readers who turned up in a kindergarten class in Hartford, Wisconsin, and intensive observation of John, a 5-year-old early reader in Atlanta, Georgia (Torrey, 1969).

A. Abilities

1. Intelligence

Perhaps the first question that comes to mind in trying to understand early reading is whether it takes any unusual ability. Do some children read early because they are simply more intelligent than the others? The answer seems to be yes and no. Table I shows that in most studies early readers on the average had higher intelligence scores than others. Intelligence, then, seems to help, but from the existence of very intelligent children who have great difficulty with reading, we already know that it is not sufficient. Now if we look at the distributions of IQ scores among early readers, we find that superior ability is also not a necessary condition. Most of the studies included some average and below average scores. Especially relevant to this question are the data of the Silberbergs (1967) on a sample of early readers taken from among children who had been referred to a psychological clinic. The lowest tested IQ was 34, while of the 26 children whose IQs could be tested, 16 were below 100. Intelligence is therefore not a crucial factor in reading.

2. Special Abilities

Several other special abilities that are plausibly related to early reading have been studied. Verbal ability would be an obvious hypothesis in spite of John's 96 on verbal intelligence (Wechsler Primary Scale of Intelligence). Evans and Smith did find evidence of special abilities in the Illinois Test of Psycholinguistic Abilities (ITPA) scores of their early readers and matched controls. All the readers showed superior abilities on two of the subtests. One of these was "sound blending," which consists of having the tester pronounce the phonemes of a word separately, as in $sh-i-p$ to determine whether the testee can identify the word. It would seem to be a useful skill for "sounding out" unfamiliar words. The other subtest (part of the Detroit Test of Learning Aptitude) was visual letter memory, in which the testee is shown a series of lowercase letters for as many seconds as there are letters and then required to tell what they were. The matched nonearly readers' scores were significantly lower on both these subtests. The early readers also all scored at least above average on the subtests of auditory reception, visual memory for geometric designs, auditory association, verbal expression, manual expression, and auditory closure. Briggs' and Elkind's second study also found a large and significant difference between early readers and

TABLE I

Study	N	Selection	IQ mean (Range)	Superior abilities	Percentage upper-middle class
Durkin (California)	49	All entering first grade in Oakland	121 (91–170)	—	14
Durkin (New York)	30	All entering selected New York City schools	133 (82–170)	—	40
Evans and Smith	19	Teacher nomination	Mostly superior	Sound blending Visual letter memory	—
King and Friesen	31	Teacher nomination	111 (SD = 10)	Visual discrimination Letter names Word recognition Learning rate	62
Plessas and Oakes	20	Teacher nomination	128	—	55
Briggs and Elkind	16 & 33	Advertising	—	Sound blending Perceptual decentration Conservation Reflection Ambiguous pictures Creativity	Higher than matched nonreaders
Morrison et al.	58	Teacher nomination	—	Pattern copying Identical forms Phonemes Letter names Learning rate	0
Silberbergs	28	Clinic referral	(34–126)	—	—
McCracken	8	Teacher nomination	132	—	—
Mayne	2	Teacher nomination	140	Verbal meaning	—
Torrey	1	Teacher nomination	104	—	0

nonearly readers on the ITPA sound-blending subtest and a smaller significant difference in the auditory closure subtest. Although these data certainly suggest that these particular verbal abilities contribute to early reading, the authors also point out that the causal relation could be the other way around. The ability to read might make possible the high scores on these tests. An already reading child could know how to sound out words as a result of being able to read without having used that technique in acquiring reading skills. King and Friesen found their readers significantly superior in some subtests of the Gates–MacGinitie

Reading Skills Test: visual discrimination, letter-name knowledge, and word recognition. They also did significantly better on the learning rate subtest of the Murphy–Durrell Reading Readiness Analysis. Morrison *et al.* found their disadvantaged "readers" much superior to controls in the Thurstone pattern copying and identical forms tests. They were also far superior in the Murphy–Durrell subtests for phonemes, letter names, and learning rate. The purpose of both of Briggs' and Elkind's studies was to find out whether there is a relationship between early reading and a Piagetian measure of perceptual decentration. In the first study they found the readers significantly superior on tests of conservation as well as on the Kagan reflection–impulsivity tests, and tests involving ambiguous pictures and creativity. Through factor analysis they identified a factor they called "operativity," which had a heavy loading on the Piagetian and the impulsivity tests and significantly differentiated the early readers. In the second study the results confirmed the differences for conservation and creativity, adding the ITPA differences mentioned earlier. The picture ambiguity and reflection–impulsivity tests did not differentiate the groups this time. Mayne's two bright kindergarten readers were given the SRA Primary Mental Abilities test, which includes a developmental age score for "verbal meaning." They scored 7 years, 10 months and 8 years, 2 months respectively. Of the special verbal abilities tested the ITPA sound-blending subtest seems to differentiate early readers the most strongly and consistently. Whether this ability is the cause or the effect of reading remains to be seen. Other variables are significantly different for readers and nonreaders, but the two groups still overlap considerably. The data on differentiated abilities generally suggest that early readers may owe their achievement in part to a number of small advantages in ability, but they do not point to any identifiable factor that alone explains fully their unusual learning ability.

Before leaving the subject of abilities, it is worthwhile to consider the Silberbergs' (1971) hypothesis that ability to read is a "normal psychological variant," that is, an ability separate from intelligence and other verbal abilities which is distributed normally in the population. Their proposal is based on the fact that dyslexia can exist in high ability individuals while what they call "hyperlexia," or superior word recognition coupled with low comprehension, is found in some of very low ability. Early readers, then, could be people with an inherited trait that made reading especially easy for them without regard to their intelligence. For those with very low reading ability, high intelligence or other verbal abilities would not always compensate.

B. Socioeconomic Status

Another commonly expected correlate of early reading is socioeconomic status. Since upper-middle-class occupations generally require considerable education and since education is therefore valued in middle-class families, it makes sense to suppose that their children will have more encouragement, more materials, and more help in their spontaneous efforts in the direction of reading. It was somewhat surprising, therefore, when Durkin's California study showed only seven children (14% of the 49) whose families could be called upper middle class. About a third were "lower middle" while more than half were "upper lower." Most of the other studies found some tendency to conform to expectation. Table I shows an estimate of the percentage of upper-middle-class children in each study based on various kinds of socioeconomic data. Morrison *et al.* had selected only "disadvantaged" children, so we infer that none were upper middle, but their criterion of reading, being able to identify one or more words, makes the group not comparable to the others in reading level. In assessing the influence of socioeconomic status, it should be remembered that Durkin's California study is the one least susceptible to socioeconomic bias in the original selection of subjects, since almost all the children in a large urban school system were tested, and this is the study in which the higher levels were least well represented. Even if we assume, however, that the other studies show a more typical situation, we will still have to say, as in the case of intelligence, that socioeconomic level (which includes parents' education) is apparently only a minor factor in early reading.

C. Family Reading Experiences

Turning from general demographic family variables to more specific home factors, the family characteristics that directly concerned reading were another subject of several investigations. Durkin found in California that all the parents could read and that in a majority of the families at least one parent thought she/he read more than average. However, in about 20% of the families, neither parent made this claim. In New York, with a control sample for comparison, Durkin found that more mothers of early readers said they read oftener than the average adult. Early readers were also read to more often at home. The attitudes of parents toward their children's early reading seemed relevant in the California study, where the lower socioeconomic levels were overrepresented among early readers. At the time of that study (1957) it was the conventional wisdom that children should learn to read in school, not before. Upper-middle-class mothers were usually aware of this and some said that they had refused on this ground to help when their child asked questions about words. Among the working-class parents of early readers, however, Durkin found few who knew about or subscribed to this idea. It seemed possible that these people had more early readers because they were less unwilling to give the necessary help. In the New York study, done in 1961, when it was no longer so fashionable to discourage home instruction, she found more early readers from the higher socioeconomic levels.

More mothers of early readers were college graduates and fewer believed that reading should be left to the schools.

Durkin found in her California sample that parents and older siblings had contributed materially to early reading in a variety of ways. Many read to the children, sometimes pointing out words and telling the children how to sound them out. They also answered many questions about what words were and how to spell them. They bought books, school-type workbooks, blackboards, and other writing materials. In the New York study, where comparison with nonearly readers was possible, she found that the readers were more likely to have been sent to nursery school. The mothers of early readers also never described themselves as "busy," suggesting that they were easily available when help was wanted. Parents of early readers were read to extensively at home and in kindergarten. Their parents as well as the parents interviewed by King and Friesen often reported teaching letter sounds and providing workbooks and materials.

D. Behavior of Early Readers

The background information so far described for early readers has been the environment they grew up in and the people they had contact with. In discussing help given to children, however, we are beginning to look at another possible set of factors, namely the behavior of the early readers themselves, since for the most part the parental help, especially in answering various kinds of questions, was actively solicited by the children. There are several characteristics of the children and their activities that seem relevant. Durkin asked her New York families about the play habits of their children. Early readers more often tended to play quietly and alone with fewer toys. Briggs and Elkind also mentioned sedentary activities in their early readers. Early readers were more likely to have attended nursery school and less likely to watch nursery school type television programs, perhaps because these come during nursery school hours. Durkin's children were also reported to watch less television than others, whereas Plessas and Oakes reported much television viewing among their group. King and Friesen compared age of walking and talking and found no difference for early readers.

Summarizing the home data so far there is nothing very conclusive in these home habits to enlighten us about early reading. However, several other activities commonly reported do seem related. Briggs' and Elkind's early readers were significantly more likely than nonreaders to watch The Electric Company where reading is consciously taught. In California many of Durkin's early readers were reported to have played school at home, usually on the initiative of an older sister who was already in school. Early readers typically were reported to have asked for all kinds of help from family members, and her New York study showed that parents had more often given such help to early readers than to nonearly readers, probably mostly because the former were more apt to ask for it. Durkin's California children often made use of the words that surrounded them on signs, labels, and television, especially commercials. New York parents of early readers very frequently mentioned interest in words being aroused by television, with many of the children's queries about words originating there. Another kind of activity that figured prominently among early readers was writing and printing. Durkin described all her subjects as "paper and pencil kids." King and Friesen also reported more drawing and painting by early readers. John, in Atlanta, had been much more interested in commercials than in other television fare. His mother reported that she could never get his attention until a commercial was over and that he knew them all by heart. This was, in fact, the only clue to how he might have learned to identify words, since his mother said no one in the family taught him to read or read to him. Inspection of commercials during children's programming reveals about 40 printed words per half hour that are simultaneously pronounced by voice. Many of these words are brand names which often have common or regular spelling patterns and are easily pronounceable.

E. Motivation of Early Readers

This discussion of children's activities suggests not only ways in which new information and practice with already learned material have been obtained, but also the underlying patterns of motivation that dispose certain children to engage in these learning experiences at sufficient length for reading. Prominent in all reports of these activities is the amount of motivation. Durkin collected the adjectives most often used in describing early readers in the California study. "Persistent" and "perfectionist" were included in half or more of the cases. Competitiveness and eagerness to keep up with a sibling were also prominently mentioned. Other motivational descriptions were mostly comments on the unusual interest the early readers showed in being read to, in printing, in spelling, and, of course, in reading. On television, commercials, weather reports, and quiz shows were often mentioned, all material in which written words appear frequently. What is most important about the learning process with these children is that the initiative came overwhelmingly from the children. Only 11 of Durkin's 49 California parents admitted having deliberately set out to teach their children reading, and in many of those cases the children may have prompted them by their own curiosity about words.

The findings on the histories of early readers might be summarized by saying that they were not taught to read, they just learned in an environment that contained enough stimulation and material. They took the initiative and reached out to find just the specific help they needed in solving the problem of how to read. If we are to make use of their experience, we must now ask exactly how they went about piecing together this great puzzle of written language. What teaching technique did they use on themselves? To understand how they solved it we must first examine again just what the puzzle is. What does it mean to read? What is the system to be understood?

II. THE NATURE OF READING

A. Decoding from Alphabet to Speech

One obvious fact about reading is that our own writing system is alphabetic, that is, written symbols represent individual sounds on the phoneme level, not syllables and not words. The system suggests that it can be solved on a part-to-whole basis, starting with the small set of letters representing sound units, piecing together words on the basis of the phonemes corresponding to each letter or grapheme, assembling larger units like phrases and sentences and so on from the individual words, and finally interpreting the meaning of the whole after it has been rendered into spoken form. The theory implicit in this view of reading is similar to the one that underlies the audio-lingual method of foreign language teaching, namely that because oral language is the first in time that it is the essential basis for all learning and understanding of other linguistic systems. According to this notion of reading, the ideal writing system would be a close grapheme–phoneme correspondence so that the written word could be readily translated into the spoken word, which would make it easier to understand. This situation is approximated in several European countries, where academies of letters keep updating the spelling to keep pace with oral linguistic change. English spelling, of course, departs considerably from such a plan, but it is still possible to relate the spelling of many words to the sounds that compose them in spoken English, provided spelling units of more than one letter are apprehended. Leonard Bloomfield (1961) devised a method of teaching reading in English that was based on the assumption that reading consisted basically of translating letters and other spelling units into spoken sound. The same assumption underlies all of the so-called "phonic" approaches to teaching reading as well as spelling reforms and the Initial Teaching Alphabet.

There are, however, a number of reasons to question the assumption that all language education must work primarily through the spoken medium. In respect to second-language learning, Scherer and Wertheimer (1964) found that, in beginning German, students taught by the audio-lingual method did not have the expected advantage in reading and writing the new language. Their superiority in speech did not transfer directly to reading, and students trained in written language without particular oral emphasis did better on those skills than the audio-lingual group. In respect to native language reading, there are several reasons for questioning whether decoding to speech is the key to learning. One is that alphabetic writing systems do not exactly represent speech even if we ignore spelling irregularities. English words that are spelled quite regularly often cannot be pronounced without knowing the context. To modify an example given by Smith (1973) the words in the following list do not contain enough clues for either vowel sounds or emphasis patterns:

read   minute   permit

until we have placed them in a sentence:

We should have read the minute print on the permit.

Intonation patterns, which are sometimes crucial to meaning, are not represented in writing except in a very limited way by punctuation. Sometimes to go from print to meaningful speech it is even necessary to know more than one sentence of context. The question, "Who are you?" for example, would require different patterns as a reply to each of the following:

"Joe will take the part of the butler. Amy is the lady."
"Who are you?"

or

"Answer me one question: Who am I?"
"Who are you? You are somebody important."

The first is said with a falling intonation characteristic of declarative sentences and **wh** questions. In the second, where confirmation is asked for, a rising intonation makes it into a yes–no question, meaning, "Is this what you are asking?" Neither words nor punctuation are enough to decide the meaning or the intonation from the question alone out of context.

Not only is decoding to speech made difficult by the limitations of the writing system, it is also sometimes easier to derive meaning directly from print without trying to articulate. Often writing contains linguistically relevant information not represented in speech. German, for example, capitalizes all nouns in writing, and French verb inflections are much more explicit in writing than in speech. English spelling often departs from phonemic representation in the direction of keeping constant the spelling of lexical units. C. S. Chomsky (1970) listed pairs like *medicate–medicine, sagacity–sage, expedite–expeditious* to support her argument that English spelling is a more accurate representation of meaning relationships between words than a strictly phonemic writing system would be. Even in Russian, where spelling is close to the phonemic, vowels in unemphasized syllables are more differentiated in writing than in speech in a way that preserves relationships between morphemes that would otherwise be obscured.

Another reason for questioning the primacy of "decoding to sounds" in reading is that the process is a slow and difficult one. Readers finding a new word seldom spontaneously try to sound it out letter by letter. Rather they use at most the first letter but mainly context to guess what a word is or what it means. Another reason for the failure to sound out is that naive individuals such as children and other illiterates often do not hear phonemes separately, so it is hard for them to form associations between letters and sounds. The ITPA sound-blending subtest is one on which early readers are superior, but there are considerable numbers of readers at the other end of the scale, unable to listen to separate phonemes and identify the word. This is not too surprising when you realize that the syllable, not the phoneme, is the acoustic unit of speech (Savin and Bever, 1970), and that many sounds, such as stop consonants, cannot be pronounced separately from some kind of vowel sound. (This may be the reason why in Japan there are very few reading problems with the "kana" symbols, each of which represents a whole consonant–vowel syllable rather than an individual phoneme [Makita, 1968].)

A final reason for doubting the importance of decoding to sound in reading is that fast reading does not permit either letter-by-letter or word-by-word conversion of writing into speech. Skillful readers apprehend much faster than they could read aloud even subvocally. In fact, Smith (1973) pointed out that since speech sounds often cannot be known until meaning is apprehended, even subvocal speech could hardly help in reaching meaning. Further, the fact that people seldom recall word for word, but instead remember the meaning of what they read, suggests that readers may not process speech sounds at all, but apprehend meaning alone.

B. Writing as Alternate Surface Structure

Instead of regarding writing as a secondary artificial transcription of oral language that has to be translated back into speech in order to be understood, both Smith (1973) and Carton (1976) have suggested that we think of it as an alternative set of surface structures, parallel and no less directly related to the same meanings as speech. With this idea in mind it is worth comparing the learning of reading with the learning of a foreign language. The two situations are not exactly alike, but their likenesses and differences are enlightening.

1. Foreign Language Learning

In a foreign language the learner encounters a new system of expressing the same meanings. Few would question that these systems are parallel and independent. Both are natural, oral languages. Learning a second language will make it possible for the learner to translate from one to the other, but translation is not likely to be its most important use. Each language will be used in appropriate situations to express meaning without reference to the other.

The learning process for a foreign language can be described in terms of three levels of linguistic analysis: sounds, words, and sentences. A new language uses a new set of phonemes, and the beginner will need auditory and motor practice in articulating and distinguishing them. However, there is no simple relation between the two phonemic systems that will help the learning. At the level of words, on the other hand, there are clear parallels between the two languages in that many words or phrases express the same concepts. In a glossary, expressions with equivalent meanings can be laid side by side and used to learn meanings of the new set of words. However, as anyone who has tried to translate with the aid of a dictionary knows, separate words do not a sentence make. Words can express concepts, but only sentences can express propositions, statements that can be true or false. Since many, if not most, of our communications are propositions, it is essential that a new set of syntactic rules be acquired along with the sounds and the vocabulary. The only interrelations that exist between two languages are through the meanings that their structures represent. The relations between these meanings and the structures that represent them are completely arbitrary, that is, there is nothing in the language forms themselves to tie them to their meanings, no way to predict from the sound of a word what it will mean. It is this characteristic of language that makes it possible to express any meaning (more or less) in any language. Nevertheless, within the language systems themselves there are many understandable grammatical relations. Acquiring a new language amounts to learning these relations, and there are two distinct approaches to the task. One is to study explicit grammars of both languages and compare them item by item in a contrastive analysis. At the same time the learner must also make a large number of associations between words in the new language and their meanings. In this way it will be theoretically possible to translate words and sentences into the native language and thus to understand them. This method depends upon conscious and explicit knowledge of abstract principles of grammar. This kind of knowledge is not adequate in itself for any effective use of the new language. A person who has this kind of explicit knowledge knows **about** the language, but this is not what we usually mean by "knowing" the language. Explicit knowledge can help to decipher one language into another, but before a person can speak or understand or even read a language, its rules must be incorporated at an unconscious level into a linguistic competence not unlike that of the native language. Words and sentences must be directly related to their meanings without the confusing mediation of abstract rules or words from another language. The recognition of this fact together with the observation that children speak their own language well without any explicit instruction or grammatical knowledge has inspired language teachers over many years to advocate various "direct methods" of second-language learning patterned after the childhood acquisition of the native language. The "direct methods" avoid explicit teaching of grammatical rules as well as use of the native language as a medium of teaching. Learners deal only with the relations between meaning and the new language, and they acquire the grammar through direct practice with information-bearing structures, through everyday uses of languge, much as children learn their native language. In contrast to school learning, this is normally a very active process. Children derive rules from what they hear, apply them in speaking and understanding, and gradually change them until they conform to the language around them. In "direct methods" of foreign-language teaching, students develop their own competence through similar practical use of the language.

2. Reading as a New Language

Now let us examine the written form of language as though it were a different language, one with a visual rather than an auditory medium. Again the reader can "translate," in other words read aloud, but that skill is of minor importance compared with the ability to understand quickly and directly. Written language can be analyzed on levels corresponding to those used for spoken language. In alphabetic writing systems there are letters corresponding to the phonemes of speech. In this case, however, there **is** a systematic relation between the two "languages" at this level. This relation could conceivably be used as a means of translation between speech and print with no intervening reference to meaning. In ideographic writing systems, like Chinese, this is not true. Word meanings are represented by symbols which cannot be pronounced without knowing their meaning. Although this difference at first seems to mean a fundamentally different process of learning to read, if reading is compared at a slightly advanced level, the difference between identifying an ideograph and sight reading of an alphabetically spelled word all but disappears. Sounding out is not very useful at any functional level of reading. Even unskilled beginners at reading quickly associate words with meanings rather than sounds. For example, a child who was having trouble with reading was heard to pronounce "l-i-t-t-l-e" as "small." Goodman (Smith, 1973, p. 80) reported that better readers make errors that preserve the meaning rather than the sounds of what is before them.

In reading, as in speaking, propositional meaning can only be apprehended by perceiving units composed of many words. "Word-calling" in reading can be compared with word-for-word translation between languages in that it often involves failure to understand the meaning of the sentence. A skilled reader, like a fluent speaker, must organize the elements into phrase and sentence units automatically and quickly. To achieve this, beginners must learn to make active use of their existing grammatical competence in perceiving the new medium. At the level of syntax the written language, unlike a foreign language, is almost the same as its spoken form except for minor changes in style, but what the reader must learn is to see as well as hear phrase and sentence units.

In contrast to the relation between languages, where meaning is the only link, the alphabetic writing system also provides a second potential bridge between speech and the language of print, one which, in principle at least, has no relation to meaning. In some written languages this system is quite simple in that each letter represents a phoneme. Even in English there are many useful rules that relate letters and spelling patterns to sound. This makes possible an approach to the teaching of reading that builds upon these regularities through teaching explicit rules. Like the grammar-and-translation approach to foreign-language learning, the phonic approach provides a rational and systematic basis for the first steps of learning. It also has the same drawback, that it cannot serve as a basis for progress beyond the initial stages to any functional use of written language. It is also an "unnatural" method in that it bypasses the all-important language–meaning relationships by a set of indirect rules governing the phonemic level of analysis, in which meaning plays no part. The approaches that correspond to the "direct methods" of language teaching are those that emphasize the use of reading for meaning. Since there is no way to "recognize" the meaning of a new word from the word itself, reading for meaning requires an active problem-solving attitude on the part of the readers. They must find their cues in the semantic and syntactic context and form hypotheses to test against the visual data. Thus what the reader already knows, consciously or intuitively, is as important in deriving meaning as the marks upon the page.

C. "Cue Systems" in Reading Instruction

Goodman (1973) summarized the "cue systems" of reading as being threefold: graphophonic, syntactic, and semantic. Graphophonic cues are used to "decode" from written to spoken language, and phonic reading instruction is designed to teach a child explicitly how to use these cues. However, the two other cue systems are more useful to skilled readers. Syntactic cues are essential in apprehending grammatical meaning, that is, meaning that is represented in larger-than-word constructions including propositions, which must be expressed in sentences. Syntactic cues are also no doubt very important in apprehending word meanings in that grammatical structure reduces the uncertainty as to what any given word in the sentence may be. Extracting the meaning of written text relies upon much of the same grammatical competence as any other use of language. Since this competence is largely an intuitive sort of knowledge, below the level of explicit awareness, it is not easy to make explicit use of it in reading instruction, as we can do with grapheme–phoneme correspondence. This may be the reason why most programs for teaching reading seem to concentrate on "word-attack skills" and reading vocabulary lists. Attempting to teach explicitly the use of syntactic cues is impossibly difficult with young children who have little conscious grammatical knowledge. It is also unnecessary in that they are naturally disposed to use their already well-developed native language competence as soon as they begin to recognize written text as a form of language. Semantic cue systems differ from the other two in that they are based outside of written or spoken language. Semantic cues to the meaning of any segment are inferred from the already understood meanings of other segments of the material, in other words from semantic context. In this sense they are purely cognitive or extralinguistic. The knowledge used in semantic inference is also largely conscious knowledge, so that it is possible to teach children explicitly to use meaning cues. Several reading techniques, for example, instruct children to "guess" at meaning from context, including pictures on the page. Our question is how early readers learn to use these cue systems, and which are most useful to them.

III. SELF-TAUGHT READING

If we put together what we know of early readers and what we know of the nature of reading, we can make some informed hypotheses about how their learning process may differ from that of school-taught readers. In terms of Goodman's cue systems, it seems reasonable to suppose that in the first stage early readers rely less than others upon graphophonic cues and more on semantic ones. If we can use the term graphophonic to cover any teaching strategy that involves translating graphic symbols into sound in order to reach their meaning, it would cover a variety of methods from straight grapheme–phoneme association through Bloomfield's spelling patterns to "look-and-say" insofar as the last implied that the "saying" part is essential to understanding. Some such method is part of most reading instruction especially when reading aloud is used to demonstrate success. In line with the "word-attack" strategy of learning to identify individual words by articulating them, many primers limit the vocabulary to a short list of "known" words and measure progress in terms of expanding this list word by word. The result is that it is difficult to compose interesting stories in normal sentences. It is assumed that children will tolerate the dull and stilted language until they "know enough words" to read things that are more interesting. Meanwhile it is assumed that learning to read is pursued as an end in itself rather than as a way of getting useful information, and the immediate rewards for progress must be largely extrinsic.

A. A Functional Approach

In contrast, the first lessons of self-taught readers are the words that surround them in the world outside of books. Smith (1976) followed 4-year-old Matthew around observing the large number of printed words he encountered at home, on the street, and in stores. Matthew was not a reader, but he could identify many of the words he saw. He used mostly context cues, although he was able to name the individual letters. Perhaps the most important fact about these signs and labels was that they were useful. The child could pick out the cereal he wanted and find the toy department. Words we encounter outside of printed text, on packages, on street signs, and in commercials, also usually occur in a context that contains cues to their meaning. Matthew knew many words he saw in the supermarket by the objects they were on or the pictures on the labels. He guessed wrong on many, too, but his guesses were nearly always based on the context, such as "reading" the name of his own street from a street sign that said something else. Other signs that appear on the street are often located near things that give cues to their meaning, e.g., CAR WASH and DRUGSTORE. Matthew did not seem to sound out words, although he knew the letter names. Asked how he knew the word on the stop sign, he said he knew because it was spelled P-O-T-S.

A child who grasps the principle that printed words give information can readily find motivation for learning them. When John (Torrey, 1969) was 3 years old, he picked out the kind of soup he wanted by reading the label. He was fascinated by letters and numbers, but would have nothing to do with nonsense shapes in the "reading readiness" test. Letters and numbers, especially numbers, are a direct route to meaning. Interest in numbers is reported very often in Durkin's early readers, perhaps because, unlike letters, numbers represent meaning directly, like Chinese characters. John delighted in identifying long numbers and even identified people by them, as when he once referred to a neighbor as "that lady (who) live(s) at number 16." Downing (Carton, 1976) observed that young children often do not distinguish between pictures and writing, as though they expected to find meaning intrinsically represented on the page.

Television is another source of words in contexts that tell what they mean. On the screen, words grab attention by changing before the eyes, and television is superbly informative because the words are very often shown with a voice that pronounces them and the things they refer to. In commercials words are shown and pronounced repeatedly both within the commercial and when the same commercial is seen several times a day. The spoken word is loud and often sung with a catchy tune. The style of commercials has been borrowed by the makers of teaching programs such as Sesame Street and The Electric Company, which are widely viewed by children and provide a wealth of printed material at their level.

In addition to being exposed to the print that is visible to any child in everyday activities, many children, of course, whose parents read to them look at the pictures as the parent holds the book. A curious child can also see the print and learn to identify the words either from the pictures or from the parent's reading. Pages of text may be hard to follow, but if the story or poem is read over and over until the child knows it by heart (a common situation), it would not be hard for a child who already had some start in reading to follow the text and expand his or her knowledge from it. The purpose of reading to a child is not to teach him or her to read, however, but to tell the story, so that the meaning of the print remains the prime focus of attention. Reading as such is only a means to another end. John seemed to have this attitude toward reading. He was always reluctant to read aloud to an adult because, as he always said, "You can read." His mother said he read stories aloud to his brother, who was somewhat below grade level in reading. He also entertained himself by reading. The notion of reading aloud merely to show someone you could do it was not in his ken, perhaps because he had never been taught to read in school.

John had the same practical attitude toward writing. Like many other early readers described by Durkin, he could use his knowledge of the writing system productively. Durkin reported that many of her subjects were paper-and-pencil scribblers and that many of them used toy blackboards a great deal for printing letters and words. John enjoyed writing messages, and he also loved to dictate sentences to a typist and watch his words come out in print faster than he could print himself. He even changed his style in this situation to sentences more characteristic of written than spoken grammar. For example, he dictated, "May I go outside?" though he never used *may* spontaneously in his usual speech. As in reading, he seemed to think of writing as producing sentences, not individual words. If asked to spell something, he typically answered by spelling out the whole sentence in which he had used the word, pausing between words and ending with a falling intonation to signify the end. Most of his written production took the form of direct communications. They were questions or orders to the person who was to read them. Once when he was being badgered by his parents to read aloud to someone, something he never wanted to do, he quietly wrote on a paper where only that person could see it, GET OUT. Writing, like reading, was for him a means of conveying messages. His attention was on this purpose and not upon written language as such, either grammar or spelling. When he could not remember how to spell a word, he never appeared to guess by sounding it out, he just said, "Ask (i.e., tell me) how to spell *laugh*." It may be inferred from his lack of concern with any aspect of written language other than its meaning, that he would also be likely to look for reading cues in the semantic context rather than in graphophonic rules.

B. Possible Use of Phonics

Although self-taught readers may get most of their word information from the semantic cue system, it is certainly not impossible for them to get graphophonic information. In the research cited, a number of parents mentioned having told their early readers "the sounds of letters," although none mentioned that the child used this information. In addition, the first words to which children are exposed are frequently especially useful for making phonic inferences. Brand names, which make up a large proportion of the words that are simultaneously shown and pronounced on television and of the words on package labels, are often nonsense words spelled in very regular patterns: *Quisp, Krispies, Crackos, Racerific, Slaptrap, Chex, Slo-poke, Creeple Peeple,* and *Quik* are examples from children's show commercials. The real words shown and pronounced in the same commercials are, of course, no more regular than words in English at large, but even in those there are a number of reliable phonic cures, especially initial consonants, which may be the most useful to a child. It is possible, then, that inferred phonics may figure in the first steps of self-taught reading. Most of the research on early readers antedates Sesame Street, but explicit phonic instruction is now available there and on The Electric Company. One mother of two early readers reported that the son who learned reading from those programs did much more "sounding out" than the one who learned from being read to. John had some sense of sound–spelling relationships. On those occasions when he tried to pronounce a word before giving up and asking what it was, his attempts were obviously guided by the spelling. He had some trouble with the word *pipsis-sewah* even after he asked what it was. In trying to imitate what he heard, he made several unsuccessful tries, one of which was "pipsewash." The final /sh/ sound did not occur in the word he heard and might have been the result of seeing a series of the letter *s* in the word ending in *h*. For the most part, however, John showed little evidence of using phonics. When he came to a word he didn't know, he did not rely on sounding out. Although he sometimes began by pronouncing sounds suggested by the letters, he usually simply asked, "What's that word?" "Whassat word?" was almost a chorus to any difficult material he read aloud. His spelling also never descended to the phonic level. He spelled everything correctly, although he often asked how to spell, especially in the case of words like *laugh* that have unusual spellings for the sounds. After reading a story about a boy named *Jonny* [sic], he wrote a sentence about the same boy spelling it JOHNNY, more correct, in a way, than what he had used as a model. (His own real name was not John.) It was also noticeable to a speaker of a different variety of English from his own that he could spell words which he pronounced in ways that were unintelligible to speakers of other dialects. One word, which could be mistaken for *churches* or *turkey,* he carefully articulated as "chrns," and finally spelled "c-h-i-l-d-r-e-n." Neither this nor any other discrepancy from a perfect grapheme–phoneme correspondence ever deterred him from standard spelling.

Unfortunately few of the other reports of early readers give any information about the extent to which they seemed to be using phonic cues. The only evidence that can be cited is the informal recollections of three mothers of five early readers. They said, when asked about their children's use of phonics, that most of the children had not spontaneously sounded out words letter by letter. One child did some of this after receiving some instruction in kindergarten, however, and another, mentioned previously, after similar instruction from television. None of these children relied much on phonics in spelling. Most of their spelling was standard. In view of the individual differences in sensitivity to phonics that are found among children generally, it would not be safe to infer from so few cases that phonics would generally play so small a role in early reading. We can only say what a handful of cases can show, that it is possible to become a skillful reader without ever showing much reliance on phonics.

C. From Words to Sentences

The kind of semantic and phonic information that is available on television and in the supermarket usually does not cue much more than single words or short phrases. A child could get a start on reading from them but not much more. The vocabulary is limited. Function words are few because there are few sentences. John certainly knew far more than he could have picked up from signs and labels. A test given him shortly after he entered first grade placed him at nearly fifth-grade level in reading and spelling. One can picture many children expanding their capacity to read through being read to, especially the same story over and over. In John's case we cannot be sure he had this help since his mother said they did not read to him. (John was sometimes able to identify words for his father, who had completed about eighth grade.) His mother did say, though, that John had shown great interest in books that his older sister brought home from the library. His mother had taken them away from him at first, not knowing he was able to read them. It may not be too much to imagine that, with a good start in reading vocabulary from everyday life and television, children's books with simple stories and pictures to help with meaning could provide enough context for a child to use in expanding his reading. In a test for silent reading, John looked at a picture of a set of flags with the sentence, "Here are some _____." He filled in FLAGS without speaking or moving his lips. Under a pair of women's shoes, he filled in "These are SHOES. They belong to a LADY." Since in his oral reading he always read with sentence intonation patterns, he could provide a grammatical framework for words which he could not read correctly. This patterning extended even to nonsense words, as in the verse,

> The bunny now gets twenty hops
> While in the woods the lolly pops.

which he read fluently with an intonation and stress pattern that made the noun *lolly* the subject of the verb *pops*. He also used correct expression in sentences which were arranged in very unusual grammatical form to achieve verse, for example,

> Two more hops for the bunny and then
> Look out for the Pipsissewah in his den.

His errors in reading occasionally took the form of changing the grammar to something more like his own variety of language, for example, reading "When you eat breakfast?'' when the text said ''When **do** you eat breakfast?'' but usually he read correctly whether or not the sentence conformed to his own usage. His grammatical competence in the spoken language seemed to provide a clear yet flexible framework within which different varieties of written language could be interpreted. A child with a definite expectation that written text will say something understandable need actually know only some of the words in order to reduce greatly the uncertainty about what remains. Combining a large enough basic reading vocabulary with his own established grammatical competence through the insight that writing is language provides a powerful means of expanding the ability to read both through new individual word recognition and through increasing ability to grasp by the eye the larger-than-word meaningful structures in sentences and discourse. That John was doing this is suggested by the fact that he always read text with sentence intonation patterns even when he had to mumble several unknown words. It seems a reasonable guess that all readers progress primarily through means like this whether they are in grade school expanding their native language reading or are students of foreign languages developing both reading and speaking ability through the printed page. It does not seem likely that asking the teacher or searching in a dictionary are the main sources of new knowledge in reading. Syntactic and semantic contexts not only give cues to meaning, they also provide for immediate and intrinsic feedback to check for errors. If the interpretation is grammatical and makes sense, it is likely to be correct. The self-taught reader especially, without a regular source of outside information, would have to rely even more on his own knowledge and linguistic competence to advance and correct his reading.

IV. IMPLICATIONS FOR RESEARCH

Most research on reading tells more about the behavior of teachers and psychologists than it does about that of beginning readers. Professional adults decide the criteria for assessing reading and they design the tests for intelligence and special abilities according to what factors they think influence children's reading. They ask questions about socioeconomic levels and early experiences, which they expect to be relevant. If we were to take seriously the problem of discovering the ''natural'' method of learning to read, we would have to spend more time and effort observing what children actually do. We would have to focus on their spontaneous behavior in free situations and less upon their responses to our predetermined questions. We would need to study their errors as carefully as their ''correct'' responses. Goodman's (1968) research into reading ''miscues'' in which he traced progress through a typical sequence of stages is an example of this orientation. Present research on early readers contains almost no information about **how** they read, for example, what intonation patterns are typical of the first stages and whether and how much they rely upon phonics. We are told what materials are offered to them but not which they choose themselves, so we do not know whether they read mainly for meaning or mainly to learn phonic cues. We are told they are highly motivated, but not what their motives are. If we knew what use they made of their first reading, we might infer their specific motives, whether it is to use what they already know or to increase their skill. We need to know what rewards they get from their reading. Is it the pleasure they get from reading stories, the instrumental value of being able to find things, or is it a sense of achievement in simply possessing the skill and being praised by other people?

It might be profitable to ask these questions about learners who are being taught in school as well as about early readers. Although the behavior of the children would no doubt be influenced by their lessons, it is possible that adults overestimate the influence of the lessons. At very least it would be worthwhile to examine individual differences in the use made of teaching and learning materials. Some children seem to get nothing out of instruction in phonics and others do not seem to grasp the principle that written material is a form of language comparable to speech. In this day of television instruction it will be hard to find children who have had no exposure to what adults think is the way to learn reading. Sesame Street lays some groundwork and The Electric Company is a conscious reading lesson. However, these new influences may not have changed the reading environment of preschool children qualitatively as much as quantitatively. Most, if not all, early readers learned through teaching by sisters and mothers and had books and workbooks that conformed to what adults thought they should learn. The Electric Company is purposely eclectic in its array of methods from narrowly phonic to strictly functional. All readers, early or late, have a chance to pick and choose what and how they will learn. It would be useful to know more about the nature and variety of those choices.

V. POSSIBLE PRACTICAL IMPLICATIONS

A. Age of Readiness

The existence of early readers suggests a question about whether the customary age of beginning reading is later than it needs to be. Six years is believed in this country to be the earliest age when most children have sufficient "readiness" to read. In Russia the instruction begins at the age of 7 years (Bronfenbrenner, 1970). If some children learn at 4 or 5 years, however, it does not prove that the schools are too late. Individual variation exists in most traits, so it is expected that occasionally children will be "ready" much earlier than the mass of others. On the other hand, it is also possible that if we had appropriate techniques, instruction could be begun earlier for many children. Durkin's follow-ups on her early readers found them benefiting from their head start far into their school careers. Although most of the early readers studied learned on their own initiative, this may be because so few children are given any reading lessons prior to first grade. It is possible that these and many others would have learned if there had been appropriate stimulation and more opportunities. Some who have attempted reading instruction with younger children have reported success, although many of them have not used the standard system of instruction used in first grades, but invented special methods. It is interesting to compare these with what we can infer about the learning processes of spontaneous early readers.

B. Methods of Teaching Younger Readers

Four principles seem to have guided teaching programs designed for younger readers. All are consistent with the reported learning experience of self-taught readers. First, they have tried to provide external stimuli that would attract attention and interest to appropriate material and make possible a guided discovery of the necessary principles. Second, in every case the **meaning** of written material has been emphasized as much as possible and as early as possible. Third, it has been a policy in all these attempts to avoid coercion. Younger children have been given a free choice whether to learn reading at all, so that those who learned could be said to have done it on their own initiative even though they were in a training situation. Finally, systematic attempts have been made to keep the children active rather than passively receptive. Both physical activities, such as writing, and mental activities, such as inferring meanings from context, have been deliberately encouraged as part of the learning procedure.

Montessori (1965) was one of the first who advocated earlier instruction in reading as in other knowledge. She devised techniques for the preschool level that would gradually lead children through their own devices to the threshold of reading and writing. She began by introducing cursive letters as solid patterns around which the children traced on paper and then colored in like shapes in a coloring book. This was a familiar and enjoyable activity that also gave them motor exercise for controlling a pencil. The next step was to give them the same shapes cut out of sandpaper to be traced with the finger in the same direction as in writing. A teacher taught them to associate each of two vowel letters with the appropriate sounds. Consonants, printed on cards in a different color from vowels, were introduced in syllables with the vowels the children already knew. In this way they could begin to form a few meaningful words from the very first handful of letters they learned. (Probably the knowledge of grapheme–phoneme correspondence is much more useful in learning to read Italian than English.) After they had begun to make many words by placing letter cards side by side, the transition to writing came almost spontaneously, since they had already had much practice with tracing the sandpaper letters with their fingers. She describes the moment when one child suddenly discovered for the first time that he could write with chalk and communicated the discovery to his whole class. To their delight and excitement, they were all instantly able to write for the first time. The Montessori method combines the principle of complete prior preparation for every step with the policy of making each step meaningful and interesting to the child. She also warns her teachers never to pursue a phonics lesson if the child seems not to respond readily, so that nothing will be imposed against the child's immediate inclination.

Another innovator in early teaching of reading has been O. K. Moore. His work has not been comparable to Montessori's in its extent or influence, but he has reported (1963) some success using similar underlying principles. Most of his subjects also were preschool children, and, like Montessori, he had a policy of making every step of the way easy and interesting and of never imposing learning against the natural inclination of the child. Instead of teachers he used a mechanical device called a "responsive environment," including a "talking typewriter," which could show a letter or a word on the screen and then pronounce it after the child typed it. In the case of a word, it could also spell it aloud and show a picture presenting its meaning. Children were allowed to sit at the machine as long as they continued to operate it, but no longer. By permitting the children to "make full use of their capacity of discovering relations" and by being "structured" so that "the learner is likely to make a series of interconnected discoveries . . ." (Moore, 1963, p. 2) the machine led all the children who used it to make considerable progress in reading. Since they ranged from retardates to especially bright children, the progress varied, but the group of preschoolers who used it prepared, typed, and published their own newspaper. Moore's report on the role of phonics in their learning is also suggestive. He says that he was surprised by the children's ability to spell nonphonetic words, adding that, "I have concluded that there must be some subtle lawfulness holding between the spoken and written forms of English" (Moore, 1963, p. 25). As the program moved ahead into stories, Moore used Aesop's Fables rather than conventional primer texts on the grounds that such stories had stood the test of time as interesting material for children and would thus provide automatic and intrinsic reward for success in reading them. Moore calls his responsive environment "autotelic," meaning that everything is learned for its own sake without extrinsic rewards, which he feels only confuse the issue. With no motive other than curiosity stimulated by a clever sequence of events, the learners were led to a self-directed learning process similar to that which early readers create for themselves out of more ordinary circumstances.

A third program for teaching younger children to read has been reported by the Denver Public Schools (McKee, Brzeinski, and Harrison, 1966). In this case a special program of reading instruction was provided for a sample of kindergarteners. The program included some phonic training, training in distinguishing letters, and collecting words beginning with the same sound, but it also explicitly taught the children to use context together with first letters to guess words. In this way it attempted to teach the children to do what we have inferred early readers must do in increasing their reading vocabularies without much outside assistance. The reported results of the Denver experiment (Brzeinski, 1964) suggest that it may have been fairly effective. No apparent harm was done to the children, and their progress was maintained provided that their first-grade instruction was designed to follow up on the initial training.

Sutton (1964, 1965) reported another attempt to have kindergarteners learn to read. In this case the class began with a high level of measured "reading readiness," so a pile of preprimers was left on a table where they could use them. No pressure was put on anyone to learn to read. The only instruction consisted of having the teacher answer questions when asked. Several children showed initial interest, and when two who could already read began reading to their friends, the collective interest developed. Later they began to read together in groups and send a delegate to the teacher to ask qustions. When a child had read a book she or he was allowed to take it home to read to the family. Of the 134 children who had these opportunities 46 had reached a measurable level on the Gates Primary Reading Achievement Tests, with a mean level for the 46 of 1.78, well into the first grade, in about 20 hours of instruction.

Appleton (1964) reported a summer kindergarten program where a similar opportunity was offered, this time with a little more formal instruction. A room separate from the more traditional kindergarten facilities was open where blackboards, books, and a teacher were waiting for any child who cared to wander in. The teacher held lessons in visual discrimination (matching pictures), auditory discrimination (selecting words beginning with the same letter), and sight vocabulary for a few children at a time as they chose to come. Those who learned enough words were given books containing the same words, and they expanded their vocabulary from the context. Many wanted to make their own stories by arranging word cards or writing with the teacher's help. Most of the 26 children took some part in the reading activities, and a few had read several books by the end of the summer.

The most striking similarity in all these early-reading training programs is the policy of keeping participation in them **voluntary.** The "open classroom" model is the nearest equivalent technique for grade school. Voluntary participation is easy to justify in the preschool, where there is no pressure for anyone to learn. It may also be that the nature of younger children themselves tends to make it necessary. Cohan (1961) described an extreme case of Cindy, a 2½-year-old, which illustrates this possibility. Cindy asked for "her own" words, and she was given two cards with her name and BABY printed on them. Since she learned to tell them apart, Cohan made more cards and Cindy learned about 30 words in all. However, when she reached the end of her interest, she simply refused to cooperate with her teacher, giving deliberately wrong answers. Cohan reported, ''Any efforts to cajole Cindy into more extensive reading were fruitless'' (p. 508). The lesson for teachers, perhaps, is that children are like horses, you can lead them to letters, but you can't make them read. There are more tools for coercing an older child, but the main difference may be that later on they are better able to see some use in reading and are thus more willing to try.

C. Should Reading Be Taught Earlier?

The existence of early readers together with the limited studies of early reading instruction do not in themselves prove that it should become a general practice to teach reading before age 6. The Denver study (Brzeinski, 1964) gave evidence for the largest group of public school children, and although it reported success, the conclusiveness of the data has been questioned (Mood, 1967). Furthermore, even if the analysis were beyond criticism, it would take more than one large-scale study to decide on the value of kindergarten reading. There are many who have argued that teaching reading before the age of 6 years is useless and can be harmful. Keister (1941) reported that the younger children in first grade, although they made normal progress in reading during the year, forgot much of it during the summer and remained behind those who had been older at the time of first instruction. Sheldon (Durkin and Sheldon, 1963) argued that too early reading instruction was a threat to mental health, although Durkin, in the same pair of articles, saw no objection to kindergarten instruction. Her own extensive studies of early readers (Durkin, 1966) had shown that they maintained their advantage for several years. Sutton (1965, 1969) also found that, contrary to Keister's results, children who had been allowed to start reading in kindergarten remembered what they had learned and continued until third grade to gain faster than their classmates who had started in first grade. The Denver study (McKee, Brzeinski, and Harrison, 1966) reported that with appropriate instruction their kindergarten beginners were able to build upon their earlier learning. MacLeod, Markowsky, and Leong (1972) found that children selected on the basis of readiness to begin first grade a few months early learned as well as older ones and adjusted as well socially. However, even after the possibility and desirability of earlier reading instruction have been decided, there will still be the question of feasibility. Is it worthwhile? Is the benefit worth the cost? It is not the purpose of this chapter to draw conclusions about such a policy matter except to say that earlier reading is probably possible for more children than now accomplish it, if anyone should decide it was worthwhile to give more of them the opportunity.

VI. READING THAT COMES NATURALLY

The other possible practical implications of the research on early readers are some suggestions about how to teach reading. If we regard the learning processes of self-taught readers as revealing some "natural" kind of learning like the learning of a native language at mother's knee, it is a plausible hypothesis that it might be a model for a good teaching method. From the fact that early readers have no obvious common training or experiences that distinguish them from others, it is tempting to suggest that readers are born, not made. In that case there would be no pedagogical implications of the phenomenon beyond perhaps measurements of abilities. The extraordinary motivation of early readers is another trait that often has the appearance of being innate since it obviously occurs at the initiative of the child. Let us choose, however, to believe that whatever native abilities and motives may participate in the development of reading, the right kind of environmental stimulation could elicit a similar response in a much larger number of children with lesser degrees of those traits. This will make it worthwhile to look for some suggestions for teaching strategies.

The most striking characteristic of early reading is that it comes at the **initiative** of the child, which seems to be almost the opposite of reading as it is learned in school. Yet there are ways in which schools can make use of pupil initiative in instruction. Several of the programs for early readers stressed the need for all the activities to be voluntary and for the materials to be attractive and interesting so that the learners would be eager to read them. The open classroom operates on a similar principle for all school learning.

There is another characteristic difference between nonreaders and readers whether early or not, and that is **a certain insight that print is a form of language like what you speak and hear.** This understanding is what makes it possible to take an active role in using the context with its semantic and syntactic cues and thus read for meaning. Children who are just beginning to be taught reading or who are having trouble learning often seem to lack this basic insight. They recite the words from a page as though they were an arbitrary list of puzzles to be solved, and then stop in mid-sentence at the end of a line to look up and get feedback on how well they are doing. If a child reads, as John always did, with sentence intonation, it is safe to infer that he not only knows he is reading language, but actually understands the structure of the particular sentence. Without that understanding there would be nothing to tell him the proper expression. It is possible to learn a basic vocabulary of sight words together with words conforming to a limited set of spelling rules whose sounds and patterns have been memorized without really grasping the principle of written language or at least without having any idea of using cues beyond the letters of the particular word in question. Montessori made a point of the difference between this and reading: "I do not consider as reading translating signs into sounds. . . . What I understand by reading is the interpretation of an idea from the written signs'' (1965, p. 296). It is possible that some teaching, by an overemphasis on graphophonic cues and single word identification at the expense of semantic and syntactic context, could mislead young learners into a strategy of trying to absorb passively something that is completely given on the page and divert their attention from the cue systems that require active use of their existing background knowledge and grammatical competence. This is not to advocate avoidance of phonics instruction, but only to suggest that children be made aware very early that the graphophonic cue system is not all there is to reading. Practice in using semantic cues has been built into several of the early reading instructional programs described earlier in this chapter and is also part of many first-grade reading programs. Like graphophonic cues, semantic ones deal with explicit and conscious knowledge and are thus easy to explain. Syntactic knowledge is another story. Grammatical competence is largely unconscious, especially with young children. We know the grammar of our native language intuitively. Children and many adults have no understanding of grammatical terminology or rules. (Even linguists understand it only imperfectly.) Thus explicit instruction on the use of syntactic cues would seem to be impractical. On the other hand by the time children start learning to read, their grammatical competence at the intuitive level is well developed. Techniques like the **cloze** procedure, which substitutes blanks for every tenth word, for example, would bring that competence into play without having to explain in grammatical terms how to do it.

If reading is seen as the use of these three cue systems, then the task of reading instruction is to help the learner to form useful hypotheses to be tested against these cues (Goodman, 1973). Which are most important will depend upon the individual and the stage of the learning process, but at all stages success will depend upon enlisting the active mental processes of the learners and engaging all of their relevant knowledge and competence. In Goodman's words, ''The child is already programmed to learn to read. He needs written language that is both interesting and comprehensible, and teachers who understand language-learning and who appreciate his competence as a language-learner'' (p. 180). Goodman's view is that the ''psycholinguistic method'' of teaching reading at present consists of just this insight. What we learn from early readers would seem to confirm this opinion.

REFERENCES

Appleton, E. Kindergarteners pace themselves in reading. *Elementary School Journal,* 1964, **64,** 248–252.
Bloomfield, L., and Barnhart, C. *Let's read.* Detroit: Wayne State University Press, 1961.

Briggs, C., and Elkind, D. Cognitive development in early readers. *Developmental Psychology,* 1973, **9**, 279–280.

Briggs, C., and Elkind, D. *Characteristics of early readers.* Unpublished manuscript.

Bronfenbrenner, U. *Two worlds of childhood, U.S. and U.S.S.R.* New York: Russell Sage Foundation, 1970.

Brzeinski, J. E. Beginning reading in Denver. *Journal of Educational Research,* 1964, **18**, 16–21.

Carton, A. *Orientation to reading.* Rowley, Mass.: Newbury House, 1976.

Chomsky, C. S. "Reading, writing and phonology." *Harvard Educational Review,* 1970, **20**, 287–309.

Cohan, M. Two and a half and reading. *Elementary English,* 1961, **38**, 506–508.

Durkin, D. *Children who read early.* New York: Teachers College Press, 1966.

Durkin, D., and Sheldon, W. D. Should the very young be taught to read? *NEA Journal,* November, 1963, 20–24.

Evans, J. R., and Smith, L. J. *Some psycholinguistic and perceptual–motor characteristics of precociously reading children.* Unpublished manuscript.

Goodman, K. S. The psycholinguistic nature of the reading process. In K. S. Goodman (Ed.), *The psycholinguistic nature of the reading process.* Detroit: Wayne State University Press, 1968.

Goodman, K. S. Psycholinguistic universals in the reading process. In Frank Smith (Ed.), *Psycholinguistics and reading.* New York: Holt, Rinehart & Winston, 1973.

Keister, B. V. Reading skills acquired by five-year-old children. *The Elementary School Journal,* 1941, April, 587–596.

King, E. M., and Friesen, D. T. Children who read in kindergarten. *The Alberta Journal of Educational Research,* 1972, **XVIII**, 147–161.

MacLeod, J., Markowsky, M. D., and Leong, C. K. A follow-up of early entrants to elementary schools. *Elementary School Journal,* 1972, **73**, 10–19.

Makita, K. The rarity of reading disability in Japanese children. *American Journal of Orthopsychiatry,* 1968, **38**, 599–614.

Mayne, L. An individual study of the reading acceleration of two kindergarten children. *Elementary English,* 1963, **40**, 406–408.

McCracken, R. A. A two-year study of the reading achievement of children who were reading when they entered first grade. *The Journal of Educational Research,* 1966, **59**, 207–210.

McKee, P., Brzeinski, J. E., and Harrison, M. L. *The effectiveness of teaching reading in kindergarten.* Cooperative Research Project No. 5-0381. Denver Public Schools and Colorado State Department of Education, 1966.

Montessori, M. *The Montessori method.* Cambridge, Mass.: Robert Bentley, 1965.

Mood, D. W. Reading in kindergarten? A critique of The Denver Study. *Educational Leadership,* 1967, **24**, 399–403.

Moore, O. K. *Autotelic responsive environments and exceptional children.* Hamden, Conn.: Responsive Environments Foundation, 1963.

Morrison, C., Harris, A. M., and Auerbach, I. T. The reading performance of disadvantaged early and non-early readers from grades 1 through 3. *Journal of Educational Research,* 1971, **65**, 23–26.

Plessas, G. P., and Oakes, C. R. Prereading experiences of selected early readers. *The Reading Teacher,* 1964, **XVII**, 241–245.

Savin, H. B., and Bever, T. G. The nonperceptual reality of the phoneme. *Journal of Verbal Learning and Verbal Behavior,* 1970, **9**, 294–302.

Scherer, G. A., and Wertheimer, M. *A psycholinguistic experiment in foreign-language teaching.* New York: McGraw-Hill, 1964.

Silberberg, N. E., and Silberberg, M. C. Hyperlexia: Specific word recognition skills in young children. *Exceptional Children,* 1967, **34**, 41–42.

Silberberg, N. E., and Silberberg, M. C. Hyperlexia: The other end of the continuum. *The Journal of Special Education,* 1971, **5,** 233–242.

Smith, F. *Psycholinguistics and reading.* New York: Holt, Rinehart & Winston, 1973.

Smith, F. Learning to read by reading. *Language Arts,* 1976, **53,** 297–299, 322.

Sutton, M. H. Readiness for reading at the kindergarten level. *The Reading Teacher,* 1964, **17,** 234–240.

Sutton, M. H. First grade children who learned to read in kindergarten. *The Reading Teacher,* 1965, **19,** 192–196.

Sutton, M. H. Children who learned to read in kindergarten: A longitudinal study. *The Reading Teacher,* 1969, **22,** 595–602, 683.

Torrey, J. W. Learning to read without a teacher: A case study. *Elementary English,* 1969, **46,** 550–556.

THE CHILD'S SOCIAL ENVIRONMENT AND LEARNING TO READ

DORIS R. ENTWISLE

Department of Social Relations
The Johns Hopkins University
Baltimore, Maryland

I. INTRODUCTION

Reading is a pivotal skill for all persons in society. One must read to use a telephone book, to find one's way through a town or city, to pay one's bills, and to buy groceries. Even simple social transactions between persons rely on reading—telephone messages, mail, traffic tickets, children's report cards, all require reading. Small wonder then that educators have paid more attention to reading than to any other aspect of education, and at times they have had help from psychologists, from specialists in linguistics, from clinicians of various kinds (including speech pathologists), and from other specialists as well. Despite all this effort we still do not understand much about how children learn to read, but the help offered from such a wide assortment of social scientists makes it all the more surprising that educators have paid scant notice to how the child's social milieu affects learning to read. So-called "reading models," to the author's

145

knowledge, model the process of learning to read always in terms of a **single** individual (see Davis, 1971). The lone child is pictured with his text and his teacher and not much is said about peers, parents, or classmates. Perhaps this has happened because reading, once learned, is an activity that can be pursued in isolation. The learning of reading, however, is highly social and the reasons for learning to read are almost entirely social.

The elementary schoolroom contains many children, often divided into "reading groups." Everyone in the classroom knows which is the "fast" group and which the "slow," no matter whether "1" is high or "1" is low. Before coming to school children "play school" or "play library." Why? Because they see school and library activities as important social activities. Most parents have a consuming interest in their child's reading, and if there is a reading problem physicians, speech therapists, guidance counselors, and psychologists are called. In short, the sources of motivation for any child's learning to read are almost entirely social and the likelihood of a child's learning to read easily and well is strongly conditioned by social factors, particularly the family.

What about motivation, granting that it is social? For some children motivation is high because learning to read offers large rewards. Middle-class children, for example, find learning to read exciting and pleasurable because reading is woven into the fabric of their daily lives. They are pleased to be able to read menus in restaurants and signs along the highway. For other children, both the inducements for learning to read and the rewards for doing so may be problematic. Often the social structure of the school and of the out-of-school environment of less-advantaged children causes learning to read to be painful rather than pleasurable. Many times these children fird that reading leads to negative rather than to positive social sanctions. If one child in a class gets pleasure from reading while the others are poor performers and find it taxing, the interested child may suffer ostracism—be tagged as a "rate-buster." There is no more potent motivator than social approval for any human being. Most young children learn to read because they receive social approval for doing so and social disapproval is a strong disincentive. This being the case, it is astonishing that so few reading specialists have thought carefully about social motivation, its nature, and its sources for children of different groups.

Marks in school are motivators if they evoke praise from significant others. Marks are strong nonmotivators if they lead to social disapproval. Marks can be meaningless (vacuous as motivators) if a child doesn't know what marks mean and/or parents are confused by them. Rewards are defined by the receiver, in other words.

Exactly how differences in reading achievement arise between children of various social groups is not well understood. As the reader might suspect, however, this chapter will cover some topics closely related to social motivators because of what has already been said. It is one thing to say that children who learn to read best are the ones for whom reading makes the most sense. It is quite another thing to trace out the causal mechanisms that lead to this outcome. Also, "social class" implies a multitude of differences, besides those in motivation, ranging all the way from differences in health status to subtle differences in the way language is used. What is beyond dispute is that there **are** large differences by social class in how well children learn to read (see, e.g., St. John, 1970; Stein, 1971) and likely much of the explanation for reading differences is therefore related to social factors.

In a short chapter one can indicate only a few of the ways that children's social environments may affect how they learn to read and much of what will be said here is conjectural—yet to be carefully researched. Furthermore, any remarks must be incomplete because reading is a complex activity, one made up of many subskills, and how these subskills are organized undoubtedly evolves as children's reading proficiency increases. Thus a social factor having an impact on reading in first grade may be less important or absent later on, for example, having people read aloud at bedtime. Other social factors, however, may assume prominence in higher grades, such things as having a good friend who likes to read, for example.

This chapter is incomplete for another reason, namely that reading, writing, and speech are all intertwined and interdependent in ways still obscure, and the social environment impinges differently upon each of these language components. Speech, for example, certainly influences reading acquisition, and probably social factors affecting speech also cause differences in the way persons from different speech communities learn to read. If so, we know little about it. Differences in speech as sources of difficulty in learning to read, if anything, have probably been overrated lately. Variations in speech may matter only if they are closely linked to critical discriminations of morphemes. In the past decade sociolinguists have mapped some of the more common dialects in an effort to pinpoint features (like dropping of final consonants) that may affect reading. These problems are now much better understood than formerly.

The most important cause for limiting coverage in a chapter of this sort, however, is that the social milieu of the child and how that milieu affects learning—the sociology of learning—is a rapidly developing and complex area of study. Many factors can be seen as primarily social (sex-role socialization, belief systems, cultural values, and other things) and they all affect how, and how well, children learn to read. Only a full-length monograph could do justice to such a comprehensive set of factors, and since much research related to these problems is currently in progress, a monograph would be premature at this time.

II. LANGUAGE AS A CUE TO SOCIAL CLASS

The interdependence between social stratification and speech forms, surprisingly, is something sociologists until recently ignored. But there is a close tie between speech type and every other social variable. Normal children learn to speak their native tongue without specific teaching. No one is surprised that children in France learn French as a first language or that children in Great Britain learn English. Political boundaries are easy to equate with language differences. What is less commonly recognized is that **social** boundaries also control the learning of language. Children who live in some parts of a city learn a rather different language from those who live in other parts. Moreover, language is used differently in different parts of a city.

Social boundaries often imply a hierarchy. Every known society is divided into social layers, and in a highly industrialized and complex society like that of the United States, where there is an elaborate division of labor, stratification of the society is extensive. There are upper-class whites and upper-class blacks, for instance, with subtle variations in status within each group. There are also persons of both races who are in the middle, lower down, or even at the very bottom of the social ladder. A person's speech is often a good clue as to his or her position in a layered society.

The reader might wonder why speech does not become homogeneous. Differences in speech persist because verbal interaction between persons in different social layers or groups is restricted. Amish parents actively promote their children's learning of "Pennsylvania Dutch," and they avoid commerce of any kind with outsiders. Blue-collar families in the San Francisco Bay area, and presumably in other areas, act in ways to insulate themselves from contact with middle-class persons. They far prefer contact with their kin or neighbors to contact with co-workers, for example. They would rather spend their spare time with persons whose speech is like their own. Cohen and Hodges' (1963) research showed, for example, that blue-collar workers in the Bay area go out of their way to avoid verbal interchanges with middle-class persons.

Human groups promote social solidarity and define social identity by common speech patterns. A common language (dialect, code) coordinates activities of a group and makes individuals aware of their membership in the group. Speech signals belongingness, being socially comfortable, in other words. Language customs have high value for pegging one's membership in an in-group. Persons who ignore their group's speech customs are assumed to be denying membership in the group.

Most persons in the United States have only a fuzzy recognition of status boundaries, perhaps because of the American ethic of egalitarianism. Language, however, signals status even for persons who will not consciously admit status boundaries, and it defines the character of social relations between people as well. In the United States and Canada, consistent and systematic differences between the speech of middle-class persons and of blue-collar or working-class persons, whether specifically acknowledged or not, may make it hard for children from different social backgrounds to be thrust together in a school. Language differences cannot be easily ignored even when people try very hard to ignore them. A teacher can easily judge children's social status from their speech and can use speech cues to tell middle-class children from children from poorer families (Williams, 1970; Rist, 1970). Such judgments, even at a level that may be below the teacher's awareness, **can** lead to other judgments. Bikson's (1974) work shows, for example, that teachers "hear" sentences spoken by minority-group children to be the same length as sentences spoken by Anglo children despite the fact that the sentences spoken by the minority-group children are about twice as long on the average as those spoken by Anglos. Such unconscious biases may lead a teacher to expect one child to learn to read easily or to expect another child to have difficulty in learning to read. As we will see later on, these status-linked judgments at times have far-reaching consequences because they are made early in a child's school career before there are any "real data" to use to forecast how well a child will do, and judgments, even when unconscious, make the child sense that he/she is held in low esteem. Both social differentiation of speech and social stratification in society itself, then, have consequences for reading.

III. READINESS OF THE CHILD

One might think that learning to read **should** not be any harder than learning to speak. One is forced to conclude, however, that children have "in some sense an innate ability to perceive speech" (Mattingly and Kavanagh, 1973, p. 5), that is, they are cognitively tuned to learn to speak. They are not cognitively tuned in anything like the same way to learn to read, however. Item: relatively few languages in the history of the world have been written languages—the alphabet seems to have been invented only once—and if human beings had innate cognitive structures predisposing them to read one would expect written languages to have sprung up spontaneously in several places. Communication with written symbols is intrinsically hard for human beings to learn and children usually need to be taught to read.

What else besides being a fluent speaker does the child need by way of preparation to learn to read? No pat answer can be given. Children do learn many other things besides speech that help them learn to read, however, and some social groups impart these "other things" involved in reading readiness better than other social groups. As mentioned previously, every child learns to speak the language of others to whom he is tied in social networks, and learns without formal instruction. Knowing the language is clearly one requisite for learning to read.

A. Social Differences in Linguistic Awareness

One socially conditioned factor is linguistic awareness. To learn to read, a child needs some conscious awareness of morphophonetic segments and the acoustic signals they represent. For example, the child should be aware, or be made aware, that the letter *m* denotes the sound at the beginnings of words like *me* or *man*. The child must have some notion that different marks on a page have systematic relations with sounds he already knows. Some speakers are much more consciously aware of how language is structured than others, and some families directly or indirectly encourage a high level of linguistic awareness in their children. Parents who make puns or poems easily, for example, consciously exploit the sounds and segments of language. Reciting nursery rhymes, reading aloud, listening to speech recordings, singing nursery songs and lullabies, or recording speech on tape or with movie cameras are all activities that foster linguistic awareness in children. Some children have their own record players and records. There are even talking records and books designed especially for "prereaders." Some commercial games capitalize on sounds, and many children spontaneously force their own made-up games to depend on speech or particular sounds. Children often count or recite lists when they jump rope or bounce balls, for example.

Very little is actually known about "awareness," but a hint of what may be involved is contained in a serendipitous finding by the author (Entwisle, 1966). In a study of children's word associations she found that, when asked to free-associate to the word *once,* some lower-class fifth graders wrote the word APONE. At first Entwisle classified *apone* as a nonsense word or error. Later she realized that *apone* probably meant *upon a,* as in the sequence *once upon a time*. This response revealed clearly that some lower-class fifth-grade children (11 years old) were confused about common word segmentations—in this case they did not identify the components of the phrase *upon a* as the two separate words *upon* and *a* with which they were undoubtedly familiar in other contexts. Such confusion in a fifth grader seems surprising but children, before they learn to read, may often be confused about whether some utterances are one word or several words. This confusion may hinder reading to a greater extent than is commonly supposed. We would expect a child hearing a "single word" for a sequence of syllables like *upon a* to have trouble in decoding or in understanding the words in written form, if only because we repeatedly see the confusion generated by a word like *misled* which many children pronounce "*mizzled*" and consequently misunderstand.

Other examples of linguistic awareness involve word roots and homonyms. Young children actually inquire, for example, on learning the word *hurricane* if there are *himmicanes*—mixing the sound *hurr* with the familiar pronoun *her*. Other young children invent a word *tenty* (derived from *eighty, ninety, tenty*) to generalize what they perceive as a system for designating larger numbers. Children build up expectancies for words that do not exist, and perhaps have no experience with some common words that they will encounter in print. I suspect that what we now know about sources of children's confusion represents the tip of an iceberg. Undoubtedly most such confusions remain buried below the child's (or parent's or teacher's) level of awareness. In families where language is a topic of interest in itself, however, and where various kinds of language arts occupy parents' attention, the sounds and meanings of language are often, if incidentally, made explicit. In such homes, one would suspect, some of the early confusions about words and word meanings are resolved as children are parties to incidental instruction in language forms and variations. Knowledge of structure and not merely knowing a great many words is what is at issue here. Command of syntax strongly predicts success in learning to read (Cocking and Potts, 1976) while an extensive vocabulary seems somewhat less crucial.

B. Social Differences and Language Type

Besides being linguistically aware, some children have an advantage in learning to read because the language they learn is "network English," the language used on network TV and by other national organizations. Vocabulary, phonology, and syntax are all modified to some degree as one moves among different regions of the country. Some modifications could be very troublesome to beginning readers, such as those in which critical inflections are lost or changed. For example, if a resident of New England says "cah" for *car* this phonological variant and others like it will probably not generate much confusion in decoding written words to speech. But if terminal consonants are dropped in speech, as in many black dialects, some verb inflections important for meaning will be lost. Thus, *He go* sounds the same as *He goed,* when the final consonant marking the past tense is left unpronounced in some black dialects. The difference in this instance is critical for meaning, so the distinction is one that must be made.

There have been many studies in the past decade of differences in dialect and of what are termed "code differences." Dialect usually means a speech variant that a speaker may be unable to speak, although he could understand it. Thus Americans who live outside Appalachia can understand an Appalachian dialect although they likely could not reproduce it.

Code implies something different. "Code" is a term popularized by Bernstein and his co-workers (see e.g., Bernstein, 1970) and it implies a differential selection of forms from within the same dialect. Most often the term "restricted code" is linked to lower-class speech and "elaborated code" is linked to middle- or upper-class speech. For example, in speaking to her children a mother may use a restricted code—short sentences with many things taken for granted. The mother might say "Cut it." The children present can tell whether she means stop right now or slow down a bit, whether she is addressing one or several of them, and so on. If the same mother were speaking to her hairdresser and she said simply "Cut it," the outcome would be very different. Two speakers of network English could switch from one code to another, speak and understand both, but choose between codes depending upon situational or social demands. A working-class person might form sentences differently when speaking with a friend (restricted) as compared with a tax auditor (elaborated), for example.

"Codes" received a great deal of attention from researchers in the United States in the 1960s following Bernstein's pioneering work with middle-class and working-class English children early in that decade. A large number of investigators in the United States were geared for finding code differences among American children of various social classes and then for using these differences to explain differences in cognitive development. There are certainly differences in the complexity and abstractness of speech of different social groups in the United States, but it is highly doubtful that these differences **in themselves** are deterrents to rapid success in reading or any other cognitive activity. Rather, like dialects, codes may decrease the likelihood of success in learning to read because they are associated with social factors, like the teacher's tagging the child as coming from a social group for whom the teacher holds low expectations, or like the child having a view of how the world operates that is different from the teacher's view.

Other language differences associated with social-class boundaries are perhaps just as important as dialect and code differences, or even more so, but are harder to pin down. These are linked to the way language is used. Middle-class children learn to use language **as an instrument,** as a means of solving problems (Bee, Van Egern, Streissguth, Nyman, and Leckie, 1969; Hess, Shipman, Brophy, and Bear, 1968).

Middle-class children also use language differently from ghetto children in interacting with adults, so-called "sociolinguistic differences." The middle-class child learns to respond to "suggestions." When a middle-class child's teacher says "I hope you will erase the board" the child interprets this as an order to erase the board and goes ahead and erases it. When the middle-class child holds a minority opinion, he may express his opinion in tentative terms, saying "Perhaps" or "I think possibly. . . ." In other words, the middle-class child has been trained to use mitigating forms. Children from less advantaged circumstances often lack experience with such forms, or even misinterpret them, equating tentativeness with uncertainty. These facts have been repeatedly pointed to by critics of standardized tests (Labov, 1966; and others).

As far as schoolwork is concerned, middle-class children, many of whom have learned to use language as a primary means of solving problems, hold a tremendous advantage. In trying to get some gadget to work, for example, they may review aloud to themselves the steps they have taken. This recitation may quickly uncover an error. Or the middle-class child, merely by translating a problem into words and thereby communicating it to another person, may be provided with help from an adult without directly asking the adult for help. Middle-class children are often specifically rehearsed by their parents in how to speak to policemen, to train conductors, or to other public servants if need arises. Ghetto children are often trained to be suspicious of adults and to conceal their own difficulties lest someone capitalize upon their weakness.

The ghetto child is not at ease using language to talk with persons outside his own social group for all the reasons just given and may justifiably react with hostility to adults outside his own group. Also the ghetto child may not have had much opportunity to observe others using language for solving problems. His parents do not use language very productively for solving problems, even for problems having to do with securing services from municipal agencies or from business firms to whose services they are entitled (see Cohen and Hodges, 1963; Hess, 1970).

A very provocative and potentially far-reaching difference between the speech of middle-class and lower-class mothers was uncovered in Hess and Shipman's (1965, 1968) study of how mothers tried to teach simple tasks to their 4-year-old children. All mothers who were observed wanted to teach their children, but of the four social-class levels of mothers included in the study, some were much more successful than others. Part of their success hinged on their speech. The middle-class mothers used fewer negatives—they said "no" less often. They also used more abstract words in trying to teach their children than did the lower-class parents. Think what this means. Fewer negatives and fewer uses of *no* may not seem important but it is ineffective, not to mention punishing, to tell a 4-year-old repeatedly, "No, don't do that." Even if the child stops what he is doing, he does not know what he should be doing instead. Also to cease one course of action does not guarantee at all that the child will know what other course of action to take that is correct. If the child is trying to learn how to run an Etch-A-Sketch toy or how to sort objects into classes as was true for the mother–child pairs Hess and Shipman studied, the child can cease one wrong approach (by responding to his mother's "no") but then take up another wrong approach. The world is structured so there are almost always a large number of wrong approaches but only a few right approaches to a problem. Middle-class mothers not only told their children what to do that was right, but gave them general "structuring" information so that in a future similar problem they might have a fruitful strategy to pursue. By helping children be successful problem solvers and by teaching them general problem-solving strategies, middle-class parents are laying the groundwork for just the kinds of behaviors that will aid in learning to read. Sociolinguistic training makes children sensitive to other cues, such as who is speaking or where. Middle-class speech in the United States tends to be considerably more context-free than blue-collar speech.

The reader may be surprised to realize how context-dependent the language used with children is likely to be. Berko-Gleason (1973), for example, in recording speech of middle-class mothers and 4-year-olds at mealtime noted that a mother would say things like "Hot! Hot!" as she set a warm plate in front of a child. Everyone understood the message, but a mother would not speak in the same way to adults or to guests. The meaning of the message, "Watch out for this plate," would not be clear unless one were there observing the activity. Speech tends to be more context-dependent the more socially intimate the speakers, and when children are being addressed context dependency may be accentuated because parents and children interact over and over in the same rituals— getting ready for school, getting ready for bed, at mealtimes, in the supermarket, and so on. Nevertheless, the middle-class child probably hears speech that is less context-dependent than the speech heard by other children (e.g., Bee *et al.*, 1969). The middle-class child, more than the working-class or ghetto child, is exposed to speech that is abstract and to speech that takes into account alternative modes of action and alternative contexts. Many of the features of middle-class speech will characterize the speech of the teacher who tries to teach the child to read, of course, for elementary teachers by and large are recruited from the (lower) middle class.

The more that speech is free of context, the more it is representative of a cognitive activity such as reading, of course. Reading is most often entirely free of specific social context. The symbols to be decoded from the printed page are usually not related to the persons who happen to be present when the child is reading. Reading successfully requires the learner to rely completely on the printed page. The reader may need to try different interpretations of what he/she is reading until he/she hits on the one that makes the most sense. By using more abstract language and encouraging more alternative modes of speech in children as well as alternative approaches to a problem, the middle-class parent encourages cognitive flexibility of a kind that should aid in reading acquisition.

C. Social Differences and Cognitive Style

More subtle differences in child-rearing practices, not as closely related to speech as any we have discussed so far, are also associated with social class. Social and ethnic groups differ greatly in how they view the world. Some groups are confident of extracting benefits, whether economic or educational, from their surroundings. Some groups feel personally responsible for their own success or failure. The middle-class person is apt to interpret events as caused by himself and as responsive to actions he can take. Persons who are economically disadvantaged are much less likely to feel that they themselves have power over their own lives. They frequently see fate or luck as the cause of what happens. Such differences in outlook upon the world, which cause differences in self-confidence, could be of enormous importance for reading. If a child senses from his/her parents that striving or effort often go unrewarded, he/she may have no interest in trying hard to reach the goals set early in his/her school career. The child may instead see school achievement as a matter of luck, as whether the teacher likes him, as whether he/she got an "easy" book, or as whether he/she just "can" or "cannot" read easily, without seeing what he himself or she herself does in an objective light.

Closely related to the ideas in the preceding paragraph is the notion of "opportunity," especially as developed in a monograph by Kerckhoff (1974). Children are offered, or not offered, many different kinds of opportunities at many different points. There are differences in the opportunities they have to learn various skills at home, differences in their opportunities to associate with various kinds of peers (including peers who themselves expect to do well), differences in whether, and how sincerely, they are offered another chance after failure, and differences in the opportunity they have to learn how society really works. Furthermore, a child who misses or who has been denied an earlier opportunity is likely to be offered fewer opportunities later on. Outlook is built up from experience and, at present at least, the experience of some social groups in learning to read is likely to be much more encouraging than the experience of others.

Other affective factors linked with social-class membership, such as whether material rewards are more attractive than verbal rewards, whether the child can work now for rewards in the future (delay gratification), or whether a child has feelings of hostility toward adults who are not of his own subcultural group, are also important. A reward such as a piece of candy may be a good way to persuade lower-class children to practice spelling. A teacher's smile may be a good way to persuade middle-class children. Even such small things as the tone of voice used to deliver instructions can have differential effects—positive intonations are reported to work best in giving lower-class kindergarten children instructions whereas middle-class children respond similarly to positive, neutral, or a negative tone (Kashinsky and Wiener, 1969).

There is also the matter of the time delay of the reward. Usually rewards are more effective the sooner they follow the event they should reinforce. But, given this, some children (often those of the middle class) have been trained to tolerate delays in rewards, to "delay gratification." They have learned through training, starting from the time they were toddlers, to postpone rewards, perhaps letting the rewards pile up. This kind of delay training can be a strong asset for children learning a complex activity such as reading, for often days or weeks must pass before the child acquires enough reading skill to derive much intrinsic pleasure from it. A child's feelings of control and a generalized expectation for success, in fact, may be crucial for success in reading because, as mentioned earlier, reading is a very complex activity and learning it takes years.

Research on how children's feelings of efficacy relate to their success in learning to read is not as tidy as a superficial look at the literature might suggest, however. Most of the efficacy studies do not take aptitude into account, and since children who have higher aptitudes could justifiably feel more in control because they more easily achieve success, it is hard to know whether the cart is before the horse, that is whether aptitude or control beliefs are causally prior. Thus control beliefs do generally differ by social class, with lower control beliefs associated with lower class, but it is hard to know exactly what the causal priorities are.

Different social groups also seem to adopt different problem-solving strategies. Lower-class children, if we judge by the data of Hess and Shipman, are taught to appeal to authority. That is, if a problem is presented, one way to solve it is to inquire the answer of someone who knows. Now certainly there are times when such a strategy is ideal. On the other hand, children will not get to be effective readers unless they develop some strong trial-and-error strategies. They need, in other words, to provide some useful feedback for themselves when confronted with a string of written symbols which must be decoded into speech.

Can the child think up and test out several solutions to a problem? Can the child endure the waiting while he/she checks various solutions? Can the child figure out which words are the crucial ones for getting the overall meaning? Can the child remain happy despite the uncertainty that accompanies trial and error? Several different kinds of research suggest that middle-class mothers, as compared to lower-class mothers, take more actions to help their children become successful problem solvers (see e.g., Bee *et al.*, 1969; Hess and Shipman, 1965). A middle-class mother allows her child to work at his own pace, and she offers general structuring suggestions on how to search for a problem's solution. The lower-class mother, by contrast, makes more highly specific suggestions that do not emphasize basic problem-solving strategies.

The task of learning to read is certainly one that will benefit from effective problem-solving strategies. The problem is to decode written symbols over and over. Each phrase or sentence is a new problem. The child must learn how to decode messages. If, first of all, the child **expects** success and if the child has the intent of persisting until success occurs, no one would doubt that the child's chances of success are improved. In decoding, the child makes use of many kinds of cues—semantic, contextual, grammatical, sociolinguistic—so that it is profitable to think up and try out various hypotheses about the message. If the child finds one set of cues in conflict with another set, he/she may wish to revise the hypothesis about the message. When the situation is structured as ''this message is more likely to be right than another one'' and when the child can tolerate uncertainty while testing out different ideas, the child improves the chance of reading the ''correct'' message. At least when cognitively attuned to uncertainty, the child comes to the classroom with the expectation that alternative behaviors are ''good'' and not ''wrong.'' Social-class differences in the way problems are seen and structured, therefore, bear heavily on reading success.

Taking this evidence altogether, what one sees is greater cognitive flexibility in the middle-class child. Such a child tries and retries solutions until a satisfactory and integrative solution is found. This is exactly what reading requires. Children who learn to read easily are more attentive (Turnure and Samuels, 1972), and we suspect from studies of Puerto Rican and other minority groups that such children are also more likely to attend to "work." In a careful study of the work responses of Puerto Rican and "Anglo" 3-year-old children to cognitive demands, Hertzig, Birch, Thomas, and Mendez (1968) found that while 82% of the white middle-class children responded with work to a verbal test item, fewer (66%) of the Puerto Rican children did so. When these same children were observed as they interacted with their own parents, Puerto Rican parents were found to place less emphasis on task orientation and task completion. One suspects that the middle-class child, in addition to possessing cognitive flexibility, is better prepared than other children for school in terms of work habits.

In summary this section points out that middle-class children differ from lower-class children in a number of respects. They are more aware of the subtleties of the language they speak (e.g., its segments and roots). They use language for different purposes and in different ways (e.g., as an aid to problem solving, as a means of interaction with persons from other groups, in less context-dependent ways). They differ in cognitive style—i.e., they perceive themselves as causal, they can delay gratification, they adopt a trial-and-error approach to problem solving, they are more flexible and work-oriented. On reflection, the possible implications for learning to read should be obvious, even though not demonstrated empirically. One would think that the middle-class child has an advantage in all these respects because reading is more abstract, it requires capacity to segment and deal consciously with language elements (e.g., words, roots), it takes a long time to learn (requiring delay of gratification) and can be approached as a problem to be solved (using a trial-and-error stragegy). Also, it seems reasonable to argue that a child who is flexible and work-oriented and who perceives himself as being "in control" has an advantage.

IV. THE SCHOOL'S ROLE

So far I have looked at "readiness" as a characteristic of children from various social groups and suggested why, or how, some children come to school more ready than others to begin reading. The question can be turned around. What about "readiness" of the school or of teachers? Readiness of the school could refer to the physical attributes of the school, that is, its facilities and equipment. Does it have suitable primers and books, audiovisual aids, a library, and teachers especially trained to teach beginning readers? In the United States special funds to help improve reading instruction have now been so widely disbursed by the federal government and so many other social action programs have been undertaken that the possession of concrete resources is usually not the problem these days.

Even if a school is well endowed in terms of resources, however, it may be deficient in other ways, in its social climate, for instance. The prevailing social climate in the classroom is crucial because learning is a social activity and the child is continually interacting with teacher and classmates in learning to read. All of early reading is embedded in social interaction. If peers are interested in learning to read and are doing well at reading, this in itself is helpful. If teachers know and understand what kinds of cultural differences characterize the children they have in a classroom, their understanding will help to make them effective as role models. If the school is an institution respected in the neighborhood and if children hear from their older siblings that school is "good" or "fun," this too is bound to help. And there is evidence, although fragmentary, that some of the cognitive flexibility the middle-class child gets before starting school can be taught after school is begun. For example, in an experimental after-school program for black children who were below grade level in reading, when rewards were stopped, children continued to work at reading because the task had been more **pleasurable** for them (Wolf, Giles, and Hall, 1968). The school's social climate, in fact, may outweigh any of the particular aptitudes a child brings with him if one considers the findings of the Coleman report or the St. Lambert experiments (discussed further on). A number of topics related to the school's social climate will be discussed separately in what follows.

A. Parent Involvement in the School

There is little direct evidence on how parent's involvement in school, or their psychological closeness to school, affects children in the primary grades. Parents who are poorly educated themselves or those whose background is culturally different, however, may have hazy ideas of what school is about. Entwisle and Hayduk (1978) have observed that lower-class parents actively avoid opportunities to establish contact with the school and, as a consequence, they often do not know what the school expects of their child or what they can do to help their child. Middle-class parents, on the other hand, were observed to have close lines of communication with the elementary school. They exert strong pressure, if necessary, on the school or on the teacher to be responsive to the child's needs. Personnel in the middle-class school know they must answer to parents. If children fail or are discouraged, the teacher will be held to account. In lower-class schools parents often find it difficult to challenge actions of the teacher or of the school because they do not know very much of what is going on or are too timid to make demands. Children no doubt have an acute sense of this power, or its lack. (After all, children easily sense, and exploit, differences in the power of two parents when such differences exist!) The child from favored circumstances has a sense of control and invulnerability while the child from a less favored background senses the gap between home and school and parents' relative powerlessness as far as the school is concerned.

The data of Entwisle and Hayduk (1978) for middle- and lower-class parents gave clear evidence of social-class differences in parents' knowledge about how schools function. When asked to guess what marks children would receive in reading on their first report cards, middle-class parents generally guessed correctly the proportion of various marks that first-grade teachers would award (40%, A; 45%, B; 15%, C). Lower-class parents, on the other hand, guessed too high. They estimated 88% of children would receive A and B, whereas only 25% of the children actually received marks this high. Put simply, the lower-class parents were at a loss to forecast what actions school personnel would take. Middle-class parents had their expectations tuned to those of the school, perhaps because they were in touch with the school, with other children's parents, and with the community at large. More than 90% of middle-class parents, for example, responded to an invitation to visit their children's classrooms. Less than 10% of lower-class parents, on the other hand, visited classrooms when similarly invited and there was no active organization of these parents such as a PTA (Parent–Teachers Association).

B. Teachers' Expectations

In considering the social climate of the school and the school's "readiness," the reader will undoubtedly call to mind the Pygmalion studies. Is it possible that teachers decide who will read well and who will not? The answer may be a resounding "yes" in some cases. Palardy (1969) asked teachers what they believed about the success of first-grade boys in learning to read. Ten teachers (Group A) believed that first-grade boys are on the average as successful as first-grade girls in learning how to read. Fourteen teachers (Group B) believed that first-grade boys are less successful than girls. At the end of grade 1, students of five Group A teachers were compared with students of five Group B teachers on a standardized reading test. The boys of Group B teachers were significantly lower than the girls of Group B teachers. The girls of Group B teachers and both the girls and boys of Group A teachers made virtually identical scores on the tests. The actual classroom events leading to these different outcomes are unspecified, but the teachers' expectations are remarkably consistent with their pupils' subsequent performance on a standardized test.

Rist (1970) provided rich observational evidence about how teachers' behaviors may determine who succeeds in the early grades. In an all-black kindergarten class he observed that within a few days after school began, actually 8 days, the class had been split into three groups. One group was continually called upon to lead the class in the pledge of allegiance, to run errands, to be in charge of playground equipment, to lead the class to the bathroom, and so on. During the school year the three groups within the class (who sat at different tables) took on castelike qualities, with the gap in their academic achievements directly and strongly correlated with their early assigned social status. Furthermore, the gap widened as the year progressed.

Rist cited detailed evidence that the speech of the children was an important criterion for this initial grouping. The three separate tables which marked the subgroups within the class, were placed at increasing distances from the teacher, and "while the children placed at the first table were quite verbal with the teacher, the children placed at the remaining two tables spoke much less frequently with her. The children placed at the first table also displayed greater use of standard American English within the classroom. Whereas the children placed at the last two tables most often responded to the teacher in black dialect, the children at the first table did so very infrequently" (Rist, 1970, p. 420).

Speech is a very good cue for estimating social class. Many things other than grammatical features signal social-class membership. Prosodic features such as intonation, or paralinguistic features such as voice quality, define what we term social-class accents. Harms (1961) showed that 10 to 15 seconds of recorded speech is sufficient for a listener to correctly judge the social class of a speaker, and Williams (1970) subsequently showed that teachers easily differentiated among recorded samples of children's speech, one of their criteria being "ethnicity-nonstandardness." Voice cues have also been shown to affect teachers' judgments about pupils' intelligence (Seligman, Tucker, and Lambert, 1972).

In other words, a child's speech gives away his social-class status almost instantaneously, and plays a role in crystallizing teachers' expectations **prior** to actual verbal interchanges in instruction. Thus speech need not affect actual classroom learning one way or the other before the teacher can use speech as a basis for forming expectations. Rist's study documents the linking of speech habits of the child to the teacher's perception of reading readiness before assessment of IQ or of reading readiness by objective tests. A study by Williams and his associates (1971) already mentioned showed much the same thing, for teachers' judgments of "ethnicity-nonstandardness" in children's speech turned out to be correlated with assignments to graded classes in language arts, where assignments are essentially a measure of performance expectations (see also Crowl and MacGinitie, 1974; Jensen and Rosenfeld, 1974). One could add to this many studies showing how teachers' expectations (judgments of educability) affect the microstructure of teaching (Rubovits and Maehr, 1971; Meichenbaum, Bowers, and Ross, 1969; Brophy and Good, 1970).

In the United States and in other countries with linguistic minorities, there is linguistic identification of status. The suggestion is that a child's speech provides a quick classificatory scheme for the teacher. Teachers may often judge children's "educability" on the basis of speech cues and other factors related to social class, and then act in ways to confirm their expectations, Rist's paper gives considerable insight into the social dynamics underlying how social-class membership mediates low achievement through teacher expectations.

Many persons have proposed that dialect itself, aside from its impact on teacher expectations, poses a barrier to early reading. If a child speaks one dialect and uses a primer written in a different dialect, what happens? In the author's opinion dialect by itself is probably one of the least important obstacles in learning to read, and a recent comprehensive review of research in the area of dialect and reading strengthens this opinion (Somervill, 1975). The strongest evidence comes from experiments in Montreal by Wallace Lambert and his associates (1969, 1970, 1972). These experiments showed that Canadian Anglophone children placed in kindergartens in 1965 where French was spoken almost exclusively, and who subsequently received almost all instruction in French up to fifth grade, read very well in both languages. Children from two independent experiments showed a high level of skill in reading in terms of comparisons against English control groups in the same school and in another school, and against a French control class in the same district. Other bilingual educational programs (Tucker, Otanes, and Sibagan, 1970; Mackey, 1971; Inclan, 1971) yielded similarly favorable results. If dialect difference were a serious deterrent to reading acquisition, one would expect severe reading problems to occur when children who know only one language, say English, received all their first-grade reading instruction in French. Quite the opposite seems to be the case. French and English differ much more from one another than a black dialect differs from standard English.

The Montreal experiments seem to parallel, at least superficially, the school experience of many children in the United States who come from homes where a black dialect is spoken, and who enter schools where standard English is spoken. Such children receive instruction in school subjects in ''standard English,'' and so hear a different dialect during school hours from what they hear at home. Why is the outcome of this bi-dialectal experience, which so often leads to repeated reading failures and dropping out from school, so different from the outcome of bilingual experiments with Montreal children?

No final answer can be given, but the social matrices of the teaching efforts differ sharply. First, in bilingual programs there is recognition by the students, by the teachers, by the parents, and by the community of the explicit task being undertaken. The task is clearly defined—to learn a second language. In the United States, by contrast, until recently there has **not** been explicit recognition of the existence of minority dialects—there has rather been pressure against recognizing ''Negro'' speech. Schools have been slow to realize that a new dialect (standard English) needs to be acquired. The United States teacher has generally viewed the problem, if a problem were acknowledged at all, to be one of stamping out errors or of suppressing ''vulgar'' speech. In other words, the need for learning a new dialect was denied or twisted.

Issues raised by controversies over teaching in dialect, or taking account of dialect, are not simple and are only touched on here. Experiments with bilingual programs, however, do suggest that **social components,** more than language components, could account for the reading difficulty of dialect-speaking children in the United States, for even when the language the child speaks at home is completely different from the language used in reading instruction, as in Montreal, children can apparently learn to read very well. The social milieus of these experiments outside the United States differ sharply from the usual social milieu of the disadvantaged American child. Studies inside the United States, unfortunately, have confounded the social and linguistic factors so it is difficult to guess about how much variance each explains separately. It appears, however, from contrasting results of bilingual experiments where language differences are maximal (the Montreal experiments) with results of education in the United States where dialect differences are thought to diminish educability, that linguistic factors are dwarfed by social factors as explanations of educational deficits. If only language factors are at issue, it is hard to understand why a child who speaks a black dialect in Washington, D.C., should fare so badly in a school where his own dialect and standard English are spoken, when a child who speaks English in Montreal succeeds so well in a school where only French is spoken. The explanation may lie in how language factors **indirectly** affect teachers, and depend very little upon how language factors directly affect instruction in reading or other language arts.

C. Evaluation Practices

With all the attention that has been given over the last decade to resources of school systems, it is hard to understand why the actual marks teachers give have been almost ignored. Grading is a very important component of reading instruction. It provides feedback to tell children (and parents) how the child is progressing. Grading also can enhance or stifle motivation. Because of this, grading can be thought of as a "control system." Dornbusch and Scott (1975) provided a model for the study of such control systems and point out that a rational model is useful in studying control systems, not because such a model is necessarily true, but because such a model serves as a means of detecting problems in existing control systems. Some first-grade classrooms studied in research of Entwisle and Hayduk (1978), it turns out, exemplify **all** four of the ways Dornbusch and Scott saw for control systems to falter. Control systems fail when low performance evaluations occur through no fault of the performer.

One way is for the participant to receive contradictory evaluations. Another way is for the participant to be evaluated for performances over which he/she lacks control. A third way involves the performer being unable to predict the relation between the work performed and its evaluation. The fourth way is observed when the performer is expected to meet unattainable standards.

These four problems were much more apt to exist in a working-class than in a middle-class school Entwisle and Hayduk observed. Working-class first graders were unable to predict the relation between their work and its evaluation. There was no congruence between their expectations and their marks in first grade (problem three). In addition the standards for the working-class first graders of this research were "unattainable" for most children, because about 40% of the children received Ds on their first report card while a large majority hoped for As (problem four).

Differences between average first marks awarded in the two schools Entwisle and Hayduk studied were enormous. In reading, the average first mark was 1.77 (a little over a B) in the middle-class school. It was 3.15 (between a D and a C) in the working-class school. Even at the end of first grade the average reading mark in the working-class school was almost a full unit below that in the middle-class school (2.59 versus 1.73). In the two schools under study, most working-class children got Ds and Cs in first grade while middle-class children got As and Bs. Children in **both** schools had average IQs considerably above 100.

The disparity in children's ability to read by the end of second or third grade in the two schools is very perplexing given the above-average IQ levels of both schools. In the working-class school by the end of the second grade, children were reading below grade level, while those in the middle-class school were reading about a year **above** grade level. In the middle-class school, it appeared the child was being "gentled" into the system—allowed a year to try his/her wings without negative sanctions. In the working-class school, on the other hand, the child's first year was an abrasive brush with reality.

These data shed considerable light on marking practices and on the actual incentive that children may consequently perceive. First of all, case-by-case differences in marking from one year to the next were amazingly large. There was no significant matching between the marks given a child at the end of first grade and those given him in the middle of second grade, even though within each grade there was considerable consistency in individual children's marks. (What a cloudy picture this must offer the 6- or 7-year-old as he or she tries to monitor behavior.) Even more surprising, very many poor marks (up to 40%) were given in the working-class school on the first report card. This was absolutely unanticipated both by parents and by children. How such negative and disappointing events affect parents and children we do not know directly. For example, parents or children were not asked how they felt about the marks given on report cards. One does suspect, however, that when feedback is extremely negative the child may insulate himself/herself against it.

A few other comments about marking are in order. First, asking teachers to evaluate each child in 22 areas, as the report cards in these schools required, is a difficult task when a teacher must rate 20 or 30 children. Earlier work suggested that most first-grade children understood what was being rated in reading, arithmetic, and conduct, but children did **not** understand other areas which were rated, such as spelling or language. Whether a child should be assigned a mark in an area he or she cannot define is a serious question, especially in light of Dornbusch's and Scott's statements cited earlier. Too many marks may also be dangerous because the child may fail to process feedback for areas which are important ones and instead process feedback for some other area which is not important. A child could pay attention to marks in physical education and music and feel he or she was doing well, for example, even though he or she had poor marks in reading and arithmetic.

This brief account of actual marks and how they are assigned leads one to think that far too little attention has been directed at what actually happens when marks are given out. The giving of a mark is a relatively simple act; its consequences are more complex. The data of Entwisle and Hayduk show that marks affect behavior of several people for a considerable time after the mark is given.

V. ATTEMPTS TO IMPROVE SOCIAL CLIMATES

The war on poverty programs, begun by the United States government in the 1960s, focused everyone's attention on educational inequalities, particularly on "school readiness." These programs were singularly ineffectual, but even now, after the war on poverty is officially over, there continue to be "right to read" programs, programs on "bicultural education," and other federal programs aimed at underachievers in reading. It is instructive to examine the thinking on which such programs are based because most of them seem to be based on the same premises as those underlying the war on poverty.

One kind of thinking that led to some programs is called the "deficit theory." It is identified particularly with psychologists such as Bereiter and Engelmann (1966). This theory holds that minority-group children experience cognitive deficits as a consequence of impoverished language and it presumes a cultural deprivation in poor children's environments. Thus black and Chicano children who grow up in poor homes are thought to develop cognitive deficits, where "deficit" implies "less ability than middle-class white children to function well in the early elementary school environment," particularly as measured by standardized tests of reading achievement. The remedy for "deficit" is thought to be strong doses of practice with standard English. Preschool programs featuring much practice with complete sentences and the like were designed and diligently tried out. Evaluations of effects of these programs when children entered school revealed no particular benefits for the children (see, e.g., Bereiter, Washington, Engelmann, and Osborn, 1969; Karnes, Hodgins, Teska, and Kirk, 1969), hardly surprising if, as Gibson and Levin (1957:508) said, "the view of Black English as a deficient dialect is based on misconceptions and inappropriate methodology."

Dialects whether spoken by blacks or other minority groups are not grammatically deficient or productive in themselves of "poor thinking." These dialects just happen to encode concepts in somewhat different terms from standard English. It is well to keep in mind that middle-class children of above-average IQ find it difficult to recall grammatical features of a dialect different from their own too (Seitz, n.d.). The "deficit theory" should be discarded.

What, though, of linguistic differences between the grammatical forms used by certain dialects and the language found in reading primers (the difference theory)? Will a black child who starts first grade saying "He come" to mean *He will come* have more difficulty learning how to read than a non-dialect-speaking child? Certainly there are abundant data to document the relatively lower reading achievement of many dialect-speaking children. But how much of a burden is imposed by the dialect itself is not at all a simple question to answer, and very little is known specifically about how linguistic differences affect learning to read. For one thing, dialect differences involving inflections signaling meaning are likely to be more important than other kinds of differences, as mentioned earlier in several places. For example, omitting the *l* and *r* sounds, as many black dialects do, could cause confusion among innumerable words—*bowl* versus *bow, foal* versus *foe,* and *mole* versus *mow* versus *more,* to name only a few. The amount of confusion caused may be a function of the teacher's dialect as well as the student's, however, and a severe, if not fatal flaw to the difference approach is that there are so many dialects. There are at least seven major dialects in the United States. Constructing programs from this starting place does not look promising.

One way to approach the problem of "school readiness" is to see the issue as that of achieving a "match" between the child's own language, cognitive style, and motivational structure and what he finds in the school (see Bee, 1976; Cole and Bruner, 1971). As Bee (1976, p. 9) noted "we need to know a great deal more about the characteristics that children from different social classes and cultural backgrounds bring with them to school. And we need to study these . . . in ecologically natural settings." Much of what has been presented in this chapter has to do with defining a "match." Instead of "difference" perhaps what is needed is more emphasis on similarities. How are children from all social groups the same? If all children are motivated by social approval, how can the social climate be made consonant with that? Researchers are trained to look for differences.

Probing a little deeper, what can one conclude from research on reading and other "social experiments"? Probably that relatively minor alterations in children's environments are unlikely to have much impact. Educational TV, given present programming schedules, can make up only a small amount of children's TV viewing. Crash programs of any kind, especially those involving children only and not their parents, will probably not be fruitful over the long run. It is becoming clearer and clearer that current models of achievement motivation are just inappropriate for a number of sociocultural systems (Mexican–Americans, blacks, and others) and that the family (parents) must be included as a target of study if children belonging to these groups are to be well served by the school (see Conferences on Studies in Reading, 1975, p. 5). Research on children's psycholinguistic development strongly suggests that **meaningful interaction** involving the child must occur if any kind of environmental change is to affect cognitive growth. Children, rather sensibly, tend to learn about things that have some meaning for them, some relation to their daily needs and activities.

As work continues on how best to serve children and especially on how to help those who most need it, a certain skepticism and conservatism are in order. Certainly money alone is not the answer. One recommendation, however, is a serious one: with every new program of whatever'sort, the means to evaluate it should be an integral part of the program from its inception. We should not read about programs started now what we read about programs started earlier! "Currently we lack complete information about the nature of the programs funded by Title I . . . we have almost no knowledge of the actual objectives and operating characteristics" (National Institute of Education, Interim Report, 1975, p. 5). New programs in reading should have built-in means of evaluating them.

VI. CONCLUSIONS AND IMPLICATIONS

The major arguments advanced in this chapter are as follows. Reading is learned in a social context and the context influences the learning in several ways. The context influences the child directly by affecting his linguistic awareness, by affecting how he learns to **use** language, and by affecting the development of his characteristic ways of perceiving and reacting to the world he experiences. Further, social class is correlated with how persons speak. Speech, being a cue to social class, elicits expectations from teachers for success (and failure) which, in turn, can influence grading and other institutional practices important for learning to read.

If these suppositions are true, then the implications which follow regarding teaching practice are many, but two stand out. First, parents' involvement with school and with their child's education should be encouraged at every step of the way. Second, efforts to broaden teachers' understanding of cultural differences, already begun in many places, should be strengthened and continued.

Obviously there are a number of areas discussed in this chapter which need further research. Among the important, and researchable, questions are the following. What are the effects of grading practices from the child's point of view? How can early reading be made pleasurable from the child's point of view? What kinds of preparation for school can parents learn to give their children which will allow these children to benefit from what the school offers? What social-structural characteristics of classrooms enhance motivation? How do a sense of efficacy and the academic self-image develop in young children?

It is time to unpackage the variable of social class and see what particular behaviors or cognitive characteristics help young children learn.

REFERENCES

Bee, H. L. *A developmental psychologist looks at educational policy.* New York: Aspen Institute Program on Education for a Changing Society, 1976.

Bee, H. L., Van Egern, L. F., Streissguth, A. P., Nyman, B. Z., and Leckie, M. S. Social class differences in maternal teaching strategies and speech patterns. *Developmental Psychology,* 1969, **1**, 726–737.

Bereiter, C., and Engelmann, S. *Teaching disadvantaged children in the preschool.* Englewood Cliffs, N.J.: Prentice Hall, 1966.

Bereiter, C., Washington, E. D., Engelmann, S., and Osborn, J. *Research and development program on preschool disadvantaged children, Vol. II: Curriculum development and evaluation.* Urbana, Illinois: University of Illinois at Urbana-Champaign, 1969 (ERIC Document No. ED 036 664).

Berko-Gleason, J. Code-switching in children's language. In T. Moore (Ed.), *Cognitive development and the acquisition of language.* New York: Academic Press, 1973. Pp. 159–168.

Bernstein, B. A sociolinguistic approach to socialization: With some reference to educability. In F. Williams (Ed.), *Language and poverty.* Chicago: Markham, 1970. Pp. 25–61.

Bikson, T. K. *Minority speech as objectively measured and subjectively evaluated.* Paper presented at the meeting of the American Psychological Association, New Orleans, 1974.

Brophy, J. E., and Good, T. L. Teachers' communication of differential expectations for children's classroom performance. *The Journal of Educational Psychology,* 1970, **61**, 367–374.

Cocking, R. R., and Potts, M. Psycholinguistics and the prediction of reading achievement. Research Bulletin, 76-20. Princeton, N.J.: Educational Testing Service, 1976.

Cohen, A. K., and Hodges, H. M. Characteristics of the lower-blue-collar class. *Social Problems,* 1963, **10**, 303–334.

Cole, M., and Bruner, J. S. Cultural differences and inferences about psychological processes. *American Psychologist,* 1971, **26**, 867–876.

Conference on Studies in Reading. *Learning and motivation in early reading.* National Institute of Education. Washington, D.C.: U.S. Department of Health, Education, and Welfare, August 1975.

Crowl, T. K., and MacGinitie, W. H. The influence of students' speech characteristics on teachers' evaluations of oral answers. *Journal of Educational Psychology,* 1974, **66**, 304–308.

Davis, F. B. (Ed.). *The literature of research in reading with emphasis on models.* New Brunswick, N.J.: Rutgers University, Graduate School in Education, 1971.

Dornbusch, S. M., and Scott, W. R. *Evaluation and the exercize of authority.* San Francisco: Jossey-Bass, 1975.

Entwisle, D. R. *Word associations of young children.* Baltimore: Johns Hopkins University Press, 1966.

Entwisle, D. R., and Hayduk, L. A. *Too great expectations: Young children's academic outlook.* Baltimore: Johns Hopkins University Press, 1978.

Gibson, E. J., and Levin, H. *The psychology of reading.* Cambridge, Mass.: The M.I.T. Press, 1975.

Harms, L. S. Listener judgments of status cues in speech. *Quarterly Journal of Speech,* 1961, **47**, 164–168.

Hertzig, M. E., Birch, H. G., Thomas, A., and Mendez, D. A. D. Differences in the responsiveness of preschool children to cognitive demands. *Monographs of the Society for Research in Child Development,* 1968, **33,** 1.

Hess, R. D. Social class and ethnic influences upon socialization. In P. H. Mussen (Ed.), *Carmichael's manual of child psychology* (3rd. ed.). New York: Wiley, 1970. Vol. 2.

Hess, R. D., and Shipman, V. Early experience and socialization of cognitive modes in children. *Child Development,* 1965, **36,** 869–886.

Hess, R. D., Shipman, V., Brophy, J. E., and Bear, R. M. *The cognitive environments of preschool children.* Unpublished manuscript, Graduate School of Education, University of Chicago, 1968.

Inclan, R. G. *Updated report on bilingual schooling in Dade County including results of a recent evaluation.* Paper presented at the Conference on Child Language, International Association of Applied Linguistics, Chicago, Illinois, 1971.

Jensen, M., and Rosenfeld, L. B. Influence of mode of presentation, ethnicity, and social class on teachers' evaluations of students. *Journal of Educational Psychology,* 1974, **66,** 540–547.

Karnes, M. B., Hodgins, H. S., Teska, J. A., and Kirk, S. A. *Research and development program on preschool disadvantaged children. Vol. I: Investigations of classroom and at home intervention.* Tucson, Ariz.: University of Arizona, 1969 (ERIC Document No. ED 036 663).

Kashinsky, M., and Wiener, M. Tone in communication and the performance of children from two socioeconomic groups. *Child Development,* 1969, **40,** 1193–1202.

Kerckhoff, A. C. *Ambition and attainment.* Washington, D.C.: ASA Rose Monograph Series, 1974.

Labov, W. *The social stratification of English in New York City.* Washington, D.C.: Center for Applied Linguistics, 1966.

Lambert, W. E., and Macnamara, J. Some cognitive consequences of following a first-grade curriculum in a second language. *Journal of Educational Psychology,* 1969, **60,** 86–96.

Lambert, W. E., and Tucker, G. R. The St. Lambert program of home-school language switch, grades K through five. Mimeograph. Montreal: McGill University, 1972.

Lambert, W. E., Just, M., and Segalowitz, N. Some cognitive consequences of following the curricula of the early school grades in a foreign language. In J. Alatis (Ed.), *21st Annual Roundtable.* Washington, D.C.: Georgetown University Press, 1970. Pp. 229–279.

Mackey, W. F. *Bilingual education in a binational school.* Rowley, Mass.: Newbury House, 1971.

Mattingly, I. G., and Kavanagh, J. F. The relationships between speech and reading. Department of Health, Education, and Welfare Publication No. (NIH) 73-475, 1973.

Meichenbaum, D. H., Bowers, K. S., and Ross, R. R. A behavioral analysis of teacher expectancy effect. *Journal of Personality and Social Psychology,* 1969, **13,** 306–316.

National Institute of Education. *Compensatory education study. Interim Report No. 1.* Washington, D.C.: National Institute of Education, August 1975.

Palardy, J. M. What teachers believe—what children achieve. *Elementary School Journal,* 1969, **69,** 370–374.

Rist, R. C. Student social class and teacher expectations: The self-fulfilling prophecy in ghetto education. *Harvard Educational Review,* 1970, **40,** 411–451.

Rubovits, P. C., and Maehr, M. L. Pygmalion analyzed: Toward an explanation of the Rosenthal–Jacobson findings. *Journal of Personality and Social Psychology,* 1971, **19,** 197–207.

Seitz, V. *Social class and ethnic group differences in learning to read.* Department of Psychology, Yale University, n.d.

Seligman, C. R., Tucker, G. R., and Lambert, W. E. The effects of speech style and other attributes on teachers' attitudes toward pupils. *Language in Society,* 1972, **1,** 131–142.

Somervill, M. Dialect and reading: A review of alternative solutions. *Review of Educational Research,* 1975, **45,** 247–262.

St. John, N. H. Desegregation and minority group performance. *Review of Educational Research,* 1970, **40,** 111–134.

Stein, A. Strategies for failure. *Harvard Educational Review,* 1971, **41,** 158–204.

Tucker, G. R., Otanes, F. T., and Sibagan, B. P. An alternate days approach to bilingual education. In J. E. Alatis (Ed.), *21st Annual Roundtable*. Washington, D.C.: Georgetown University Press, 1970.

Turnure, J. E., and Samuels, S. J. *Attention and reading achievement in first grade boys and girls.* Research Report No. 43. Center for Education of Handicapped Children, University of Minnesota, December 1972.

Williams, F. Psychological correlates of speech characteristics: On sounding disadvantaged. *Journal of Speech and Hearing Research,* 1970, **13,** 472–488.

Williams, F., Whitehead, J. L., and Miller, L. M. *Attitudinal correlates of children's speech characteristics.* Final Report OEG-0-70-2868(508). Austin, Texas: Center for Communication Research, 1971.

Wolf, M. M., Giles, D. K., and Hall, R. V. Experiments with token reinforcement in a remedial classroom. *Behavioral Research and Therapy,* 1968, **6,** 51–64.

REHABILITATION OF ACQUIRED DYSLEXIA OF ADOLESCENCE

CAROLE ANN WIEGEL-CRUMP

Miami University
and
McGuffey Laboratory School
Oxford, Ohio

I. FACTORS IN READING

A. Introduction

During the past decade, striking advancements in medical and surgical management of adolescent cases of cerebral infarct have led to an increasing proportion of these children on the case registers of speech and language pathologists. It has been necessary to evaluate the speech and language status of these young adults in depth, to examine the broad implications of their language deficits for achievement in specific academic areas, and to prescribe a program of language intervention to meet their needs. In order to fulfill, in the best way, the long-term educational needs of these students, extensive research has been done and continues to be done in the area of language skills required for total communication, including development of reading and writing skills. It is the purpose of this chapter to provide a review of one form of language disorder which commonly occurs following either surgical or traumatic cerebral insult in adolescents: deficits in the processing of written language or acquired dyslexia.

The personalized approach to dyslexia rehabilitation as it is presented in this chapter recognizes that an effective therapy program will use those materials and approaches which best fit the learning needs of the client. But it also recognizes the need for sequential facilitation and reacquisition of reading skills in order for the client to develop ease and independence in reading. To this end, each client enters the reading program on the level of readiness or reading skills he is using successfully prior to initiation of therapy. In some cases therapy may begin with the earliest steps of beginning to read. It is the hope that at the conclusion of therapy the youngsters will have returned to their pretrauma levels of performance where, as mature readers, they are able to read and understand materials they have never read before.

This chapter, then, concerns recovery of linguistic competence in adolescents demonstrating dyslexic impairment following either surgical or traumatic cerebral insult. Three personalized approaches to reeducation are described, together with a rationale of their use and a statement of the outcome.

B. Emotional Factors Inhibiting Progress

1. Effects of Withdrawal, Submissiveness and Apprehension on Recovery from Dyslexia

Increasing importance is currently being given to the idea that the language deficit in aphasia cannot be attributed solely to the physiological results of brain damage. At least part of the symptomatology attributed to the brain damage may be a function of anxiety. The causes of the aphasic's withdrawal, submissiveness, and apprehension are legion, but center in his relationship to the environment of attitudes created by those around him (Borden, 1962). If this relationship is negative, then problems develop (Aita, 1953), and permissive or indulgent relationships are often as effective stiflers of progress in rehabilitation as are more obviously undesirable punitive relations. For example, the family may so protect the aphasic that without them to ''interpret and intercede'' for him he lacks initiative and perseverance. Conversely, they may set such high standards for him, perhaps in terms of his pretrauma achievements, that he despairs. Sometimes the client's hostile attitudes toward the unjustness of his linguistic losses are transferred to his therapists, so that he resists any approaches from them; sometimes he assumes a defeatist stance—a passivity and lack of desire to achieve (Fisher, 1961). Of course, such emotional disturbances are likely to produce an inhibition of recovery and intellectual growth in general, not only of reading (Shapiro and McMahon, 1966).

Even those young aphasics who face their disability with firm resolve to strengthen verbal skills may not succeed in therapy as rapidly as they had anticipated and thus develop a sense of failure to succeed in rehabilitation, which increases the difficulties. It is fair to say that one cause of reading failure is reading failure. What we conceive ourselves to be and the abilities we conceive ourselves to have are important factors in determining the tasks we undertake and the level of achievement we reach in them. Adolescents who have reading problems oftentimes have an accompanying problem of low self-esteem. This problem can be compounded by a continued emphasis upon weaknesses. Many times the best way to improve a reading deficit is to find the client's strengths and work through them. The importance of treatment directed toward the individual and not the disorder cannot be overemphasized.

C. Intellectual Factors

1. Preinfarct Performance as a Predictor of Success in Therapy

The negative effect of even mild mental retardation before onset of aphasia is considered to be a real contraindication to language rehabilitation. Numerous authors corroborated this claim (Lebrun and Hoops, 1974). However, there are few well-documented studies dealing with the posttraumatic intellectual function of aphasic subjects.

Luria (1966, p. 462) wrote that "among the many hundreds of articles published on the subject of aphasia, hardly any deal with the investigation of the intellectual activity of aphasic subjects. Even the reports of Gelb and Goldstein do not make clear to what extent the observed intellectual defects are attributable to the speech disorders in this group of patients. For this reason, the definitive description of the intellectual disturbances arising in these patients remains to be done."

D. Educational and Social Factors

In an attempt to isolate the contributions of educational and social factors to the recovery process in dyslexia, the author reviewed case records of nine adolescent dyslexics acquired over a period of 2 years, 1974–1976, looking at child-centered factors (mental, physical, and emotional attributes and attendance at clinic), home-centered variables (socioeconomic status, stability of home, parental help and encouragement, family activities), and therapy-centered factors (organization of sessions, reading materials, and methods and contribution of the therapist). With allowances made for individual variation in severity of dyslexic impairment, it was concluded that success or failure of therapy depended mainly on the quality of the interaction between the therapist and the client and on the smooth organization of the therapy session (Wiegel-Crump, 1976). This point will be expanded in Section II, C on Retraining Programs. Suffice it here to say that those clients who responded most successfully to therapy had clinicians with whom they could communicate in a meaningful way. In order to communicate effectively, the therapist must understand who the patient is, what has happened to him, and what the dyslexia means to the client.

In addition, the successful therapists trained themselves to behave purposefully toward their clients and the clients' families. It was assumed that the youngsters come to therapy with individual needs and expectancies that the clinician was committed to serve insofar as he could. To construct personalized programs the therapist had first to determine what needs the client felt and then set about remediating those needs as directly as possible.

The identification of client's felt needs is an essential part of the therapy program. Until there is a teaching machine that will benefit all dyslexics equally, uninformed clinical activity will do more harm than good, by stifling client motivation and feelings of personal responsibility for and involvement in recovery from aphasia. The successful clinician in our experience was concerned both with the individual adolescent's symptomatology of aphasia and with the youngster's ability to channel his energies toward recovery.

The conclusion that the therapist–client interaction was the dominant factor is interesting. Socioeconomic status and other family- and school-centered factors, frequently cited as factors which can effectively make or break rehabilitation and education programs, were not so important. Other researchers on aphasics (Stoicheff, 1960) and on normally developing readers (Morris, 1966; Southgate, 1966; Ramsey, 1962) have supported this conclusion. This is not to say that some methods are not to be preferred to others, nor that some clients do not progress more rapidly under some programs than others.

E. Physical and Perceptual Factors

Clearly, the extent of the reading difficulty is influenced by the nature and extent of defects in vision and audition. Research by Brookshire (1974) defined the nature of the auditory impairments that may result in dyslexic impairment. He found aphasics tended to employ one of five problem-attack sets when responding to auditory verbal material. These attack sets logically extend to patient analysis of written verbal material, as well.

The first group of patients described by Brookshire consistently missed the initial portion of incoming messages, requiring more time than is normally required to begin processing information and formulating a response. The second group responded efficiently to the initial portion of the message but deteriorated in performance with increasing complexity of the incoming material.

The third group identified by Brookshire demonstrated poorer performance as the message increased in length. The performance of members of this group deteriorated at about the same point in all messages, regardless of the complexity of the material. Auditory verbal retention was also poor. The fourth group seemed unable to receive and process the message at the same time, evidencing greatest difficulty with embedded material and least difficulty processing the beginning and the ending of the message. Brookshire's fifth group faded in and out on a random schedule, having no discernible pattern to their errors.

To the extent that Brookshire's groups represent universal categories of auditory dyslexics recognition of group characteristics enables the therapist to personalize the organization and presentation of reading material to fit the individual client's problem attack set. Phrased in other terms, the extent of the reading difficulty is essentially dependent on the nature and extent of the aphasic impairment. It may range from the complete dissolution of reading skills to the inability to recognize or distinguish between visually and auditorily similar words or members of a specific semantic category. The client may be able to read simple phrases, but loses comprehension when the complexity of the material is increased. This difficulty with complexity may also be tied to the frequency of occurrence of syntactic structures used to express more complex linguistic concepts. The extent of dyslexic impairment may also be determined by the client's word-retrieval skills and his facility in accessing the lexical store.

In addition to their widely discussed auditory–verbal deficits, adolescent aphasics frequently evidence difficulty on tasks requiring auditory–visual integration and temporal sequencing. Since sequencing is a basic factor in reading, writing, and speaking, it is probably one of the first areas that must be considered in therapy. The dyslexic must first understand this principle: that certain letters and words precede or follow others. Without this basic information the complex tasks of spelling, reading, and writing cannot be developed. Another basic skill on which reading is dependent is the ability to make smooth transitions from the auditory–verbal to the visual–graphic coding system and vice versa (Dennis and Wiegel-Crump, 1976).

The application of the preceding data to construction of personalized reading programs results in the generation of a checklist of reading skills to be facilitated during the course of therapy. The parallels between these skills and those required of normally developing children in the process of acquiring reading expertise are obvious. A partial listing of readiness skills to be established prior to initiation of the reading rehabilitation program includes:

1. A desire on the part of the client to relearn to read and an interest in books and other printed materials.

2. An enjoyment of being read to and a listening vocabulary adequate to understand ideas.
3. An ability to reproduce auditorily presented two- and three-syllable words, to hear minimal differences between words, to hear rhyming words, and to be able to make auditory judgments on word length.
4. An ability to see likenesses and differences in colors, shapes, size, letters, and words.
5. An ability to name uppercase and lowercase letters and to pair them accurately.
6. An ability to recognize word boundaries and an awareness that printed words represent spoken words.
7. An adequate attention span.
8. An ability to remember the main ideas from stories read aloud to him.
9. An ability to sequence events logically and to follow oral directions.
10. An awareness of usual text progression from front to back, from left-hand page to right-hand page, from left to right along a line of print, from top to bottom down a page.

II. DESIGN OF THERAPY PROGRAMS: THEORY AND PRACTICE

A. In Theory

In terms of both the normal and the pathological, many authors (Luria, 1966; Becker, 9167) have emphasized the importance of auditory analysis in the process of decoding written words. Thus Luria claimed before a person can read a word he must first acoustically analyze its sound composition. Acoustic analysis and synthesis, which should occupy the whole of the initial period of learning how to read, have also been shown to include the very close participation of articulation. Beginning readers ''mouth'' or subvocalize printed material they are attempting to decipher. This subvocalization carries over to the muttering or undercurrent hum that accompanies study of difficult reading material by more advanced readers.

Analyzing the visual side of the reading process, Hill (1974) stressed the importance of the reader's establishing visuomotor habits. He saw reading and writing as mutually dependent processes, a particularly compelling argument when one thinks in terms of previously literate adolescent aphasics. Describing writing as ''delayed copying,'' Hill claimed that the writer learns to ''photograph'' the printed word in his brain, store the photograph there, and finally to retrieve it when he needs it. In many primary schools considerable weight in the early stages of learning to read and write is put on visual or visuomotor memorizing. At a slightly later stage phonics are introduced, followed at a still later stage by some rote learning of more difficult words.

This cursory description of early reading programs designed for normally developing elementary school pupils is not intended to suggest that special education and rehabilitation programs for adolescent aphasics should follow closely the lines of normal acquisition. It is recognized at the onset of therapy that the aphasic client's word attack techniques may have to be restructured but probably need not be relearned. However, selection of three provisional approaches to retraining, based on visual-kinesthetic memorizing, auditory analysis, and global stimulation techniques of elementary reading programs afforded the possibilities, first, to design reading rehabilitation programs quite different in their emphasis and, then, to compare the responses of individual adolescent aphasics to each therapy regime.

B. In Practice

1. The Subjects

The six male and three female adolescents participating in the reading rehabilitation programs to be described were between the ages of 11 and 15 years. All had a mild to trace degree of oral verbal apraxia in addition to their symptoms of mild to moderate expressive aphasia with a predominant dyslexic component.

The term "trace to mild oral verbal apraxia" denotes a slight difficulty in executing the motor movements of articulated language or clumsy articulatory movements which in the case of these subjects did not interfere with the general intelligibility of their speech. The mild oral verbal apraxic occasionally substitutes one speech sound for another or may omit or distort the odd sound as he gropes for correct positioning of tongue and lips, especially in polysyllabic words.

The term "mild to moderate expressive aphasia" is intended to suggest a speaker who may have no problems in auditory comprehension but demonstrates inconsistent difficulty on expressive tasks in dialing-up words he wants, in employing correct grammatical structure for his ideas, and in properly sequencing the phonemes within words (mild oral verbal apraxia). The students participating in this study were aware of their occasionally faulty word choices, errors in grammar, and clumsy attempts at articulation and were generally successful in correcting their own errors. In other words, the subjects had no difficulty keeping an idea in focus, but occasionally they did have trouble expressing their ideas in sentences with proper linguistic trappings.

As indicated by the diagnostic label mild expressive aphasia with a predominant dyslexic component, the major linguistic deficit evidenced by the nine adolescent aphasics participating in reading therapy was an inability to accurately decode written language on a level commensurate with preinfarct performance. In no case did a student fail to demonstrate those reading readiness skills which, in the author's opinion, must be established prior to initiation of a reading rehabilitation program. The reader may want to return to Section I,E for a cursory enumeration of these skills.

In addition to the symptoms of mild expressive aphasia with a predominant dyslexic component, all the clients had some degree of right-sided motor deficit, although all were able to use the right hand for activities of daily living and did not require any special assistance in walking, personal grooming, or other routine activities. All had been right-handed prior to cerebral infarct. All were native English speakers.

Prior to sustaining cerebral trauma, the dysphasic students participating in this study had been making normal progress in public school. Four of the youngsters were completing the sixth year of elementary school and five were enrolled in secondary school programs.

All the clients had had some speech and language therapy prior to their entering the reading rehabilitation program, but reading and writing practice, apart from copying printed texts, had played only a minor role. Earlier therapy had included drill on picture-naming, accuracy of speech articulation, stimulation of sentence production in oral speech, and accuracy of auditory verbal reception. In no case was the therapy of longer than 8-weeks duration. These activities would be seen by most speech pathologists as an effort to facilitate spontaneous recovery of verbal skills immediately postinfarct.

The written language therapy programs detailed in this chapter were initiated after the clients had been discharged from hospitals and returned to their homes. The content of each child's therapy regime was prescribed by the author. Therapy was executed by the author or by a graduate-level student trainee under the author's supervision.

Because it was our purpose to compare the efficacy of three approaches to reading rehabilitation, the subjects were divided into three groups for therapy. Subjects were matched across groups for age, preinfarct level of education, and postinfarct reading performance on the 220 Dolch Basic Sight Words and Barbe's Reading Skill Check List (Barbe, Walter, and Abbott, 1975). All subjects were of normal intelligence; none evidenced other than dysphasic deficits which could have been expected to interfere with performance (e.g., personality disorder, visual-field deficit, hearing loss). Therapy for all subjects continued for 20 weeks: 2 hours weekly instruction by the author or her student assistant at the speech and language clinic and 1 hour daily as part of their individualized special education programs. The content of the daily therapy sessions was prescribed by the author. Therapy was executed by the reading therapist or the speech pathologist serving the subject's school. Results reported here were obtained at the conclusion of the 20-week program.

C. Retraining Programs: Three Approaches

1. A Program Based on Visuokinesthetic Memorizing

In this approach to reading based on word wholes, the client was encouraged to attack words as visual patterns rather than building them up from individual letters. Emphasis was placed on the total shape or configuration of the word. The word *water* has the shape ⌐⊥⌐ which clearly distinguishes it from *coffee* ⌐⊥⊢. In the same way, one can distinguish *book* ⌐⊔ from *paper* ⌐⊓⌐ but when the task is to distinguish *book* from *look* ⌐⊔ or even from *lock* ⌐⊔ there are some difficulties. In fact total shape is only one of the visual features of words which enable readers to distinguish them; others are clearly the shape and position of individual letters.

The recognition of words by sight, from their shape, is the basis of the "look-and-say" or "key words" (Murray, 1964) method of learning to read, and could be used to justify several traditional approaches to reading rehabilitation in aphasia. By these traditional methods the client is required, as a first step, to acquire a "sight vocabulary" of a limited number of functional words. Words may be presented in a variety of ways. Objects in the home or speech clinic may be labeled (*door, chair*); pictures of labeled objects may be displayed (*house, taxi*); the shapes of the words may be traced; "flash cards" can be used to drill word recognition; word-matching and word-picture matching exercises can be used.

In the sight vocabulary program adapted for adolescent aphasics, the client was shown, one at a time, 20 printed words per session, accompanied by a simple ink-line drawing depicting the word, and was instructed to trace with his index finger the shape of the word presented on the card and then to trace each letter followed by a second trace of whole word shape. Having traced the exposed word, the client flipped over the next card in his deck and was again required to trace the word presented. The client's visual and kinesthetic examination of each word was accompanied by the therapist's reading the word aloud followed by the client's repetition of the therapist's model. The cycle was repeated for 20 weeks of therapy. Each session, including the first, was preceded by a flash card presentation of the words studied in therapy. During this drill the client attempted to read each word. He received no aid from his therapist during this drill. One week after completion of the 20-week series there was a final flash-drill to measure retention of gains made in therapy. No client made significant improvement in word recognition skills using this visuokinesthetic memory approach.

Examination of the kinds of errors subjects made over trials to see if these more nearly approximated correctness with increased practice in therapy revealed that the largest group of errors, both pre- and posttherapy, comprised substitutions, often of words whose acoustic, articulatory, or visual representations did not resemble each other closely, e.g., *toilet* for *bathtub*. There were fewer errors of transposition, e.g., *but* for *tub,* and a certain number of errors which could be attributed to aphasic dysgrammatism, e.g., omission of the plural morpheme resulting in *glass* for *glasses.*

2. Programs Based on Global Stimulation

The global stimulation method used pictures with simple accompanying texts, starting not with individual words but with groups of words and simple sentences since they, and not the individual words, are the true units of meaning. The rationale for this approach stated that the adolescent aphasic using the sentence method would have clues to the nature and meaning of individual words from the rest of the sentence which he was denied under the visuokinesthetic memorizing scheme.

One common procedure with this method was for the client to formulate a sentence, e.g., in describing a picture, which the therapist would write below the picture. The client then read the text with the help of the therapist, who drew attention to the illustration, making sure the subject understood the written words. The client then found the key or content words (nouns and verbs) on the stimulus card and repeated them aloud while writing or tracing them. There was frequent repetition of the key words. After much global exposure to the sentences, the clients were requested to read each aloud, with no assistance from their therapist. This procedure was followed for 20 weeks.

Although the literature suggests (Weigh, 1961) that the successful identification of written words in a meaningful context seems to facilitate recovery from dyslexia, the present study did not find this to be the case. The subjects' post-training reading scores were not significantly better than their pretraining reading levels.

Qualitative evaluation of clients' performances revealed that semantic paraphasias, that is, the interchanging of words which may have a similar meaning or be members of the same semantic category, as, for example, *table* for *chair,* continued to comprise the greatest number of errors. Errors of transposition ran second place. There were also errors of perseveration of previously presented words, and fewer within sentence substitutions of words closely associated in the text.

3. Training Methods Based on Phonemic Analysis

Auditory analysis of the phonemic structure of words proved to be the most powerful basis for retraining. The procedure emphasized drill of certain grapheme–phoneme correspondence rules in a selection of words. With practice, the adolescent clients were able to generalize phonics rules drilled in therapy to materials that had not been presented during the rehabilitation session. With the other approaches, the visuokinesthetic and the global stimulation programs, reading skills had not evidenced general improvement, even gains made on material drilled in therapy had been unrewarding. In retrospect, the effectiveness of rule-oriented phonics therapy was predictable in the light of a Carson, Carson, and Tikofsky (1968) study demonstrating that the learning of rules for problem solution, in contrast to learning dependent on rote memorization, greatly enhanced rate of learning and stabilized gains made during therapy for adult aphasics.

In the phonics approach, individual letters and letter blends were sounded and the sounds run together to approximate the sound of the whole word, e.g., /m-ae-t/ 'mat'. The order of phoneme presentation adopted followed conventional phonic reading schemes (Hildreth, 1958). Sounds of the single consonants were introduced first. Sounds of the consonant digraphs, e.g., *ch, sh,* followed. Short vowels were presented before long vowels and the final *e* rule for the long sound of vowels in English. Double vowels, diphthongs, and sounds of vowels with *r—ar, er, ir, or, ur*—were stressed in successive therapy sessions. Soft *c* and *g* before *e* and *i,* prefixes and suffixes, and rules of syllabification were emphasized during the final weeks of the 20-week therapy program.

In this approach to reading rehabilitation the emphasis was on phonic word-attack skills. Where they existed, rules for phoneme usage in English were stressed. Ideally, the subjects were exposed to several cases of a rule in application and asked by the therapist to formulate the rule governing the cases presented. For example, where it was the goal of therapy to establish mastery of *ai* and *oi* versus *ay* and *oy,* word lists containing the target diphthongs were presented (e.g., *join–joy; toy–oil*). The student was asked then to devise a rule covering use of *ai* and *oi* versus *ay* and *oy,* that is to say: *ai* and *oi* are used at the beginning and in the middle of a word; *ay* and *oy* are used at the end of a word.

Aside from its emphasis on sound–symbol associations, therapy encouraged the structural analysis of words, focusing in succession on endings, compound words, common word families, contractions, root words, and syllabification.

4. Qualitative Evaluation of Progress in Therapy

Of the three approaches used, visuokinesthetic memorizing seemed to be the least productive. Pre- and posttherapy administration of the 220 Dolch Basic Sight Words revealed that subjects made only limited gains during the course of therapy and complained of boredom with the task and the lack of a sense of accomplishment. This lack of accomplishment was quantified when the subjects' posttherapy reading skills levels on Barbe's Reading Skills Check List were compared with skills charted pretherapy. Again, no subject made demonstrable improvement in reading skills over the 20-week course of therapy.

Although failing to make significant quantifiable improvement in either Dolch or Barbe skills ratings over the 20 sessions of the global stimulation program, most subjects enjoyed this approach and felt the verbal drill improved their spoken if not their graphic language. Here it is difficult to say whether it was in fact the totality of the stimulation or any one component that was affecting a client's feelings of progress. There may be an advantage in this umbrella approach from the client's point of view, but it weakens consolidation of any theory of recovery.

In the absence of more and a wider variety of dyslexic aphasics with whom auditory phonemic analysis could be used, it is premature to generalize on the effectiveness of this method. However, it may be said that for those adolescent aphasics completing this therapy regime, there was significant improvement in reading skills. Prior to initiation of therapy, subjects were successful in identifying 15% of the 200 Dolch Basic Sight Words, the level of performance typifying pretherapy performance in all three groups. At the conclusion of the 20-week auditory phonemic analysis program, subjects' scores on Dolch word recognition had risen to the level of 75% correct. This rise in performance was not achieved by subjects participating in the visuokinesthetic memorizing or the global stimulation programs.

Pre- and posttherapy comparison of subjects' reading skills using Barbe's Reading Skills Check List demonstrated equally impressive gains. Although all subjects demonstrated established Readiness Level and emerging First Level skills prior to initiation of therapy, subjects following the auditory phonemic analysis program progressed to Fourth Level skills during the course of the 20-week regime, while subjects in the visuokinesthetic and global stimulation programs either maintained and stabilized First Level skills or, in the case of two children participating in the visuokinesthetic program, demonstrated emerging Second Level skills at the conclusion of the 20-week programs. Both the outcome of auditory-phonemic analysis therapy and the clients' sustained interests and reasonable levels of motivation throughout the 20 weeks of rehabilitation were encouraging.

III. CHOOSING MATERIALS FOR THERAPY

It has been established that dyslexia is a symptom common to various aphasia syndromes. Far from being a unitary disorder, it may represent the end result of one of several different pathologic mechanisms. However, clinical experience suggests that the majority of patients manifesting acquired dyslexia respond in predictable ways to changes in the level of semantic and syntactic difficulty of the material to be read. To facilitate success in therapy, rehabilitationists must concern themselves with the various ways which have been employed to choose reading material for adolescent dyslexics

A. Vocabulary

1. Frequency of Occurrence

From studies of word recognition it may be concluded that recognition occurs more readily with frequently used words than with infrequently encountered words. As Schuell and her associates noted in their text on aphasia (1969), common sense dictates that more associational linkages exist with words like *car, hat, chair,* than with words like *octopus, indubitably,* and *retrograde*. From a linguistic standpoint, one should expect that word retrieval, fundamental to the reading process, would be an easier task in response to the frequently used words in the first list than in response to the rarely used words in the second. For this reason words used in therapy should be selected from among those appearing on basic word lists (McNally and Murray, 1962).

2. Superordinate Word Category

Although several clinical reports allude to the choice of superordinate category as being a profitable area of consideration governing the selection of vocabulary for aphasia therapy, few studies objectively substantiate the clinical observations regarding the effect of superordinate category on word-retrieval tasks.

3. Concreteness

Since ease of understanding and concreteness are closely related, a higher level of recognition for highly meaningful words, that is those words which the dyslexic adolescent has experienced in a variety of contexts, would be expected. The effect of word parameters observed in numerous studies confirms the contention that the meaningfulness of a word can to a substantial degree be defined as its concreteness and that both meaningfulness and concreteness are effective determinants of auditory and visual word recognition, both processes fundamental to decoding of written material. The research further indicates that meaningful material is easy to learn, not because it is meaningful per se, but because it preserves the short-range associations that are familiar to the subjects.

B. Context

In addition to consideration of familiarity, semantic load, and meaningfulness, the selection of reading material for dyslexia therapy will be determined by the approach to rehabilitation or the reading program the therapist chooses to adopt. For those opting for a phonic schema the phonetic composition of the reading material will determine its suitability for use in therapy. Attention must be paid to the sounds of the letters, introducing new ones gradually, and reinforcing those already learned.

Instruction based on the whole-word scheme is facilitated if the words included in the basic sight vocabulary are not of the same shape and if there is not a dearth of similar letter combinations. However, these considerations are superfluous when using vocabulary in a sentence context approach to reading rehabilitation. The sentence scheme is concerned neither with phonics nor with shape, but rather with context, focusing on the sense of the sentence rather than on individual words. All types of schemes will, of necessity, include both content words, i.e., nouns, verbs, adjectives, and adverbs (Fries, 1963), and structure words, i.e., determiners, modals, and auxiliaries, negatives, intensifiers, conjunctions, prepositions, subordinatives, and personal pronouns. One salient difference between content words and structure words is that most of language is made up of the former, while there are perhaps a few hundred of the latter which enjoy understandably frequent usage since it is impossible to write or speak without them. McNally and Murray (1962) claimed that 12 members of the structure word set account for 25% of the words we read. These were *all, as, at, be, but, are, for, had, have, him, his, not, on, one, said, so, they, we, with, you.*

IV. AN ECLECTIC APPROACH

So far the discussion has treated the phonic, the whole-word, and the sentence reading programs as though they were distinct, and indeed one has been advocated to the exclusion of the others. However, in practice it is neither desirable nor possible to devise a reading scheme which is exclusively concerned with one method, although the emphasis may fall to one technique more than others.

Surveying speech pathologists actively engaged in the rehabilitation of adolescent aphasics, the author found that most therapists reported using a mixture of methods, emphasizing particular techniques at different stages of a client's recovery from dyslexia. This is understandable if each technique is assumed to contribute to the facilitation of a different basic skill required for fluent reading with comprehension.

At the initiation of therapy, the whole-word or visuokinesthetic approach was the method of choice. Therapists using this technique reported that once the client was able to identify accurately by sight several familiar, concrete words his confidence in himself as a reader was sufficient to enable him to tackle phonics. Clients reportedly felt a need to know what sound the letters stood for in order to avoid visual confusion of word shapes that were similar, and here phonics plays a role.

Therapists interacting with these clients observed that the dyslexics as a group, when presented with a series of written alternatives from which they were required to select the single word of phrase most accurately labeling a simultaneously presented picture stimulus, appeared to fix on one alternative, spending a disproportionate amount of time looking at it, and then select it as correct, without considering the other possibilities. Prior to the inclusion of phonics drill as part of their reading rehabilitation program, aphasic dyslexics had difficulty also in breaking the written alternatives into component parts, and seemed to make their decision to accept or reject the alternatives on a global basis. Attention to the individual phonemic components of words significantly reduced visual confusion of similar word shapes. When using phonic word-attack skills, clients were forced to scan alternatives more effectively, greatly reducing errors made as a result of impulsivity and inefficient scanning.

The contribution of the sentence method is best realized once the dyslexic client begins to feel confident in his ability to attack single words. Placing the words to be read in a meaningful relation to one another, so that the familiar words give clues to the recognition of unfamiliar words, enhances reading rate and improves reading comprehension. The ability to read phrases rather than single words is an important skill in reading with comprehension. Though an oversimplification of the facts, it is not unreasonable to propose that rehabilitating reading skills in the adolescent dyslexic is a matter of drawing upon his prior learning. Using the experiences of clients as part of the reading program not only lays a good foundation for individualization of materials, but heightens interest in reading as well. When clients are encouraged to relate their experiences to their clinician who subsequently uses these experiences to individualize the therapy program, each client should leave therapy having internalized the fact that his richly stocked storehouse of language experiences gives him a compelling reason to continue reading. The reading skills facilitated by therapy are part of the client's general linguistic ability, of his awareness of the possibilities of language.

REFERENCES

Aita, J. A. Modern consideration of the man with brain injury. *Journal of Neurosurgery,* 1953, **4,** 240–254.

Barbe, W. B., and Abbott, J. L. *Personalized reading instruction.* West Nyack, N.Y.: Parker Publishing Co., 1975.

Becker, R. *Die lese-rechtschreib-schwache aus logopadischer sicht.* Berlin: Verlag, Colk and Gesundheit, 1967.

Borden, W. Psychological aspects of stroke: patients and family. *Annals of Internal Medicine,* 1962, **47,** 689–692.

Brookshire, R. H. Differences in responding to auditory-verbal material among aphasics. *ACTA Symbolica,* 1974, **5,** 1–18.

Carson, D. H., Carson, F. E., and Tikofsky, R. S. On learning characteristics in adult aphasics. *Cortex,* 1968, **4,** 92–112.

Dennis, M., and Wiegel-Crump, C. A. Transcoding between phonemes and graphemes in the isolated left and right hemispheres. Sign Language and Neurolinguistics Conference Proceedings, Rochester, New York, 1976.

Fisher, S. H. Psychiatric Considerations of cerebral vascular disease. *American Journal of Cardiology,* 1961, **7,** 379–385.

Fries, C. C. *The structure of English.* London: Longmans, 1963.

Hildreth, G. *Teaching reading.* New York: Holt, Rinehart & Winston, 1958.

Hill, L. D. *English sounds and English spellings.* Oxford, U.K.: Oxford University Press, 1974.

Lebrun, Y., and Hoops, R. *Intelligence and aphasia.* Amsterdam: Swets and Zeitlinger, 1974.

Luria, A. *Higher cortical function in man.* New York: Basic Books, 1966.

McNally, J., and Murray, W. *Key words to literacy.* London: Schoolmaster Publishing Company, 1962.

Morris, J. M. *Standards and progress in reading.* Slough, U.K.: National Foundation for Educational Research, 1966.

Murray, W. *The key word reading scheme.* Loughborough, U.K.: Wills and Hepworth, 1964.

Ramsey, W. An evaluation of three methods of teaching sixth grade reading. International Reading Association Conference Proceedings, 1962.

Schuell, H., Jenkins, J., and Jomenez-Pabon, E. *Aphasia in adults.* New York: Harper and Row, 1969.

Shapiro, L., and McMahon, A. Rehabilitation stalemate. *Archives of General Psychiatry,* 1966, **15,** 173–177.

Southgate, V. A few comments on reading drive. *Educational Research,* 1966, **9,** 145–146.

Stoicheff, M. L. Motivating instructions and language performance of dysphasic subjects. *Journal of Speech and Hearing Research,* 1960, **3,** 75–85.

Weigh, E. The phenomenon of the temporary deblocking in aphasia. *Zeitschrift fur phonetik, sprachivissenschaft, und kommunikationsforschung,* 1961, **14,** 337–364.

Wiegel-Crump, C. A. Dyslexia Therapy Seminar in Toronto, Ontario, for T.S.H.A., 1976.

COGNITION AND READING: AN APPROACH TO INSTRUCTION

HILDRED RAWSON

Ontario Institute for Studies in Education
Toronto, Ontario, Canada

I. INTRODUCTION

This chapter proposes an approach to instruction that is derived from the studies of Piaget and his associates, the work of Chomsky and Halle, of Halliday and others in linguistics, and of Neiser, Norman, and others in psychology. The instruction is based on two premises: (1) that cognitive growth, the understanding of basic structures of the language, and reading, are interrelated, and (2) that an objective of instruction in reading is to ensure competence in thinking.

In instruction, cognitively oriented questions, a characteristic of Piagetian-type interviews with children, are considered an essential procedure. The questions will elicit specific operations in thinking; the responses of the children are then considered in terms of the cognitive development and understandings they represent. A response, for example, may indicate readiness for a new challenge in thinking or, alternatively, a child's need to consolidate and extend to reading the strategies in thinking he is currently discovering. Readiness, a theme of this book, is considered in this chapter to be a continuous and cumulative process of preparing children for successive advances in operational thinking, ensuring at each level that operations are extended to understanding the code and to comprehension in reading.

Children will begin the discovery of specific operations in thinking in response to questions presented as they manipulate concrete materials. Using counters, for example, questions will suggest to the children that they abstract criterial properties, construct classes, and discover class inclusion relations. These operations will be extended to abstracting distinctive features of consonant sounds, associating these spoken sounds with a symbol, and recognizing classes of consonants: voiced and whispered. Similar operations in classification will be used in presenting other aspects of the code: consonant clusters, lax and tense vowels, inflectional and derivational suffixes, and so on. Reading will provide opportunities for consolidating and extending these and other operations in thinking to new situations. Children will discover the meaning of a word as a class name and relations between structure and meaning in the sentence.

In other concrete and reading situations children will discover reversibility in thinking in response to questions involving conservation of length, weight, area, and so on, with changes in appearance of the materials. The relation to reading comprehension of operations in conservation and classification, in particular the concept of class inclusion, will be clearer as children's responses to questions in stories are presented later in this discussion. A comprehension problem for children is that meanings involving class inclusion and other operations are implicit in what is read: an author assumes that readers understand and will apply operations such as these as they read.

As operational thinking involving classification and conservation is extended to reading, and as knowledge of word and sentence structures contributes to understanding, questions will elicit operations in deductive and inductive reasoning. Materials in concrete situations and in reading will involve the concept of irreversibility and the "new reality" chance. Information will be ordered in a hierarchical structure and the structure used in speaking and writing. Hypothesis formulation and testing will be introduced in reading. These later operations, inductive reasoning, the idea of chance, hypothesis formulation and testing, approach the level of formal operations (Inhelder and Piaget, 1958), and prepare a student for a curriculum that will require combinatorial reasoning and abstract conceptual thinking. The topics that are selected here for discussion illustrate some of the possibilities in instruction in reading for challenging and developing children's potential for operational thinking.

II. LEARNING TO THINK

The stimulus of questions designed to challenge a child's potential for inventing and elaborating strategies in thinking is an inherent feature of a Piagetian-type interview with the child. A child's responses to similar questions presented by a teacher offer clues to the child's understanding, suggest activities and further questions that are likely to be helpful, and permit a teacher to monitor progress (Inhelder, Sinclair, and Bovet, 1974). The classroom presents opportunities for the social exchanges that encourage operational thinking, and reading provides for the extension of the thinking skills to organizing and remembering in another medium.

The child's initial discoveries in concrete thinking include operations in classification and conservation (Piaget, 1962). Questions in classification direct attention to the possibility of abstracting criterial properties, of identifying categories and constructing classes, and of recognizing the relations of inclusion that hold between a superordinate class and its subordinate classes. Operations in conservation alert the child to regularities in the environment: to the persistence of relations of equality, of "sameness," with changes in shape, form, and the position of objects in space. The complementary roles of teacher and child tend to be clarified in these learning situations. The child becomes the active participant in observing, manipulating, deciding, and explaining. The teacher is listener and questioner, an adult who devises the situations, selects and presents materials, and expects and permits the child to invent, explain, and defend his decisions—his logical decisions and his prelogical notions in the process of becoming logical.

In the sections that follow, dialogues between teacher and child are presented. Some of these exchanges took place in classroom situations, some in groups of six to eight children, others in individual instruction and in studies undertaken by the author. The children responded to questions as they manipulated concrete materials, examined word and sentence structures, and considered meanings in reading. Instructional sessions were organized as follows: for 10 to 12 minutes the children engaged in concrete experiments; for approximately 15 minutes they were examining aspects of the structure of the language and writing; for the remaining part of the hour they were reading and responding to questions involving comprehension.

A. Operations in Classification

For discovering operations in classification in concrete situations a child examines a pile of counters—red and white circles and squares. He identifies the features characteristic of individual counters: "That one's a red square; that's a white circle." The construction of classes is then suggested:

TEACHER: Put the counters in **two** lots, so that everything in each lot belongs together, goes well together.
How do these belong together? And these?
Now make four lots, two from this lot and two from this lot (pointing).
How do these belong together? And these . . .?

Children who are not yet reading frequently begin by putting the counters together two by two, matching by features, or by counting, trying to ensure that each lot will have the same number. When they find that this is not possible they hesitate. When the instructions are repeated, children usually succeed. (Alternative classifications are shown in Fig. 1.) The child is asked to draw chalk lines on a table or chalkboard to represent the actions he performed in constructing the classes. Questions then suggest to the child that he look back on the thinking involved in abstracting criterial properties and identifying members to be included in a class:

TEACHER: If I give you a red circle where will it belong? Why there?
If I give you a square one, where will it belong? [An undetermined situation: more information is needed.]

Next, two of the subordinate classes, consisting of seven red circles and three red squares, are selected. Questioning is directed toward the discovery of an inclusion relation in terms of *all, some,* and *more:*

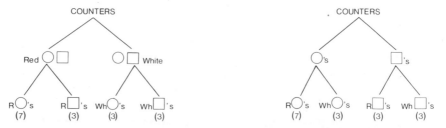

Fig. 1. Alternative classifications: counters. (Suggested number of counters in each subclass is shown in parentheses.)

TEACHER: What color are the circles? What color are the squares? What color
are they all? [An inclusive gesture.]
If you give me a **red** one, will it have to be square. Why is that?
If you give me a round one will it have to be red? Why is that?
Put the circles and squares together again in **one** lot. What name could they
be called when all the circles and squares are in one lot?
Now make the two lots, two classes. How do these belong together? And
these?
Could we say that **some** of the red ones are circles? How is that? Could we
say that **all** of the red ones are circles? Why not? Are there **more red** ones or
more red circles. How did you know that? How come there are more red
ones than red circles? [or more red circles than red ones, since the child's
decision is repeated in eliciting a justification for the decision.]

Some children count and decide: "There are more red circles, because there
are seven of them and only three squares." This response appears to represent an
early stage in coming to understand the class inclusion relation. The inclusion
concept will be discovered and generalized when questions requiring this operation are repeated in other concrete situations and in reading. Once discovered, an
operation is apparently conserved through use, that is, it continues "by virtue of
its own functioning . . . the memory of an operational schema [such as class
inclusion] . . . (in contrast to the memory of the objects that might have been
classified), coincides with the schema itself" (Piaget and Inhelder, 1973). Having been constructed, the operational schema is conserved throughout the life of
the individual except for pathological reasons. The author's research and experience in reteaching disabled readers (Rawson, 1969, 1978) suggests that delay in
developing operational schema is likely to be associated with difficulty in learning to read.

Some alternative situations involving the concept of class inclusion are presented:

TEACHER: What is the name for things in this room: the tables, chairs, book-
cases, lamps . . .? All these things in a living room?

A child will likely know the word furniture, but may not know the concept, the
meaning of the word as a class name.

TEACHER: In this room, are there more chairs or more furniture?

An initial decision, based on counting, is likely to be "more chairs." A second
decision could be:

STUDENT: Oh! I know now, there's the **same** of each, chairs **and** furniture.

The inclusion relation may be discovered during a teacher's puzzled silence:

STUDENT: More furniture, of course. Chairs are furniture too!

A child who proceeded through these sequences to arrive at an understanding of the extension of the superordinate class, decided to check if others had made this remarkable discovery:

STUDENT: I'm going to ask my mother and see if she knows that!

This boy of good potential was in grade 7, but was reading at approximately a grade 4 level. The discovery of strategies in ordering and thinking appeared to contribute to his later success in overtaking his peers, and certainly to the growing confidence he cultivated in learning.

B. Operations in Conservation

Concepts in conservation will be relatively new to a number of children. For discovering conservation of substance, weight, volume, area, length . . . the child is given materials to be measured and recognized as equal (or unequal). He is asked to judge the persistence of the relation following various manipulations. For conservation of substance, weight, volume, two balls of modeling clay are presented. The child makes the two balls equal in weight on a balance scale. Questions follow transformations of one and of both balls: one ball as a plasticine doughnut, or pancake; one ball rolled out as a snake and the other cut into small pieces:

TEACHER: Is there more clay in the doughnut than in the ball, or is there the same amount of clay in the doughnut and in the ball, or less clay in the doughnut? How did you know that?

Sequences have been observed in the development of the concept of conservation (Inhelder, *et al.,* 1974). At first, children do not have the concept of conservation of quantity. "The focus," Inhelder finds, "is on the *action* carried out (flattening, rolling, cutting) or on the resulting *appearance*. When the child becomes capable of mentally returning to the starting point, he predicts that there will be the same amount of clay when the doughnut is returned to its original shape." It will not be clear if he may still consider that as a doughnut the quantity of clay will have increased or decreased. Inhelder points out that in his thinking the child, "neither cancels out this transformation nor compensates for it." The return to the original shape is merely "a second action which, for the child, is completely independent of the first...." Finally, the child will maintain the conservation of quantity under whatever transformation and justify this decision by arguments "based on logical identity, reversibility by cancellation of the change, and compensation between dimensions... (e.g., every increase in length implies a corresponding decrease in thickness)" (Inhelder *et al.*, 1974).

During an experiment a teacher will rephrase a question in an attempt to influence the child's thinking and elicit a logical argument. A child who decides there is the same amount of clay in the ball and in the doughnut, explaining that "the doughnut is only made with a hole in it," is asked:

TEACHER: Suppose I can hardly believe you when you tell me there's the same amount of clay in the solid ball and in the doughnut with a hole in it. How will you help me?

One 9-year-old suggested an experiment that would make it "perfectly clear" and then explained the outcome of the experiment:

STUDENT: Tell you what I'd do. I'd take two glasses and put the water in each of them up to the same level. I'd put the ball in one glass and the doughnut in the other. Then you'd see. The water would go to the same level in both glasses and you'd **have to** believe me.

The child was questioned further:

TEACHER: I might still wonder how come the water went to the **same** level in each glass. What about that doughnut with a hole in it?

He explained it this way:

STUDENT: But you see, if the doughnut has the same amount of clay as the ball, it will take up the same amount of space, and the water will **have to go up** just as much.

In another experiment in which one ball is cut into small pieces, the other ball rolled out as a snake, a child is asked:

TEACHER: Will all the small pieces weigh less than the snake, or more than the snake or will the snake and pieces weigh the same?

One child recognized conservation of weight and justified his decision by a logical argument, by indicating compensation between dimensions and by proposing a demonstration. His logical argument included the premise: If nothing is added and nothing is taken away in the transformation the quantity and its weight remain the same!

STUDENT: Look, I'll do it over again and you watch me. . . . Am I dropping any? Am I taking any from the pieces to put on the snake? So you see they **must be** the same. The amount didn't change. They're only different in the way they look. Maybe you were thinking the snake **looked** longer. But it's **thinner** too.

Some of the nonconservers in the group remained unconvinced. They said:

STUDENT: The pieces are lighter, because they're little and all spread out.

At this point a visible check was made on the balance scale. The ''evidence'' appeared to be somewhat disturbing to the unconvinced. They admitted the evidence but reaffirmed their first responses:

STUDENT: They weigh the same on the scales, all right, but if you had them in your hand you could hardly feel them, because they're just little and light.

A week or so later these children seemed astonished to be asked again so ''simple and obvious'' a question. They had reconsidered the evidence, revised their decision, then seemed to have forgotten that once they did not know.

Questions requiring the conservation of volume may also be presented. A glass is partly filled with water.

TEACHER: Suppose you put the snake in this glass of water. What will happen? What else will happen? [An elastic band is placed to show the level of the water in the glass.]

Now put the snake in the water. What makes the water go up when you put the clay snake in the glass? Put an elastic band to mark the level of the water now.

Some children will be surprised to see that the level of the water in the glass is higher. They had not predicted that the water would rise. The weight of the object may be given as an explanation for the higher level of the water:

STUDENT: The snake's heavy. The weight of it makes the water go up.

Questions continue:

TEACHER: If you take the *snake* out of the water, what will happen? Let's see if it does. If you put the **pieces** in the water will the level of the water be higher for the pieces than for the snake, or will the level be the same for the pieces and the snake or will it be lower?

Some children will be surprised to see that the level of the water is the same for the clay snake and for the pieces. They may not respond to the next question:

TEACHER: Why does the water rise to the **same** level for the snake and for the pieces?

For these children alternative experimental situations that require conservation of substance, weight, length, area, and volume will be presented. For example, two blocks identical in shape, color, and size, one quite heavy, the other lighter, are presented. Two glasses filled to the same level with water are available. The questions require a prediction and an explanation of the levels of the water when a block is placed in each glass. In this situation the weight of the blocks must be eliminated as a factor in accounting for the levels of the water. Children at 9 years, who have had experience with other experiments in conservation are generally able to explain that it is the space occupied by the blocks that counts, that the two blocks are the same **size,** so the water levels will be the same in each glass. An objective in presenting questions in classification and conservation in a sequence of concrete experiments is to challenge prelogical levels of thinking and effect changes in cognitive structure by inducing children to observe, consider evidence, search for relations, and present convincing explanations.

C. Natural Development or Acceleration?

Under conditions of natural development changes in cognitive structure tend to occur gradually over a considerable period of time (Piaget, 1962). Conservation of substance, Piaget finds, is recognized by children on the average at about 7 years; weight, between 10 and 11 years; and volume at 12 to 13 years, at the beginning of the transition to formal operations (Piaget, 1962). Lovell and Ogilvie (1960, 1961a,b) in studies of children in England found comparable ages for the recognition of conservation of substance and weight. In examining the concept of volume (interior volume, occupied volume, displaced volume), Lovell and Ogilvie conclude:

> The concept of physical volume . . . develops slowly during the Junior school years . . . It appears that not until the fourth year of the junior school [approximately grade 7] do 50 per cent of pupils realize that the amount of water displaced by a single cube is independent of the size of the full container. . . .

Is this rate of progress a matter of concern? Can one depend on natural development? Is intervention justified? Will it be effective in promoting operational thinking?

Piaget raises a critical question concerning intervention: natural development, he suggests, "can serve as a basis for new spontaneous constructions"; intervention may result in continued dependence on adult help, a learner who "will no longer learn anything without such help" (Piaget xiii, in Inhelder, *et al.,* 1974). Planned intervention appears, however, to be unavoidable. There is evidence that for many students cognitive changes do not reliably occur during the period of schooling (Renner, Stafford, Lawson, McKinnon, Friot, and Kellogg, 1976). For these students the delay in intellectual development continues to interfere seriously with academic progress at the secondary and college levels. Elkind (1962) and Tower and Wheatley (1971) report that only 60% of students tested at the college freshman level believed that the volume of a clay ball remained constant when the ball was rolled into a sausage. Renner and Stafford (1976) report the results of interviews with a sample of 588 students, grades 7 through 12, ages 12 to 19 years. Only 14 students, 2.4% of the total sample, could be called fully formal operational. Including students who scored within the early concrete operational level, 75.3% of students in the secondary schools could be considered, at best, **concrete** operational. Renner and Stafford continue: "This is a stage of intellectual development, which Piaget's data have told him children begin to leave at about 11 years of age, and from which they have emerged by age 15."

By grade 7, Renner and Stafford report that 83% of the sample of 96 students interviewed scored within the concrete level; at grades 9 and 10, 82% and 73% obtained similar scores; at grades 11 and 12, 71% and 66% continued to function within the concrete operational level. The authors ask, "What do students do to survive in a system that hour after hour requires them to cope with situations they cannot begin to handle? They have only two choices—memorize or cheat." A third alternative may be the one adopted by the dropouts (Lloyd, 1976). Of the seniors continuing to graduation, Renner and Stafford found 60% to be still concrete operational. At the college level these potentially "good" students are described by Herron (1975) as still "floundering down the concrete path."

To cope with this delay, Herron suggests returning concrete level college students to the point at which changes in cognitive structure apparently came to a halt by providing manipulative materials, concrete experiences, and concrete models of abstract concepts. Herron would undoubtedly agree with the present author that questions will be needed—questions that challenge the dominance of perception, that present alternatives, and that require logical decisions and the defense of these decisions not only in concrete situations, but also in reading. Cognitive operations discovered in concrete situations may not be extended to understanding in reading. In this case a possible mutually facilitative interaction between discoveries in concrete situations and in reading—an interaction that could be crucial in the development of operational thinking—will have been overlooked in instruction.

A study was undertaken by the author (Rawson, 1969) to assess the relation between cognitive operations in concrete situations and the generalization of these operations to reading comprehension. The 100 children in the sample, 50 boys and 50 girls, mean age 9:10, had completed grade 4 in a western Canadian city. The children in the study were average to better than average readers as measured by a standardized test of reading comprehension, Cooperative Sequential Test of Educational Progress (STEP) Reading, Form 4B.

Operations in classification, conservation, deduction, induction, and probability reasoning were assessed in this study by test items in two situations, concrete and reading. The concrete tests were adapted from those originally described by Piaget and his associates. The materials for the reading tests consisted of stories written by the author. Comparability of the operations required in the concrete and reading situations was assessed by representing corresponding test items in the formulas of symbolic logic. Subjects were tested individually, first on the stories and then on the concrete tests. In administering the reading tests, silent reading of a story was followed by an interview with the child. Preliminary questions were presented to ensure that a child had read the story correctly and could recall (given assistance if necessary) the relevant factual information. These questions were followed directly by questions to assess cognitive operations.

Before considering the results, it may be helpful to elaborate a little on the procedure used in assessing classification to illustrate the general strategy employed in the study. The materials for the concrete tests consisted of counters similar to those described earlier (Section II,A). The questions were adapted from studies reported by Inhelder and Piaget (1964). For the reading tests, two stories—"The Ducks Arrive in Spring" and "A City Long Ago"—served as "materials." Questions on the concrete and reading situations assessed fundamental dimensions in classification: inferring class inclusion relations, constructing predicates which describe extensions of classes, and constructing multiplicative classes. While the specific stimuli in the two situations were not identical, the decisions and their defense required the same cognitive operations in each situation.

One of the stories, "The Ducks Arrive in Spring," describes an event familiar to children who live on the prairie. It begins like this:

Every spring the prairies become a fly-way for the birds on their way north for the summer. The first birds to arrive are the ducks, and the first ducks are the pintail. The pintail come in flocks of hundreds, long dark lines against the blue prairie sky. There is ice on the ponds and lakes and snow on the wheat fields when the pintail arrive. But the pintail can live off the land until the ice melts on the ponds. Then they will join the other pond feeders, the mallard and teal, on the shallow ponds and pools. These pond ducks are surface feeders. . . .

> The last ducks to arrive are the redhead and golden eye. These ducks are diving ducks. They come later when the ice is melted on the lakes and rivers. . . .

The individual interviews began with a discussion of the factual information given in the story, the details, the sequence of events, related observations and experiences. The cognitively oriented questions followed directly in this context. The children, however, responded differently to nonfactual questions. They seemed aware that a transition to another level of thinking had occurred. Some would pause, take time to consider, then speak tentatively, "I'm not quite sure, but I think. . . ." Others avoided offering an opinion. For example, when asked, "Are ducks birds?," some children responded:

STUDENT: It didn't say anything about birds in the story. It only talked about ducks.

From the child's point of view this could be true: operations in classification remain implicit in reading. An author assumes that the meaning of a class name and the class inclusion relation (a duck is a bird) are understood and will be supplied by the reader. Responses to the classification questions suggest that some readers are unlikely to recognize this operation in reading:

TEACHER: Will there be more ducks or more pintail here on the prairie in the summer?

STUDENT: More pintail. It said they come in flocks of hundreds.

TEACHER: Are pintail ducks?

STUDENT: No, pintail aren't ducks. They land on the wheat fields.

TEACHER: Are ducks birds?

STUDENT: A duck's not a bird. It's better than a bird, it swims and flies.

TEACHER: What is a bird?

STUDENT: Birds have wings. They can fly.

TEACHER: And mosquitoes?

STUDENT: They have wings too, but they're insects.

TEACHER: Is a bird an animal?

STUDENT: A bird's not an animal. An animal has four feet. A bird has only two.

TEACHER: Are there more animals or more birds in the world?

STUDENT: More birds. Birds have more babies and I don't see many animals around. I guess they get shot. It didn't say anything at all about animals in the story.

TEACHER: If **all** the birds flew into the far north for the summer, would there be any ducks here on the prairie?

STUDENT: There'd still be ducks here, all right. Ducks really like our ponds and pools.

(One teacher who was asking questions like these remarked, "I had no idea how much my pupils didn't know." Her pupils were saying, "Ask us some more of those funny questions today".)

An attempt also was made in the study to use questions to elicit categories and predicates which describe some extensions of classes or the subtopics that develop the main theme of a story. In the concrete situation the categories were shape—circles and squares—and color—red and white (Fig. 1). For the story "The Ducks Arrive in Spring," the categories were pond feeders and diving ducks; or ducks that come early, and ducks that come when the ice is melted on the lakes. The question was:

TEACHER: Put the ducks that come back to the prairie in the spring into **two** lots: all the ducks in the story that are alike in one way in one lot, and all the ducks that are alike in another way in the other lot. [A gesture, left and right.] Give each lot a name that will tell us how the ducks in this lot are alike and how the ducks in this lot are alike [gestures repeated].

A number of responses were of the form:

STUDENT: I remember the pintail and mallard and redheads. I forget the others.

Questions involving the construction of the multiplicative class, the familiar adjective–noun construction, were also presented in both concrete and reading situations. In the concrete situation a column of large white squares and a row of small white circles were shown attached to a display card at right angles to an empty square space. The construction of the multiplicative class involved the abstraction of criterial properties and the multiplication of these properties to form the class of intersection. The question was:

TEACHER: What could we put here? [pointing to the empty space at the point of intersection]. We want to finish the pattern. We want to put **one** thing here to finish the pattern: it must belong to the column of white squares [gesturing] and belong to the row of white circles. Just **one** thing. . . . [Two choices were elicited—a **small** white square; or a **large** white circle].

   Circumstances in the reading situation were similar. Two streets in an old city were described as meeting at a corner. The people on one street set out rafts that had brought them safely down the river. The people on the other street set out treasures that they had carried from their villages. They painted these treasures a bright yellow. A family that lived at the corner where the two streets met [gesturing] had a problem. They wanted to set something in front of their house—**one** thing to show they belonged to the street with the rafts and the street with yellow treasures. The children were asked: "What should this family put in front of their house?" Children who accepted the condition **one thing** usually suggested "a yellow raft," or "a raft painted yellow."

   Table I shows the mean percentage of correct responses obtained on two of the tests—classification and conservation. The results in Table I indicate that for these 9- to 10-year-old children operations applied in responding to questions in the concrete situations are not necessarily applied in the reading situations as measured by responses to questions on the stories. The logic of a situation can be overlooked in reading if attention is directed toward how one would feel and act oneself in the circumstances. For example, in assessing conservation of substance in one of the stories, "Jimmy Feeds the Birds," the birds are described as being given one of three **equal** pieces: one piece left whole for the chickadees, one cut into big chunks for the jays, and one cut into small pieces for the sparrows. A question was, did the jays and sparrows get the same amount to eat, or did the jays get more or less to eat than the sparrows? A frequent response was:

TABLE I

Mean Percentage of Correct Responses in Subtests in Classification and Conservation in Concrete and Reading Situations ($N = 100$)

Logical operation	Concrete tests	Reading tests
Classification		
Class inclusion	73	24
Predicates	60	30
Multiplicative class	48	27
Total	60	27
Conservation		
Substance	64	43
Weight	57	27
Volume	40	36
Total	54	35

STUDENT: The boy gave all the birds the same amount to eat, because they were
all cold and hungry. He was really sorry for them.

A child could experience emotional satisfaction in giving such a response. The
empathy he expresses could also be appreciated by the teacher. Such a reply,
however, is unlikely to add to the child's competence in logical thinking. It
should be possible in teaching reading to help children make the distinction
between logical implication and personal involvement, and to operate logically
when this is required.

As an exploratory study the research raises this question: Is the teaching of
reading adequately oriented to developing operational thinking? The difficulty
children apparently experience in recognizing comparability in processing information derived from manipulable situations and information derived from reading situations suggests that a possible mutually facilitative interaction between
the two situations has not been emphasized in instruction.

III. OPERATIONAL THINKING AND INSTRUCTION IN THE
LANGUAGE

Children who have been challenged to discover unexpected relationships in
concrete situations are likely to expect similar challenges in reading. If they find
in learning to read that the task is mainly to look and remember what one is told,
they could be wondering what is there to do, to think about, to be surprised
about? It should be possible in teaching reading to tell less and ask more questions, to provide for more social interaction, to set a pace that requires the
operations in organizing and thinking that ''move children deeper and deeper into
the concrete operational stage'' (Renner et al., 1976).

There are unexpected relations to be uncovered in learning the language,
relations that involve operational thinking. Operations in classification are basic
in understanding the meaning of a word as a class name (Anglin, 1970), in
ordering and remembering elements of the code: the consonants, consonant
clusters, vowels, and morphophonemic elements such as inflectional and derivational suffixes (Chomsky and Halle, 1968; Venesky, 1970). Other cognitive
operations are involved in relating structure and meaning in understanding sentences (Lyons, 1975; Halliday, 1975) and discourse (Grimes, 1975; Becker,
1975).

There are special difficulties for children in managing the transition to operational thinking in reading. During the early school years primitive notions are
remarkably persistent (Piaget, 1951, 1960, 1976; Piaget and Inhelder, 1975).
Teachers discover this by not assuming that children ''know,'' and by presenting
questions that challenge preoperational thinking. For example, as children are

examining a photograph of a river flowing quietly through a northern forest, a teacher could inquire:

TEACHER: What direction is this river flowing? How come it flows in that direction?

Explanations such as these have been offered by children 8 to 10 years old (Rawson, 1978):

STUDENT: The pebbles on the bottom push it along that way.

STUDENT: It's the wind. It goes whatever way the wind goes. Yes, it could turn and go with the wind.

STUDENT: It's the fish? When the fish go that way the river goes that way too?

In the beginning metaphorical expressions in reading can be taken quite literally by a child. In a series of books for young children a story begins:

Winter is coming. . . . The grass is dead and brown.

A teacher who asks:

TEACHER: Is this true? Is the grass dead? Quite dead? Does it come alive again in the spring?

may find that the notion of roots alive under the snow is not forthcoming.

Questions that require the abstraction of criterial properties, the construction of classes, and the concept of class inclusion introduce children to operational strategies in thinking that will replace the simpler notions characteristic of the preoperational years.

A. Words as Concepts

Learning a language is described by Quine (1974) as occurring in "a succession of leaps," leaps that are associated with new dimensions in thinking. One of these new dimensions is the abstraction of criterial properties. Oléron (1964) defines abstraction as a learned behavior:

Abstraire, c'est penser à part ce qui ne peut être donné à part.

Abstraction, "thinking apart," begins with description: A property, the color red, or the shape round, comes to be thought of "apart from" an object, but belonging to or a characteristic abstracted from instances in which it may be observed: "We have all learned to apply the word 'red' to blood, tomatoes, ripe apples, and boiled lobsters" (Quine, 1974).

From abstraction at this level the child moves to classifying: the operation of "putting together what belongs together" by virtue of a property abstracted from and common to all its members. Kneale and Kneale (1962) have pointed out that there is a difference of the greatest importance between a set that can be specified by enumeration of its members (e.g., naming objects that come together by chance) and one that can be specified by an indication of some features common to all its members (Birds are feathered creatures.).

There is power in the concept "membership in a class" and the notion, class inclusion. "An individual member of the class may be assigned any property of the general class to which it belongs" (Bobrow, 1975). The child begins to discover the interrelations of classes: relations of inclusion, exclusion, the additive relation between subordinate classes and a superordinate class that properly includes them (e.g., reptiles, fish, insects, birds . . . are animals). Observation, pointing, does have a basic role in learning the language. "We learn the language from other people in shared circumstances. Though we learn it largely by learning to relate strings of words to strings of words, somewhere there have to be non-verbal reference points. . . . Ostensive learning is fundamental and requires observability" (Quine, 1974). In ostensive learning someone points and says:

TEACHER: That's a squirrel. Those are nuts.

There is a considerable distance between interpreting sentences at an observational level and understanding sentences that involve abstracting attributes, constructing classes, inferring and quantifying inclusion relations. In the sentence, *The squirrels are storing nuts for winter,* words represent concepts. As concepts their meanings involve operations in class inclusion, relations expressed in terms of . . . *is a . . . , . . . is a kind of . . .* , and . . . *is a member of . . .*, and by quantifying expressions such as *some, more, all, other:*

TEACHER: What is a squirrel? What kind of animal is a squirrel?
            What are nuts? Are they a kind of seed? What is a seed?
            Find the words "seed" and "fruit" in the dictionary.
            What does "store" mean in this sentence? Where do squirrels store nuts?
            What does "for winter" **imply?** Where do the nuts the squirrels store, come from? What is a tree? [One response to this question was a thoughtful: "You know, I really don't know".]

Questions such as these will begin to occur to children as they read—perhaps only as a fleeting awareness, as a challenge to search for meaning. Answers will begin to come too, some tentative: "You know that . . . remember?," "Read on, you may find out. . . ."

B. Word Structure

A child's early impression of a word is likely to be that it is a single sound, a whole. Children examine the words they speak and discover that words are made up of elements, of units. They abstract distinctive features of a number of the units, initially consonant units, and associate the features abstracted with a letter and its name. Units having certain features in common will fall into groups, classes that will have a name—which is an operation in classification. Gerard (1969) describes the sequence in operational thinking that appears to be involved: "Attention moves from the initial unit up to the superordinate units and down to the subordinate ones." That is, the child's attention will move from single units whose distinctive features are known, to the superordinate classes that include these units—the classes consonants, vowels, letters—and down to the subordinate classes, lax and tense vowels, voiced and whispered consonants (see Figs. 2 and 3).

In abstracting, categorizing, and structuring, the child is adopting behaviors characteristic of adults. "As humans we belong to that component of nature

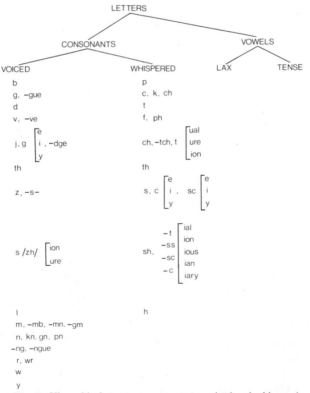

Fig. 2. Hierarchical structure: consonants, voiced and whispered.

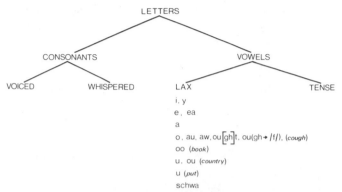

Fig. 3. Hierarchical structure: lax vowels.

given to organizing and structuring. We not only physically organize ourselves and our environment . . . we also organize our perceptions of the physical world into abstract structures'' (Whyte, 1969). Children **discover** operations in organizing and structuring as they manipulate objects and concrete materials. It will be through language that these operations are extended to understanding, perhaps to creating, structures that humans live and work in and impose on their knowledge and experiences.

1. Consonants

The first unit to be identified in the word is the consonant. The production of consonantal sounds is not the concern; the child masters this at an early age. What is important to the child is an awareness of how he says the consonant sound. Piaget's word for awareness is ''cognizance,'' the linking in consciousness of action and concept (Piaget, 1976). For most children, a linking of consonant sound and symbol is quite easily accomplished. Underachieving readers also recognize consonant–symbol associations, but their continued attention to these in reading and their confusions of voiced-whispered consonants (*g/c, d/t, b/p* . . .) in spelling suggests that they have learned in some nonspecific manner. It is the **features** of a consonant sound which are represented by a symbol, the feature ''points of articulation,'' and associated features such as voice, nasal, vocalic, back, front, and continuant. A printed symbol represents a particular set of features. The letter *b,* for example, represents the distinctive features consonantal, anterior (front), voice (Chomsky and Halle, 1968). Since a child pronounces consonant sounds and discriminates between them in the speech of others, he need only become aware of a minimal set of distinguishing features and give this set a name. The operation is comparable to one in classification: the abstraction of criterial properties, identifying and naming the class and the superordinate class that properly includes it.

The identification of distinguishing features of consonants proceeds at a rapid pace. **Putting together what belongs together** on the basis of common properties facilitates learning and recall (Miller, 1956). A minimum of six to ten voiced consonant sounds are presented in sequence to make it possible to recognize common features and construct a class. The common feature, "two things touch to close off a space," suggests that these sounds "belong together," that the class will have a name: consonants. There are two kinds of consonants, as there were two kinds of shapes: circles and squares. Some consonants are voiced, some are whispered.

Procedures in eliciting features of the voiced consonants are illustrated:

TEACHER: Everyone say, music. Get ready to say, music, don't say anything. Just get ready. I'm ready. What touches?

Make the first sound you say when you begin to say music. Listen. Put your hands over your ears and listen. Do you hear it? /m—/

Put your fingers on your throat and say /m—/. Do you feel the vibration? You are using your voice box.

There is a letter to tell you to put your two lips together, like this, to close off a space in your mouth, and say /m/. Do you know it's name?

Write the letter *m*. It goes like this: one, two, three, *m*.

Tell me when I say a word that does not begin with the sound /m/: *museum, mix, matches, melting . . . lunch.*

Voiced and whispered consonants are compared using similar procedures:

TEACHER: Say, come. Say, go.

Get ready to say, come. What touches? Get ready to say, go. What touches? You see they are the same.

Say the first sound you say in, go. Put your hands over your ears and listen. Do you hear a sound? Put your fingers on your throat. Is there vibration? You used your voice-box.

Say, come. Say the first sound you say in come. Put your hands over your ears and listen. Is there a sound? Perhaps you whispered. Put your fingers on your throat. Is there vibration? No vibration in your voice-box! You did whisper!

Other contrasting voiced–whispered consonant sounds are compared in this way (see Fig. 2).

To reinforce the notion of consonants as a class with subclasses, voiced consonants and whispered consonants, cards with a single consonant printed on each may be sorted. The action in establishing the subclasses can be shown by lines drawn on the tables and chalkboard. Naming the classes, and class inclusion questions follow:

TEACHER: What name goes here, What are they all? What name goes here? and here? Are **some** of the consonants voiced? Are all of the consonants voiced? Are there more consonants or more voiced consonants? Why is that?

"Spelling" initially for beginners will be writing the letter for the consonant sound heard at the beginning of a word pronounced by the teacher and repeated by the children, words such as:

laugh, book, chin, museum, . . .

As each letter is written it is checked with a model on the chalkboard. Children identify and sometimes explain an "error." They say:

STUDENT: I wrote *b,* for *p; b,* for *d;* or *t,* for *d, . . .*

The nature of the mistake is discussed—a voiced–whispered confusion, a directional problem, perhaps both. The correction is called "editing." The children are modeling behavior characteristic of adults when they are writing. The work of each child will be perfect at the end of the exercise.

Pace and the vocabulary will differ in reteaching older students. These students also need to recognize elements of word structure, including the consonants, and apply operations in classification in describing and ordering these elements.

2. Lax Vowels

Vowels are voiced sounds. Lax vowels are spoken with facial muscles relatively relaxed. Space is shaped in producing the vowel sound but without closure. This feature identifies members of the class, vowels. To assist the child in discrimination and recall, five lax vowels are presented together as a class of speech sounds, in the sequence high front to low back:

i e a o u

A gesture, the hand moving downward from the lips to the throat as each vowel is pronounced, reinforces awareness of the position from which each vowel is spoken. Alternative spellings for lax vowels, the pronunciation of the schwa vowel, /ə/, as in *a book, alike, alone,* and of /u̇/ as in *put, push,* are introduced later (see Fig. 3).

Children listen for the vowel sound in a spoken word. The teacher points from left to right along the line of vowels:

TEACHER: Say stop! when I point to the vowel you hear in this word: *top (sit, get, run, bat . . .).*

The word *top* is printed on the chalkboard and a procedure for blending is introduced that approximates saying the word slowly:

TEACHER: Put your mouth this shape [pointing to the letter, *t*]. Now, if you move your tongue very fast you can say the consonant and vowel sound /ŏ/ [pointing] right together. Are you ready? Try it. Feel how fast your tongue moves. You have a clever tongue! Say /tŏ . . ./ together again. Hold it! Now close the vowel sound with the whispered /p/.

Gesture may be used by the children to illustrate the action in blending. Two fists held together represent readiness to pronounce /t/; the right fist moves slowly to the right as /tŏ/ . . ./ is pronounced and held briefly. The right fist drops to complete the word, as /p/ is pronounced, closing the vowel sound. The gesture appears to suggest blending as an **uninterrupted** action rather than a sequence of isolated sounds. As the gesture is discontinued the vowel sound tends to be seen as a critical clue in recognizing a new word. The pronunciation of a consonant changes infrequently with the change in position in the word.

Children now spell "by ear" words of the form CVC and CVCC. They listen, repeat the spoken word, and select the vowel they hear from the series on the chalkboard. They write the first consonant sound they hear, the vowel they have selected, and the consonant or consonants that close the vowel /fa . . . st/. Two downward gestures represent final consonants in sequence.

The child's spelling of a word is immediately compared with a model on the chalkboard. A child identifies an "error" he may have made, explains it if he can, and rewrites the word correctly. Spelling includes words such as:

 shut, dish, sand, last, left, camp . . .

The lax vowels are included in a hierarchical structure that puts in order what has been learned about vowels (see Fig. 3).

Class inclusion relations are elicited:

TEACHER: Are there more letters or more consonants in the alphabet? Why is that? Are some letters, vowels? What is a letter? Is this a letter? Why not? It's an interesting mark. Are some letters consonants? Are all letters consonants? Why is that?

3. Consonant Clusters

Consonant clusters at the beginning of English words present an interesting regularity (Fig. 4). There are clusters in which the initial consonant(s) is followed by an *l*, or by *r*. A third group begins with the letter *s*. There is a nonregular group, a class with few members.

Children discover these regularities by consulting a dictionary or by sorting a set of cards on which consonant clusters are printed. They "put together what belongs together" on the basis of a common characteristic. As words are pronounced they listen and write the cluster they hear at the beginning of the word. The cluster is then pronounced together with the vowel that follows it. The child is asked to anticipate the adjustment that will be made during the transition to the vowel sound. Spelling then includes words such as these:

>   *stump, flat, drop, crash, think . . .*

A hierarchical structure such as that shown in Fig. 4 facilitates recall of the individual items. Indeed, a child need not memorize all the individual items. Once the child becomes familiar with the four categories, he may recover whatever specific information he requires regarding initial consonant clusters in English.

There are other predictable consonant spellings. Instances of the spellings of the final consonants for the spoken sounds /v/, /ch/, /j/, /k/, directly after a lax vowel in one-syllable words are examined. Visual discrimination and operations in inductive reasoning are involved:

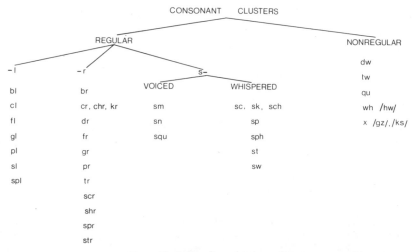

Fig. 4. Hierarchical structure: consonant clusters.

TEACHER: What letters spell /v/ at the ends of these words: *have, give, love, glove, shove, live, arrive* . . . /v/ is spelled, *ve,* at the end of a word.
What letters spell /ch/ in these words: ditch, scratch, watch, latch, stitch, crutch, . . .
In these "person-who" words: *pitcher, catcher, dispatcher, watcher,* . . .
In *kitchen?*

Children observe that the spelling -*tch* in the preceding words follows directly a lax vowel. They find other instances of this spelling and the exceptions:

   much, such, rich, and *which*

They examine words in which the final spelling of /ch/ is *ch,* and explain the difference between the two situations:

   church, lunch, bench, search, screech

Words in which /k/ is spelled *ck,* in one-syllable words directly after a lax vowel, are examined:

   truck, trick, luck, lock, neck, . . .

These words are compared with words in which *k* spells /k/:

   thank, drink, think, trunk, milk, silk, . . .

Children will later consider and account for the spelling of /k/ in *picnic, picnicking, trek.*
   Recognizing variations in consonant spellings that are predictable and functional in the language reduces the load on memory and suggests an attitude of inqui.*y* in examining word structures.

4. Inflectional Suffixes

   Inflectional suffixes are syntactic features indicating tense, agreement with a third person singular subject when added to verbs, number when added to nouns, comparison when added to adjectives:

   -ing, -ed, -s, -es, -er, -est . . .

Children apply these suffixes in their spontaneous speech, in general correctly, to word classes to which they may be added. They now examine these words in print, note the meanings that the suffixes contribute to a word and the spelling pattern that applies in adding them to one-syllable words. The pattern to be discovered is "1,1,1, and you double": that is, if the word is a **one**-syllable word, has **one** vowel, and **one** consonant after the vowel, double the last consonant before adding the suffix. A proviso will be added: do not double if the suffix begins with a consonant, as in *nets, gladly, cupful*.... The extension of the rule to two-syllable words will present a later challenge: double only if the second syllable is 1,1, and the vowel in this syllable is **stressed:**

> *ópening, músical, refér̃ring, equípped, occúrred...*
Children now write by ear and by rule words of the form:

> *jumped, running, dashing, thicker, bigger, dropping...*

They note that vowel contrast, consonant contrast, and word contrast, indicate past-time in words such as these:

> *sing–sang;   sleep–slept;*
> *keep–kept;   catch–caught;*
> *grow–grew–has grown*
> *make–made–has made;*
> *go–went–has gone.*

5. Tense Vowels

Voicing is a feature of both lax and tense vowel sounds. In speaking the tense vowels, the muscles of the throat and face are tensed.

Children will be familiar with the pronunciation of "open" tense vowels in one-syllable words that have already occurred in sentences:

> *go, no, me, be, you, I, to, so, my, our...*

and perhaps also in two-syllable words in which a tense vowel is stressed:

> *óver, músic, méter, Ápril, ísland...*

Tense vowels also occur as clusters (see Fig. 5): **apart,** as in ride, and **together,** as in rain. Tense vowel clusters written as two vowels apart may be presented first:

TEACHER: How many vowels do you see in this word—count them:
> *slide*

Point to the two vowels, you see, like this [the child points, using one finger of each hand]. Which vowel is written first in *slide?* So you will say /ī/:

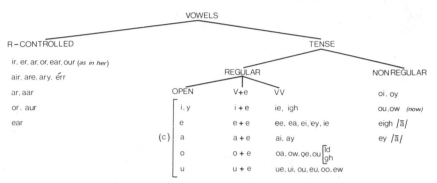

Fig. 5. Hierarchical structure: tense and *R*-controlled vowels.

/slī ... de/. Get ready to say /sl/ [pointing]. Just get ready. Now think about saying /ī/. Say them together—/slī .../ Hold it! Close the vowel sound with /d/ [pointing]. You have said the word.

The procedure may be repeated for words of similar form:

rope, tape, shine, chimes, use, fuse, refuse, taste, here, these, grebe, mere...

The children note that /k/ is spelled *k* between two vowels that are written apart:

make, flake, shake, hike, smoke, duke...

The plus *e* vowels are listed on the chalkboard:

$$i + e$$
$$e + e$$
$$a + e$$
$$o + e$$
$$u + e$$

As a word is pronounced for spelling, the children select the vowel they hear and write the word.

The suffixes *-ing, -ed, -er, -s* are added to the plus *e* vowel words and the spelling patterns are identified:

slides–sliding;   uses–using–used;
makes–making;   dive–diver–diving...

The final *e* is first discarded, then the suffix is added. It is observed that the cluster *u + e* may be pronounced /ü/:

rude, flute, crude, brute . . .

Tense vowel clusters are also written **together:** the first vowel that is written is regularly pronounced by name:

dream, tried, stain, clay, road, throw . . .

Children discover that the vowel cluster, *ie,* may be pronounced by the name of the second vowel as in these words:

chief, thief, grief, believe, fiend

A few vowel clusters are **not regular:** neither vowel is pronounced by name (see Fig. 5).

oo/ew; oi/oy; eigh; ou/ow (as in *how, round*), *ey/ā/*

Two older spellings, *-igh* and *-eigh,* appear in a limited number of words. The children search for instances and find that the spelling, *eigh,* occurs in these words and their derivatives:

eight, weight, freight, sleigh, neighbor

A number of alternative spellings and alternative pronunciations for these spellings occur for the tense vowel clusters (Fig. 5). There is a tendency for the tense clusters (pronounced as glides) that end in *-y* and in *-w* to occur at the **end of a word** or at the **end of a syllable:** for example, the clusters

ay, ey, oy,   aw, ew, ow

The clusters *ow* and *aw* may be followed by *l,* or by *n,* at the end of a word. The cluster *aw* also occurs followed by *k.* Other spellings of the tense vowel clusters more often occur **within a word:** for example, the clusters

ai, au; ee, ea, ei, eu; ie; oa, oe, oi, oo; ue, ui

Some of the preceding clusters occur in either position, for example:

ee, ea; ue; oa, oe, ou

The positions of tense vowel clusters in words are illustrated as follows:

ai/ay   remain, portrait, daisy, sailor, delay, essay, portray, array . . .
ee   see, flee, speech, screech . . .
ea   sea, tea, treat, speak, repeat . . .
ei   receive, deceive . . .
ie   chief, grief, belief, believe . . .
ey   honey, money, monkey, key . . .

oi/oy   toil, foil, coin, spoil, royal, voyage, oyster, enjoy, toy . . .
au   autumn, haul, fault, saucer . . .
aw   hawk, awkward, straw, law, claw . . .

oo   too, zoo, cocoon, moose, moot . . .
oe   shoe, canoe, loess, shoemaker . . .
ue   blue, Tuesday . . .
eu   Europe, neuter, neutral . . .
ui   fruit, suit, bruise, nuisance . . .
ou   through, caribou
ew   pewter, jewel, slew, threw . . .

oa   cocoa, boat, float . . .
oe   hoe, floe . . .
ou   shoulder, boulder . . .
ow   shallow, follow, sorrow, borrow . . .

ou/ow account, noun, ounce, town, crown, crowd, tower, towel, now . . .

It will be noted that the inflectional suffix *-ing,* may be attached directly to a word ending in a tense vowel cluster, for example:

staying, seeing, fleeing, journeying, enjoying, canoeing, hoeing, following, knowing

These and other recurring spelling patterns are observed and ordered by the child as he examines instances of their occurrence in words in reading and spelling and as they are presented for word study. The child infers and describes the regularities and variability he observes. One of the values of variability in an orthography that still shows considerable predictability is the opportunity it provides for making decisions under conditions of not completely certain predictability, but with an acceptable degree of probability. Children are encouraged to distinguish between these conditions and conditions in which regularity, and therefore certainty, is assured. In the absence of certainty both flexibility and risk taking are likely to be involved.

6. R-Controlled Vowels

The R-controlled vowels are introduced as a class of vowel sounds (Fig. 5), a procedure that was followed in presenting the lax vowels, the tense vowel classes, consonants, and consonant clusters. One advantage of this procedure is that features common to all members of a class may be abstracted, reducing the load on memory. This advantage is not available if only one or two instances are shown, if uniqueness is emphasized, or if a consonant and then one vowel is presented. A further advantage is the emphasis on organization for understanding: the procedures suggested here are designed to make clear the relatedness of members within the group and the relation of the group within a larger context.

The R-controlled vowels are presented as a class of vowel sounds having the following characteristics: an r is added to vowels that are already familiar; in pronouncing an R-vowel, the sound /r/ is the final sound.

The lax vowels and alternative spellings of lax vowels are shown on the chalkboard:

>   *i   e   a   o   u   ea   ou*   (as in *rough*)

An r is added to each vowel:

>   *ir   er   ar   or   ur   ear   our*

Each of these R-vowels may be pronounced /er/, as in *her:*

>   *doctor, armor, earth, learn, early, courage, birch, particular, return, terráin . . .*

The R-vowels *ar, aar,* may be pronounced as in *car, bazaar.* The vowels *aur, orr,* are pronounced as in *or, aura, borrow. . . .* The following R-vowels are pronounced as in *fair:*

>   *air   stare   scary   érrand   pérish*
>   *stairs   parents   canary   érror   térrible*

For most children it will be sufficient to hear R-vowel words pronounced in conversation. Context clues will be used in reading. Other children, however, will need to examine words with R-vowels in some detail.

C. Understanding Sentences

Words in a sentence are considered as concepts—as class names having inclusion relations (Section III,A). A sentence is presented as a structure based on a whole–part relation. The implication of a whole–part relation is that there will be subordinate units, parts that relate to each other and function together in giving meaning to the sentence, the whole. The relation between the parts is topic-comment (Grimes, 1975). The development of the child's awareness of the topic–comment relation between the parts of a sentence contributes to his understanding of the meaning of the sentence as a whole.

A sentence in print has a second characteristic that can easily be made explicit as the child begins to read: print proceeds in a left–right linear direction. The child may walk and read left to right and respond to a message printed on the chalkboard, for example, a sentence such as this: COME, SUSAN, I HAVE A . . . FOR YOU. A toy is held in lieu of the printed word.

1. The Basic Sentence

The parts, topic–comment, in the following sentences are elicited by *wh*-questions:

> Robins are making a nest in our tree. The mother brings mud for the nest. The father brings sticks for the nest.

The questions are:

TEACHER: Who is making a nest in our tree? What are the robins doing? Who brings mud for the nest? What does the father bring?

Gesture, an arm extended to the left and an arm extended to the right as the child is reading a sentence, helps to dramatize the two parts of the sentence. The questions direct attention to the topic–comment relation between the parts and the function of the parts in determining the meaning of the sentence. The children are asked to listen and repeat sentences using the left–right gestures. They also suggest sentences:

STUDENTS: Children are watching the birds. The baby robins will be safe in the tree. The parents will bring food for the young robins.

A sentence is diagrammed. The parts of the sentence, topic–comment, are represented by the symbols NP   VP (Fig. 6). Children draw the diagram and use the terms, S, NP, VP. When they ask what S, NP, VP, stand for they are told—NP: 'Noun Phrase'; VP: 'Verb Phrase'; S: 'Sentence'.

Frequently occurring words appear early in sentences the children are reading, words such as:

> *I, he, she, me, my, we, our, you, come, went, will, saw, want, who, where, they, . . .*

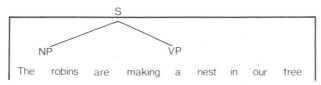

Fig. 6. The sentence: topic–comment; NP VP.

These words are read in context, not in isolation. They are pronounced for the child as needed until he recognizes them. The emphasis in reading is on understanding and in oral reading on a performance that helps others to understand.

2. The Topic Sentence: Anticipating Style

The form of a topic sentence if it occurs at the beginning of a story or article can provide a clue to the style of the writing likely to follow. Children consider the questions:

TEACHER: Is it possible that the sentence—**The squirrels are storing nuts for winter**—is a comment spoken by someone walking along and noticing what the squirrels are doing? Who might this person be? Who might he be speaking to? Where are these people?

If this sentence is introducing a conversation could the author have let you know this, perhaps by writing the sentence another way?

STUDENT: If that person was talking to me, I think he'd just say: **"Look! The squirrels are storing nuts for winter."**

TEACHER: If you had first asked that person a question, "What are those squirrels doing?" would he say: **The squirrels are storing nuts for winter.**

STUDENT: Well . . . he might say that, kind of surprised like! But maybe not. It wouldn't sound quite right. He might say: "They must be storing nuts for winter. Let's go and see."

TEACHER: If the conversation continues, and you are the writer telling us about it, would it be possible for you to include comments of your own about the people and what they saw? What would you tell us?

Suppose the sentence is **not** the beginning of a conversation. Instead, it is the first sentence in an article about squirrels: a topic sentence for a paragraph. What kind of sentences would you expect to come next?

STUDENT: I'd expect to read more about squirrels, sentences about other kinds of squirrels, like the gophers on the prairie. They hibernate in the winter.

TEACHER: Could this information be included in a conversation?

STUDENT: Yes, I think so. But I think I'd remember it better in an article, and maybe you could tell more.

TEACHER: Write a short piece about squirrels. Choose the style you prefer. It may be a conversation, with comments of your own; or it may be in the form of an article.

The teacher will read a number of these compositions to the group. They will be presented as interesting effective pieces of writing. When this atmosphere and audience participation are established, children may read their own work.

3. Relations between Elements in the Sentence

In speaking, children observe a correct positioning of nouns, verbs, adjectives, adverbs, and prepositional phrases. "In some sense the broad categories that make up the parts of speech are distinct for the child at a very early age" (Anglin, 1970). Children also employ cleft sentences in casual conversation, for example, during the above discussions, one child remarked:

STUDENT: What I would really like to know is how they find those nuts they've buried.

Complex embedded sentences, with pre-positioning of adverb clauses and phrases also occur in children's speech. The structures and relations of sentences in print are likely to be more complex. The relation of elements within the printed sentence may be made explicit.

a. NOUNS AND VERBS

This sentence:

My friend is riding her pony at the fair.

is diagrammed, NP VP, to indicate the topic–comment relation (see Fig. 7).

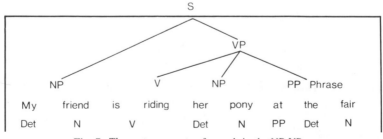

Fig. 7. The sentence: parts of speech in the NP VP.

TEACHER: **My friend,** the NP directly under the S, is the noun phrase selected
as the subject of this sentence. This noun phrase has an N, a 'noun'. Which
word is the noun in the noun phrase, **my friend?**

There are two noun phrases in the VP. Can you find them?

Which word is the **noun** in the noun phrase **her pony?** In the noun phrase,
the fair?

The VP will have a V, a verb. My friend is doing something. Two words tell
what she is doing.

So, **is riding,** is the verb in this sentence. She might have been doing
something else: eating, or laughing, or thinking, or watching. We couldn't
know until we read the verb **is riding.** Then we could think, "So that's
what she's doing," and perhaps begin to think, "What is she riding?"

The noun phrase, my friend, tells us who **is riding.** How is the noun phrase
her pony linked with the verb **is riding** in meaning? How is the phrase **at
the fair** linked with the verb in meaning?

b. THE PREPOSITIONAL PHRASE

TEACHER: There is a word before the noun phrase **the fair.** Which word is in
the **first** position in the phrase, **at the fair?** The first position word in a
phrase like this is called a **preposition,** a first position word. The phrase is
called a **prepositional phrase.**

Find the prepositional phrases in the VP in this sentence: Our class is going
in a bus to the zoo tomorrow?

How is the prepositional phrase, **in a bus,** linked to the verb in meaning?
And **to the zoo?** The word, **tomorrow?**

Here is a sentence with a prepositional phrase in the NP: The driver of the
bus will wait for us.

How is the prepositional phrase **of the bus** linked to the noun phrase, **the
driver,** in meaning?

How is the NP, **the driver of the bus,** linked to the verb in meaning?

c. DETERMINERS

TEACHER: Look at the words that come before the nouns in these noun phrases:
a bus; the zoo; our class; the children. These words are called **determiners.**

Suppose we rewrite the sentence: Our class is going in a bus to the zoo
tomorrow.—

like this: Our class is going in the bus to a zoo tomorrow.

Which words are different? Is the meaning of the second sentence the same
or different with the change in the determiners? How is the meaning different?

d. ADJECTIVES

TEACHER: A word may come between a determiner and the noun. Suppose you
tell me, "We will be riding in a big bus. . . ." Then I can think of a
particular kind of bus, one that is quite big.
If you told me: Our new friends are coming with us.
Which is the larger group of people I will think of, **your friends** or **your
new friends:**
So an adjective can make the group referred to, the smaller one; "new
friends," the smaller group, is included in the larger group, "your friends."
Find the adjectives in this sentence: We will see long-legged birds feeding in
a small pond near the road.
Are there more birds or more long-legged birds?—More small ponds or
more ponds?

e. PRE-POSITIONING AN ADVERB

TEACHER: Suppose we rewrite the sentence: Our class is going to the zoo
tomorrow.—
like this: Tomorrow our class is going to the zoo.
Is the meaning of the new sentence the same or different? How does the
meaning seem "a little bit different"?

f. PROBABILITY

TEACHER: Suppose we write the sentence like this: Tomorrow our class might
go to the zoo.
Is the meaning still the same or is it different? In what way is the meaning
different? Which word expresses probability?
How is probability expressed in this sentence: Tomorrow, perhaps our class
will go to the zoo.

g. CONDITIONAL PROBABILITY

TEACHER: Consider these sentences:
1. If it doesn't rain tomorrow, the teacher will likely take our class to the
zoo.
2. If it rains, she might take us to a movie.
3. That will be fun.
In the second sentence, who is "she"? Who are "us"? How did you know?
In the third sentence what does "that" refer to? How could you tell? Where
did you find the meaning of the word, that?
Read the sentences again. Suppose it is **not** raining tomorrow. Is it certain

the class will go to the zoo?

Suppose it **is** raining tomorrow. Is it certain the class will go to a movie. Which word indicates that going to a movie is a possibility? How else could this possibility be expressed?

Write a sentence that tells what will probably happen if something else happens. You make it up!

h. EMBEDDED SENTENCES

Embedded sentences are used by a writer to avoid repetition, to emphasize or clarify relationships among events or ideas, and for contrast with shorter simpler sentences. Some of the operations likely to be involved are subordination, compounding, deletion, and pre-positioning.

Several short sentences that tell a story are presented:

1. We saw three baby racoons yesterday.
2. They were huddled together beside the road.
3. They were waiting for their mother to take them safely across the road.

TEACHER: Could these three sentences be written as *one* sentence? Which words need not be repeated? ''They were'' occurs twice. Could both be eliminated? Is there a noun phrase that need not be repeated? Is there an adverb that could be pre-positioned? Write these sentences as one sentence.
Here are two sentences in the same story:
1. The mother returned.
2. She led them safely across the road.
How can these sentences be rewritten as one sentence?

Two patterns will be elicited: a compound sentence (two sentences joined by **and**) (Fig. 8); and a complex sentence (Fig. 9) with the option of pre-positioning the subordinate clause. In the complex sentence the noun phrase, **the mother,** may occur in the main clause or in the subordinate clause.

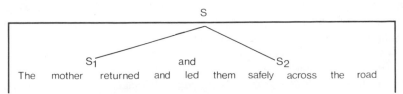

Fig. 8. A compound sentence: S_1 and S_2.

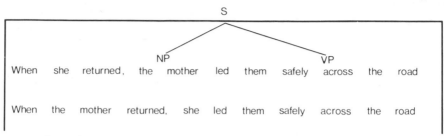

Fig. 9. A complex sentence: S_1 (Fig. 8) is embedded in S as an adverb clause and pre-positioned. Note: the NP, "the mother," and the NP, "she," referring to the mother may occur in either of two positions: directly under S or as NP in the adverb clause.

In the following sentence, two sentences are joined by *or,* indicating a choice:

We could take a picture of the little family or make a drawing.

TEACHER: What are the alternatives? What word indicates that there are choices? Is there a third choice? Does *or* leave open the possibility of doing both, of taking a picture and making a drawing, or is there just one choice? What choice does *or* leave open in this sentence: Dive, Jimmie, or come back off that diving board.
So *or* may mean *either . . . or,* but **not** both, and *or* may mean *either . . .or,* **and** *both*. Which of these meanings does *or* suggest in the following sentences:
1. We could write our friends a letter or call them long distance.
2. We could have our dinner first and then go to the show or go to the show and have dinner later.

D. Vocabulary Development

Children aged 11 to 12 years will have had considerable experience in abstracting criterial properties, in constructing classes, in combining classes in more inclusive classifications, and in recognizing the extension of classes. In reading they will be developing operations in deduction and induction (Section IV, A,F). These are experiences that help children become aware of the importance of thinking in deriving meaning, and of their responsibility for recognizing and inferring relations implicit in what they read. Operational thinking in these respects will be moving some distance from its concrete beginnings, achieving a measure of independence from the content of experience, becoming capable of "dispensing with the concrete as intermediary" (Piaget, 1972). At this point preparation for the transition to the formal level of "operations on operations" will be under way. These developments will be extended as children examine a vocabulary that includes abstract nouns derived from verbs and adjectives, and make an effort to comprehend and verbalize abstract meanings. Derived nouns, as abstractions, refer to qualities, characteristics, processes, phenomena, that are to be considered **apart from** any application to a particular object, or a specific instance. Words such as kindness, honesty, caution, triangularity, survival, amazement, justification . . . are abstractions. As abstract words, these nouns appear to be cultural constructs, abstractions imposed on experiences.

An understanding of the roots of words that are abstractions develops at a concrete level. The verbs and adjectives from which the abstract nouns are derived become known through awareness, by associating a name with one's own behavior, feelings, thoughts; by observing that persons like oneself are kind, honest, cautious; that an object may be pointed to and called a triangle and described as triangular; that people survive in difficult situations; that some achievements are amazing; that an action may be justified. Understanding the meanings of nouns that are abstractions implies a transition between hierarchical levels, a reorientation and reorganization of thinking that requires cognitive operations relatively new to children still reaching for competence in reading.

1. Abstract Nouns Derived from Verbs and Adjectives

Abstract nouns derived from verbs are marked by the addition of one of the following noun-forming derivational suffixes (Quirk, Greenbaum, Leech, and Svartvik, 1973):

-ion, -ment, -al, -ity, -age, -ing, -ance, -ness, -ery, -ism

(The classes, derivational and inflectional suffixes, are shown in Fig. 10).

Procedures previously introduced for ordering other word elements—consonants, vowels, inflectional suffixes—are appropriate in presenting noun-forming derivational suffixes. Instruction begins with auditory and visual recognition of the derivational suffix:

TEACHER: What is the **last** syllable you hear pronounced in these words: *collection; attention; action. . . .* [The words are shown on the chalkboard.] What letters spell /shən/? Count the vowels you hear in *collection. . .*
Do you hear /āshən/ as the last **two** sounds pronounced in: *determination; imagination; operation. . . .* What letters spell /āshən/ in these words:
What is the pronunciation of the consonant, *t,* in the word *operation?* Of the suffix *-ion?*

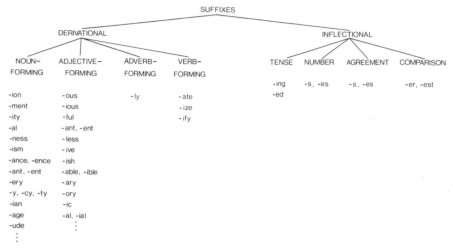

Fig. 10. Suffixes: derivational and inflectional [see Affix Index, Chomsky and Halle (1968)].

The parts of speech, verb and noun, are identified:

TEACHER: What part of speech is **operate** in this sentence: The doctor will operate as soon as possible.

What part of speech is **operation** in this sentence: The operation is scheduled for tomorrow.

Why is the final *-e* of **operate** discarded in spelling **operation?**

From what verbs are these abstract nouns derived: *investigation, application, indication* . . .

In these words, which vowel in the verb and in the derived noun receives the primary stress:

Verb	Derived noun
connect	*connection*
interpret	*interpretation*
derive	*derivation*
continue	*continuation* and *continuity*

Inflectional suffixes may be added to a verb. What are these inflectional suffixes? Write the verbs in the preceding list adding inflectional suffixes.

What inflectional suffix may be added to a noun? Add the inflectional suffix to each of the derived nouns in the preceding list to form a plural noun.

(Determiners and a determiner-plus-adjective construction may also be suggested by the children for the singular and plural forms of derived nouns.)

TEACHER: What part of speech is *absorb* in this sentence: Roots absorb moisture and minerals from the soil.

Add a noun-forming derivational suffix to these verbs: *absorb, describe, conclude, evolve.*

What changes in pronunciation and spelling do you observe?

What changes in pronunciation and spelling occur in deriving abstract nouns from these verbs:

Verb	**Derived noun**
repeat	*repetition*
deceive	*deception*
relax	*relaxation*
recede	*recession*

Mark the vowel that receives primary stress in the verb, and in the derived noun.

Noun-forming derivational suffixes are shown on the chalkboard:

-ion, -al, -ity, -ing, -age, -ence, -ance, -ment

(Children note that the vowel in these suffixes is pronounced /ə/.)

TEACHER: Which of these derivational suffixes is selected by the verb in deriving an abstract noun: *measure; involve; survive; distribute; identify; decide; destroy; appear; appreciate; cover; arrange; perform; open; drive; drain; obey . . .*

What is the pronunciation of the consonant, *c,* in *appreciate?*

The final *-e* of measure, is retained in adding the suffix *-ment.* Is this a regular pattern? What is the pattern?

The children examine two exceptions:

argue–argument; judge–judgment

Abstract nouns are also derived from **adjectives** by adding a noun-forming suffix to the adjective. These suffixes are shown on the chalkboard:

-ness; -ion; -ity; -ce; -y -ty cy; -ism

TEACHER: Which of these noun-forming suffixes is selected in deriving an abstract noun from these adjectives: *stable; mature; evident; useful, decent; generous; active; curious; anxious; harsh; honest; cruel; dense; rapid; confident; delicate; electric; desperate; national . . .*

Take the words, *generous* and *generosity*. Write two sentences, one sentence in which *generous* is an adjective and one sentence in which *generosity* is a noun. How are the words *generous* and *generosity* different in meaning? Or are they different in meaning?

Children who are beginning to be aware of the meaning of a word as an abstraction find this understanding difficult to express. The following response illustrates an early attempt to provide an explanation:

STUDENT: They're different... because if I tell you about somebody I know and I say he's generous, I'd be remembering some real things he did that I thought were pretty generous. But generosity! That's not really about a person, is it? It's about something bigger, I think. You put a lot of generous things you know about together and then you think, 'That's generosity.' It's more like something people get to know about, and talk about, and then you get to know about it too.

TEACHER: Suppose we compare the meaning of the verb *destroy* with the meaning of the derived noun, *destruction*. Are these words the same in meaning or are they different in meaning?

This child's response appears to follow a similar argument in explaining the meaning of the verb. Abstract meaning is compared with the specific instances that may be referred to by the verb:

STUDENT: Well, when destroy is a verb in a sentence you can say who did it, and then whatever it was that got destroyed and even when it happened, because it is a happening that you know about. When it's a noun you can still think about it because you know what destruction is but it won't be something definite like before. It'll be more like an idea in your head.

2. Adjective-Forming Suffixes

Adjectives are derived by adding adjective-forming suffixes to a noun or to a verb. The adjective-forming suffixes include the following (Fig. 10):

-ous, -ful, -al, -able, -ary, -ory, -less, -ive, -ic, -ical...

Children identify the adjective-forming suffix that is selected by a noun and by a verb from a list such as the following. They pronounce the words and mark the primary stress:

tumult; exception; legend; progress; pity; drama; angel; reason; avoid;

accept; proverb; speech; history; experiment; rebél; economy; peril; intro-duce; illustrate; rest; industry; horizon; fable; volcano . . .

TEACHER: The *-l* in the verb rebél is doubled in adding the suffix *-ious?* Why is that?

The meanings contributed by the derived adjectives to nouns they are linked with in a sentence are illustrated and discussed.

3. Adverb-Forming Suffixes

Vocabulary will be extended as the derivational processes in forming adverbs and the meanings contributed by adverbs to verbs and adjectives are made explicit. Most adverbs are formed by adding the adverb-forming suffix *-ly* to an **adjective.** The adjective may or may not be marked by a derivational suffix. If the adjective ends in *-le,* the *-le* is dropped before adding the suffix *-ly.* If the adjective ends in a consonant-plus-*y,* or vowel-plus-*y,* the *y* is changed to *i,* and *-ly* is added. Examples of adverb-forming processes are illustrated in the follow-ing list:

strangely; openly; vaguely; densely; simply; capably; possibly; responsibly; daintily; ordinarily; gaily; daily; generously; progressively; historically . . .

A few adjectives ending in *-ic* add the adjective-forming suffix *-al* (or do so optionally) before the adverb-forming suffix *-ly* is added:

dramatically; realistically; frantic(al)ly; basically; democratically . . .

The children note that a **derived adjective** is formed by adding the suffix *-ly* to a **noun:**

lovely; worldly; brotherly; friendly; cowardly; beastly . . .

4. Prefixes

Prefixes are important for the **meanings** they contribute to the words and word stems to which they are attached. When familiar prefixes including those that add the meanings *not, the opposite of, reversing an action, make (more),* are at-tached to a known separable word, the meaning and pronunciation of the word is likely to be recognized, certainly in context. For a first look at a new word in which the sequence is prefix, known word, derivational suffix(es), and/or inflec-tional suffix, decoding may appropriately begin in the middle of the word, move left to include the meaning added by the prefix, then right to take into account the suffixes. Words such as these may be recognized in this way:

un-	dis-	in-/im-
untie	disagreement	inside
unfairly	disappearance	improperly
uncovered	distrusted	inactive
uncertainty	disappointments	inaccuracy
unharmed	dislocation	incomplete
unheard of	disconnected	immobility
unknown	disloyal	
unkind	disobedience	
unguarded		
unleash		

ir- (before r)	re-	en-	de-
irreversible	replace	enlarge	decode
irresponsible	reforming	enclosure	defrost
irregularity	return	encirclement	decentralization
		entitled	desegregation
		enforce	

The difficulty is greater in understanding words of the form: prefix + verb stem + (suffixes). In words such as *uniform, unify, unity, uniformity, universe, universal*, the prefix, stem, and derivational suffix contribute semantic and syntactical meanings. When the same prefix is attached to **different** verb stems, the prefix will contribute a similar meaning to the verb stem. The verb stems will contribute different meanings to the prefixed verb. Examples include:

    pre-   — precede, preside, presume
    trans- — transfer, transact, transmit
    re-   — resemble, resent, resume
    dis-   — dissent, disturb, dispense
    con-   — consist, consume, condense
    de-   — deviate, detain, deter . . .

When **different** prefixes are attached to the **same** verb stem, the prefixed verbs will also have different meanings:

    -sist   — persist, insist, subsist, desist
    -fer   — prefer, defer, infer, confer
    -sign   — consign, resign, design, assign
    -pel   —expel, compel, repel, impel
    -clude   — exclude, conclude, include, preclude
    -cite   — excite, incite, recite . . .

The prefixes *ab-, ad-, sus-, sub-, in-, . . .* "undergo assimilation of the final consonant under certain conditions" (Chomsky and Halle, 1968):

ad- — adhere, admire, admit
ab- — abhor, absent, abdicate
sub- — subdue, subsist, subside
sus- — suffice, support, succumb
sub- — suspect, suspend, suggest
ad   — attribute, assign, assume
ad- — alleviate, abbreviate, annex
in-   — irregular, illiterate, immerse . . .

Derived words will become part of a child's listening and reading vocabulary as their meanings are illustrated concretely or dramatically, when they are read in short episodes, quoted or specially prepared, and are used by the teacher in discussing or describing incidents and situations.

IV. COGNITIVE OPERATIONS AND COMPREHENSION IN READING

"Some of the relationships that we find *between* sentences are the same as those we find between elements of a single sentence (e.g., topic and comment)" (Grimes, 1975). "At the same time," Grimes continues, "The organization of a text above the level of the sentence has more to it than can merely be extrapolated from relationships within sentences." It is this "more" that is of interest.

A. Operations in Deduction

In reading, comprehension involves relating ideas encoded in propositions. A "text," an ordered sequence of propositions, presents the material to be manipulated in thinking. To the extent that the cognitive operations required are known and used appropriately, comprehension is possible. But some of the operations discovered in a concrete situation, may not yet be generalized to reading. In reading, an operation may function but only in response to questions requiring the specific operation. For some children these questions will be only mildly disturbing to their present level of thinking, and will need to be rephrased and repeated. In this situation, a child will "read" but not yet understand.

Children will be familiar with the **unit** in deductive thinking, the proposition: a sentence that expresses what is true or false, believed, disbelieved, doubted, or supposed. There are singular propositions and general propositions. Quine (1974) refers to these as "occasion sentences" and "eternal sentences." A singular proposition attributes a property to a thing (an object, an individual). It has two parts, a name, and what is asserted to be an attribute of what is referred to by the name:

> That counter is square.
> The consonant, *m,* is voiced.

The **form** of the attributive sentence is productive: it is used again for the general proposition. The general proposition has two parts: it is a statement that mentions a member or members of a class, and the class to which these members belong (are included in):

> Ducks are birds.
> A duck is a bird.

Two propositions, joined, express conjunction, disjunction, or implication. If two sentences, say *p* and *q,* express propositions, then *p* & *q* expresses their conjunction, as in the following:

> That counter is square, and this one is a triangle.
> The suffix *-ion* is a noun-forming suffix and the suffix *-ous* is an adjective-forming suffix.
> Birds are animals and fish are animals too.

Or, symbolized as v in *p* v *q* expresses their disjunction:

> A prairie is a wide open plain, or a rolling plain with clumps of trees called "bluffs."

If *p* is the antecedent and *q* is the consequent in an implicative proposition, then *p* → *q* expresses an implication as in this sentence:

> If that word is a 1, 1, 1, word, the final consonant will be doubled before adding *-ing*.

Children generally understand and produce, in their own spontaneous speech, singular and general propositions and sentences in which propositions are joined to express conjunction, disjunction, and implication. These understandings do not represent an operation in deduction. Deduction involves the coordination of propositions according to a "Truth of Logic" in the "Logic of Propositions" (von Wright, 1965); the law of **modus ponens;** the law of **modus tollens;** the principle of transitivity; the inferences, possible, not possible, and the inference

undetermined (i.e., "one may not validly infer," the information is insufficient). Implication, derived by a rule of logic, is the fundamental relation between propositions, as inclusion is the fundamental relation between classes.

The law of **modus ponens** may be symbolized:

$$[p \ \& \ (p \rightarrow q)] \rightarrow q$$

This may be read:

The conjunction of the proposition, p, and the implicative proposition ($p \rightarrow q$), entails q.

In the story "The Ducks Arrive in Spring," an inference follows from the rule **modus ponens:**

There's no ice on the rivers and lakes.	$p \ \&$
When the ice is gone, the ducks have returned.	$(p \rightarrow q)$
It follows that the ducks have returned.	$\rightarrow q$

The law of **modus tollens** may be symbolized:

$$[\sim q \ \& \ (p \rightarrow q)] \rightarrow \sim p$$

This may be read:

The conjunction of the proposition $\sim q$ (q is not true), and the implicative proposition if, p is true than q is true ($p \rightarrow q$), entails $\sim p$ (p is not true).

In the following question, the inference follows from the rule **modus tollens:**

TEACHER: Its the first of April and there are no ducks on the prairie.
Has the ice melted on the ponds and lakes?

The following response is derived by the rule **modus tollens,** the inference being stated first:

STUDENT: No, it hasn't melted.	$\rightarrow \sim p$
If the ice was melted, the ducks would be	$(p \rightarrow q) \ \&$
back and there aren't any ducks back yet.	$\sim q$

Some children defend the inference, "It hasn't melted," by using a nonlogical argument: it may be an "authority." In this case a child referred to the weather:

STUDENT: It's not melted. The story said it hadn't melted.
  It's too chilly yet for it to melt.

In these instances the rule **modus tollens** is not yet used in reading.

An inference that follows from the **principle of transitivity** may be symbolized:

$$(P \rightarrow Q) \ \& \ (Q \rightarrow R) \rightarrow (P \rightarrow R)$$

This general principle may express the logical relation of equivalence, the relation serial order, the transitive relation that holds between a superordinate class and its subordinate classes, and the implicative relation by which judgment on propositions may be formulated. The relations are transitive and the structures parallel:

$(a=b) \ \& \ (b=c) \rightarrow (a=c)$ The transitivity of equivalence.
$(a>b) \ \& \ (b>c) \rightarrow (a>c)$ The transitive relation of serial order.
$(a \supset b) \ \& \ (b \supset c) \rightarrow (a \supset c)$ The transitive relation of class inclusion.
$(p \rightarrow q) \ \& \ (q \rightarrow r) \rightarrow (p \rightarrow r)$ The transitive relation of propositons.

Each of these expressions of the principle of transitivity may be involved in reading comprehension. The transitive relation between a superordinate class and its subordinate classes may be illustrated:

$$(ducks \supset birds) \ \& \ (birds \supset animals) \rightarrow (ducks \supset animals)$$

The inference **undetermined,** follows in a situation in which one may not judge with certainty between possible alternatives. This situation is presented in the following question:

TEACHER: The lakes and ponds are frozen over. Are there ducks on the prairie?

In the following response, the premise is noted and circumstances given in the story are recalled. The decision is: this is not a "yes" or "no" question; in fact, it could be **either** "yes" **or** "no." The **undetermined inference** is then explained:

STUDENT: Well, they can be and they can't. Some come back when everything is frozen and go to the wheat fields. Some come back when it's not frozen. For sure they won't be here in the winter, but you didn't say if it was winter or nearly spring.

Two operations in thinking appear to come together in deriving the inference, **undetermined:** the disjunctive class inclusion operation $B = A + A'$; $(B_x,$ that is, any member of the class B can be **either** an A or an A'), and the inference **undetermined,** an operation in deduction.

Operations in deduction yield necessity, certainty, and inferences that provide new information. The extension of these operations to reading provides understanding and contributes to cognitive growth. The instructional procedures outlined in the following paragraphs will include questions that require deductive inferences. A child's responses will be considered in terms of the evidence they provide of his progress in learning to think.

B. Deductive Reasoning in Reading

The story, "The Prairie Blizzard," written by the present author for 9- to 10-year-olds, suggests questions requiring inferences based on the rules **modus tollens, modus ponens,** the inference **undetermined,** and an inference that follows from the **principle of transitivity.** Inferences derived by these rules provide information that will be **implied** but **not expressed** in the text. While the story, summarized as follows, describes an incident from pioneer days in the west, even today in a world of "all weather" roads, helicopters, and all the rest, children "know" the hazard to life in a blizzard.

"The Prairie Blizzard"

Jimmy's father was a doctor in the early days of settlement on the prairie. Many of the doctor's patients lived across the river on farms far from the village.

One cold night there was a loud knock on the door. A man wrapped in a heavy buffalo robe stumbled into the room.

"Could you come right away, doctor. My neighbor's wife is having a baby. They need you."

The doctor wakened Jimmy. "We must go, Jimmy. You'll need to help with the horses. There's a terrible blizzard."

Jimmy put straw and warm robes in the sleigh and hitched up the horses. They drove down to the river and started across. The snow had completely covered the trail and visibility was reduced to zero. The doctor was concerned.

"It's going to be up to the horses to get us across, Jimmy, and you know they could turn in the wind and circle back home. If we do get across, do you think we can get up the bank on the other side?"

Jimmy knew the banks on both sides of the river. He had fished and hunted prairie chicken and this winter he had hunted rabbits.

"The horses won't make it up the banks, Dad. But there's a cut in the river bank and a farmhouse right after you get through the cut. The people at the farmhouse keep the cut open all winter. The road that goes past that farmhouse goes right to your patient's house. We'll have only another three miles or so to go."

"I hope we can find that cut, Jimmy."

They pulled the buffalo robes over their heads and waited.

In the story the writer, as writers do, assumes the reader will interpret the meanings of unfamiliar expressions from context and will understand the inclusion relations of the class names that are mentioned: *prairie chicken; a cut; circle back; visibility.* . . . The writer also assumes that the reader will derive information not "spelled out" in the story: for example, the character of Jimmy's father; Jimmy's courage and competence in an emergency; the relation of mutual respect and confidence between the two—a relation implied but not elaborated by the writer. One child, understanding this, combined his insight with a derived inference in this remark:

STUDENT: They **could** be at the wrong house, if the horses turned in the blizzard. If that happens what they'll do is just turn around and try again. I know!

The following questions require inferences that follow from the rule **modus tollens:**

TEACHER: 1. Jimmy and his father have **not** gone through the cut in the river bank. Have they reached the farmhouse? How did you know that?
2. They have **not** reached the farmhouse. Have they gone through the cut in the river bank? How did you know that?

The first sentence in each question calls attention to the danger in the situation, and by association to its urgency. Concern appears to interfere with "selecting out" the logical elements in order to consider the problem from this point of view. Concern may have influenced these responses:

STUDENT: I don't think so, because they could go through the ice and drown.
They could freeze to death out there. One of the horses could break a leg.
I don't know if they should even be out there in that blizzard. If they don't find the cut, maybe the father could help the mother get the baby.

No answers will be considered "wrong," certainly not these sensitive responses. They will be "accepted." A child must continue to **believe in** his capacity to think if he is to make progress. As mentioned before, questions will be rephrased and repeated in other situations. Some children, also concerned with the emergency were able to respond to the questions logically:

STUDENT: No, they're not there yet, because the farmhouse is right by the cut and that's the only way they could get through. If they'd gone through the cut they would see the farmhouse. It's going to be tough to find that cut in a blizzard.

Difficulty in inferential reasoning could extend to deriving an inference based on the **principle of transitivity.** In the following question the premises are expressed as implications:

TEACHER: If they reach the farmhouse, they will reach the road. If they reach
the road, they will be on the way to the patient's house. If they reach the
farmhouse will they be on the way to the patient's house?
The transitive relation may be represented in symbols: *FH,* 'Farmhouse'; *Rd,*
'Road'; *PH,* 'Patient's House'.

$$[(FH \rightarrow Rd) \ \& \ (RD \rightarrow PH)] \rightarrow (FH \rightarrow PH)$$

These statements may be seen to involve an ability to visualize spatial-temporal
relations in reading. Some children telescoped into one place the farmhouse and
the patient's house, eliminating the road. Since the spatial–temporal considerations in the premises no longer applied, the if . . . then relations in the premises
could be overlooked:

STUDENT: They already reached the patient's house, right after they came
through the cut. So now they can begin to help the mother.

Other children explained the transitivity relation quite clearly:

STUDENT: If they reach the farmhouse, they're on the right road so now it'll be
O.K. They can just drive on to the patient's house.

A first sentence in a question can be reassuring; it can also be a contrary-to-fact
statement as in the following questions 1 to 4. (In the story the people are still on
the frozen river.) In questions 1 and 2 the inferences follow from the rule **modus
ponens:**

TEACHER: 1. Jimmy and his father have gone through the cut in the river bank.
Is there a house in front of them?
2. They have reached the farmhouse. Have they gone through the cut in the
river bank?

Questions 3 and 4 require the inference, **undetermined.** These questions also
begin with contrary-to-fact statements:

TEACHER: 3. they have reached **a road.** Is it **certain** they have gone through
the cut in the river bank?
4. There is **a house** in front of them. Is it **certain** they have reached the
road to the patient's house?

It is of interest that 9- to 10-year-old children accept, apparently without hesitation, that it is appropriate to reason from contrary-to-fact premises. The following responses also recognize the undetermined inference:

STUDENT: Well, if they've reached a road, they'd at least be off the river. But it could be a different road if the horses turned in the blizzard, and if they haven't gone through the cut.
They **could** be O.K. but that house would have to be the right farmhouse. The horses could swing around and take them back home. If that happens I guess they'll just have to turn around and try to get across again.

Conditional and conjectural thinking, a willingness to speculate on the possible and not only on the real, is not, apparently, a universal achievement. In some cultures young adults, to only a limited extent, are willing to reason from contrary-to-fact propositions (Spindler and Spindler, 1965). Studies of the classification system of the languages of these cultures suggest one possible source of the differences. Languages apparently differ widely in their manner of ordering the environment (Sturtevant, 1964; Bright and Bright, 1965; Murdock, 1945). In not all languages are exclusive and exhaustive terminological systems used. Murdock has pointed out that "the assumption that cultures . . . have in common a uniform system of classification . . . a single basic plan, has led to much confusion in describing cognitive orientations." The classificatory pattern, "A is included in B; A is a B," was found to be inadequate for describing a number of folk taxonomies. It has been suggested that these taxonomies are better represented by a "sphere of influence" model (Bright and Bright, 1965). Exclusive and exhaustive classification and the logic of class inclusion would likely be learned most effectively if these were already incorporated in the language. The development of inferential skills, the ability to reason from "as if" premises may depend on a mastery of class structures and class inclusion relations since these appear to be related in form to the logic of propositions. Progress in inferential reasoning may also be observed in the growing acceptance by children that an intellectual operation can be substituted for perceptual evidence in arriving with certainty at knowledge of a state-of-affairs. Children may resist employing intellectual operations in this way. One 9-year-old, for example, in a concrete situation declared, "I can't tell if I don't **see.**" He decided to try.
It is possible that a number of children in our culture who have difficulty in learning do not assimilate basic components of the classification system as they are learning the language: components such as the abstraction of criterial properties; the concept of a class name; class inclusion relations and the expression of these relations in implicative propositions. It would seem that operations in

classification hold a position of some priority in the on-going process of cognitive development. Delay in recognizing class inclusion relations, if it remains unrecognized, could adversely affect progress toward inferential reasoning.

C. Imposing Structure: An Operation in Mapping Information

The structuring of information is another essential operation in understanding meaning that is largely a responsibility of the learner. Structure is **imposed** on knowledge and experience, imposed **by us.** "The world is the way it is. Only an observer can simplify it" (Pattee, 1969). Simplifying involves operations in describing and ordering observations and information. "... a description in terms of a hierarchy [or other structure] comes from *us* and not necessarily from the system we are describing" (Becker, 1975).

Children are introduced to operations in hierarchical structuring as a means of ordering and simplifying what is observed as they separate out and examine elements that make up a word. They abstract criterial features of subunits within the word, recognize that the features abstracted are common to a number of subunits, group subunits that have features in common as a class of units, and combine classes to form superordinate classes. At each level, one rule is applied in determining membership in a class: the class inclusion relation. A hierarchical structure, based on the inclusion relation, is built from the bottom up (see Fig. 2).

There will be other approaches to imposing hierarchical structure in reading that will contribute to understanding relations within the whole, approaches that also go beyond the dictionary meaning of the term hierarchy. The dictionary defines the word *hierarchy* as a relation of dominance, of command, that is, as a unidirectional or "bossing" relation. An example of this relation is the line of command in an army. The current extended meaning of the term hierarchy entered "exact human thought more than a hundred years ago" (Whyte, 1969). Whyte points to the present, "immense scope of hierarchical classification," and describes it as "the most powerful method of classification used by the human brain-mind in ordering experience, observation, entities and information." As evidence of the scope of this concept Whyte cites the hierarchical classification of:

numbers, scales, times . . .
symbolisms, sentences, and languages of all kinds
logical types, concepts, principles, information, quantities and abstractions
of many sorts.

Basic yet distinct concepts of hierarchical structuring, coordinating, and sequencing provide working hypotheses in the social, physical, and biological sciences and in the study of language. Students need to develop similar skills in mapping information presented in reading, in lectures, and in discussions. In discussion, communication proceeds as a succession of declarative statements, the natural and efficient way of communicating information to others.

> Much of what we know is most easily statable in a set of declaratives. Natural language is primarily declarative and the usual way to give information to another person is to break it into statements. (Winograd, 1975)

In a class discussion, this "set of declaratives" may present a considerable body of relevant information. Consider a class discussion that follows a week of independent reading on the topic, "Survival in Winter in the Boreal Forest." The students will have some background knowledge of life on the tundra, and on the plains, and some general information of conditions in the boreal forest. The focus now is the survival of animal life in this forest region in the winter. A general reference is available (Fuller and Holmes, 1972). Other sources will be chapters in books, articles, and reference materials. Discussion proceeds more or less in this fashion:

STUDENTS: I read that caribou **shovel snow** to get at the plants they eat.

Did you read that it is *warm* under the snow. That's hard to believe. But animals make tunnels and live in them—miles of tunnels. They even have chimneys to get to the top and look around.

It said that bears don't really hibernate like other animals. They go out and move around sometimes.

Our newspaper said a boreal owl was seen in Toronto last week.

I never heard of voles, but there was a picture of one.

It was a surprise to me that chickadees could pack away seeds and stuff on the **under** sides of branches. I wonder how they find them again. It said they had to do it in just four or five hours of daylight.

I think the predators have the best of it. There are lots of animals to hunt.

Contributions such as these will continue for some time. Eventually the contributions begin to slow down. This appears to be partly from the confusion of so many disparate impressions, partly from a sense of frustration, "What does all this add up to?" "What does it **mean?**"

The problem will be in part the lack of shape, of continuity and relatedness. It could also be a consequence of the way the students are seeing the events: they seem to think of each behavior as proceeding in a **linear** order, day after day, month after month. Caribou begin by shoveling snow and keep on doing this; foxes hunt, voles live in tunnels, and life goes on in the forest week by week as it has from time immemorial. Details are interesting—up to a point—but the "whole" is escaping them. Structure is needed for relations in the data to become visible and productive.

A teacher may reorient the discussion by pronouncing a simple summarizing, finalizing word: "So." *So* will refocus attention, suggest the possibility of a new direction, and convey approval and appreciation of what has been going on. It says in effect:

TEACHER: All is well. You have done a good job of reading. You know many things and everything you have told us is new and interesting.

What the teacher **actually** says is:

TEACHER: So!... Animals **do** find ways to survive in winter in the cold northern forest. Different ways! How **do** animals survive?

A response that begins with *some* will be helpful.

STUDENT: Some of them just sleep through it all.

If a next response introduces *all,* as in this response,

STUDENT: But they don't **all** of them hibernate the same way. Some of them only partly hibernate. . . .

structuring can begin from the top down. The top branching nodes of the hierarchical structure may be set up and extended as dichotomies. To survive—some: a dormant phase—hibernation—and semihibernation; others: active (see Fig. 11).

TEACHER: You were saying that not all animals hibernate the same way. What does that mean?

STUDENT: Well the ground squirrels hibernate, and I think they said the woodchucks do too, but their brains get some extra oxygen. They sometimes move around for a bit, and they can waken if there is danger.

TEACHER: What kind of animal is a ground squirrel? A woodchuck? How will you show in the hierarchical structure that these small mammals hibernate? [One child drew the line, then asked: Will I write the animals' names under mammals?] What about the reptiles, frogs, insects, in the forest? What do they do? [This group is identified as "other animals" and included in the structure.]
You mentioned the bears. Do they have a dormant phase?

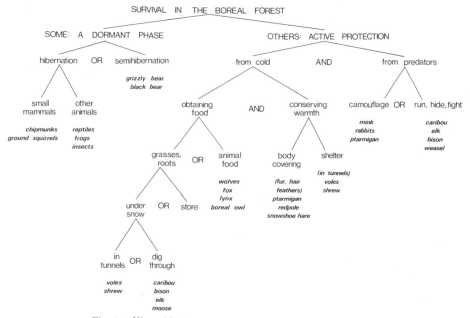

Fig. 11. Hierarchical structure, reading: ordering information.

STUDENT: Bears eat a lot in the fall, and find a cave or something, and sleep a lot. But they go out some too.

There are other large animals in the forest. What do they do in winter?
The mother bear has her young there in the den. They'll be ready to come out when it's warmer, maybe by June.

TEACHER: Could we call this semihibernation—a half-in-half affair? Where does this information belong in the hierarchical structure? Put it there.
There are other large animals in the forest. What do they do in winter?

STUDENT: Oh they just keep going. They're all over the forest.

TEACHER: These active animals, do they have problems surviving? What are their problems?

STUDENT: The cold for sure. And enemies.

TEACHER: What is the name for animals that prey on other animals? [The node—Others: active, need protection; and the nodes—from cold—from predators, are added.]

At the end of this discussion, two main nodes, and alternatives at these nodes have been established. For the following week, the children decide to share the reading, one group following the problems of active animals in coping with the cold; another group, the problem of escaping from predators. When the structure is completed most of the topics the children have discussed are included in a relationship within the structure (Fig. 11).

So far there has been no writing, except additions to the hierarchical structure. The first use of the structure will be in speaking rather than writing. Speakers may choose to speak to the topics from the top down; or top across down; or bottom up. Or a speaker may choose to expand on one aspect of winter survival, referring briefly to others. It is a case of "speaker's choice." The second use of the structure will be to demonstrate its effectiveness in providing new information: the development of "*a causal chain* between the original conceptualizations" (Shank, 1975). Questions based on the structure follow:

TEACHER: What are the consequences for the predators when small mammals and other animals hibernate during the winter. Are there advantages for the predators, too?

There's shelter from the wind under the snow, but only a dim light. How can it be "warm" there for the animals? Where does the warmth come from? What else is alive down there under the snow?

Few birds stay in the forest in the winter—the owls, willow ptarmigan, redpole, chickadees, stay. But most birds migrate. These migrating birds have warm feathers too. Why do some birds stay and others leave?

There is usually a brief warming period in the forest during the winter and this leaves a hard sharp crust of frozen snow. Will this be a problem for the animals? How will the different animals react to this?

Foxes in most parts of the world have rather high wide ears. Look at these pictures. Why should the foxes of the boreal forest have small ears?

At this point writing may begin. The project will be prepared "for publication," in this case, presentation to the school library. An extended effort such as this proceeds better when there are a purpose and a product in view. The writing is shared, individuals developing topics, writing, rewriting, and editing, and consulting with others to prepare links that provide continuity. The hierarchical structure will indicate the main themes, provide headings, and suggest paragraphs. The joint effort is assembled, edited, and typed. An introduction, conclusion, and bibliography are added. All work is shared.

The exercise as a whole brings together and focuses on a specific task operations in classification, organization, and inferential reasoning. Imposing a structure and writing clarify for the students some of the contrasts between the two modes of communication—natural communication in declaratives, and the more formal communication in writing that requires structuring and includes understandings derived from the order imposed.

D. The Idea of Chance

For some time during the early school years the discovery of operations in classification and in deduction will provide confidence and competence in understanding and learning. A decision recognized as undetermined, can still be explained. Eventually this confidence will be challenged by an awareness that there are events and outcomes that are unpredictable and irreversible and seemingly impossible to explain. As one child said, "Maybe nobody knows. Maybe things just happen by themselves."

The idea of chance as opposed to miracle, caprice, occurs, Piaget suggests, as an awareness of a conflict with recently acquired notions of deductive necessity. "The idea of chance and the intuition of probability constitute almost without a doubt secondary and derived realities dependent precisely on the search for order and its causes" (Piaget and Inhelder, 1975). Chance, for the child, is then a "new kind of fact," and he begins looking for a hidden cause, a regularity or explanation under appearances. The search, in the case of conservation of substance, weight, length, and so on, led the child to the discovery of reversibility. But the essential characteristic of chance is irreversibility, a completely new reality to the child. This reality will come to be understood by way of contrast with reversibility, and in contrast to necessity, the status of inferences derived by operations in deduction. In deduction, however, he has come to recognize the inference undetermined, an understanding that if $B = A + A'$, and x is a B it must be either an A or an A'. Add to this equation a much greater number of alternatives and it becomes possible to conceive of the **indeterminate** inference, a condition not reducible to a deductive operation. Observation may support the notion of **irreversibility,** that is, of an irreversible mix, the outcome of multiple interacting forces: leaves, for example, scattered by winds, and the impossibility of a return to their original places in a pile. The sequence of operations leading to the discovery of irreversibility and chance may therefore be traced from the initial discovery of reversibility, through operations in deduction yielding necessity, to the undetermined inference as the "possible," and finally by way of contrast with the necessary and the undetermined, to the notion of the indeterminate and irreversible, as the outcome of multiple interacting forces.

E. Probability Reasoning in Reading

The story, "Home from School" written for 9- to 10-year-olds, describes a sequence of events, each the outcome of multiple interacting circumstances.

Given that such events are reported as occurring in sequence on a particular day, as in the story, the probability that they will occur again, on another day, and in the same sequence, may be considered to be zero. A child will **list** these events, in the order they happened, without difficulty. Recognizing and explaining the chance nature of the events and the probabilistic factors involved will be more difficult. These understandings are assumed by the writer; they are not made explicit in the story. Children may not, however, be required to make clear what is implicit in a story. A teacher will not know if a child understands unless questions require specific inferences. Clymer (1968) points out that a child "may or may not be asked to verbalize the rationale of his inferences." It could also be the case that the child has not been required to verbalize a logical inference. Inferences that seem obvious to an adult are not necessarily obvious to a child. Formulating questions that require specific inferences, accepting a child's responses, and reintroducing the questions if necessary are important procedures in facilitating cognitive development.

The story "Home from School," describes a series of chance events:

> One afternoon Mary got off the school bus and walked along the gravel road to her house. Suddenly she tripped and fell. Her books were scattered all over the road. She was covered with sand, and her hands hurt. She got up, brushed off the sand, picked up her books, and walked on.
>
> In a few minutes a small green snake scuttled across the road in front of her. It disappeared in the tall grass at the side of the road. As she passed the old pine tree a flock of crows settled noisily in its branches.
>
> A few minutes later Mary opened the kitchen door. There was mother. She had just baked a lovely pan of muffins.

Questions on the story require what may be called "subjective probability reasoning": applying to a present situation an awareness based on one's experiences in the past, that what happens can be subject to conditions of uncertainty. Subjective probability in reasoning would be used in recognizing that the events described in the story would be the outcome of a great number of interacting chance happenings. Preliminary questions ensure the recall of the events in the story:

TEACHER: What happened when Mary got off the bus? . . . What happened as she walked along the road? . . .

Questions requiring subjective probability reasoning follow:

TEACHER: Is it possible that each of these things will happen again just like this **tomorrow** when mary gets off the bus? (Next week?)
Why is that? Why is it likely (not likely) these things will happen again like this tomorrow? (Next week?)

Can you explain how it is that events like this are likely (not likely) to
happen just like this again the next day? (Next week?)

In the following response the child recognizes that the events are unlikely to
happen the next day, but seems unable to explain the chance factors that account
for this. One explanation offered was "every day is a little different." This child
is referring to past experience in judging the present situation:

STUDENT: No, because it would be very funny if the same things happened over
again.
Not very many things happen like that if it ever does.

TEACHER: Next week?

STUDENT: Well, . . . I don't think . . . well no, you get up in the morning and
things are a little different and well . . . every day's a bit different from the
time you brush your teeth.

TEACHER: How come every day things are a little bit different?

STUDENT: Well . . . I don't quite know . . . but they **are.** Life's like that.

Some responses begin by recognizing uncertainty for a particular event, then
become confused in considering the probabilities in the situation as a whole:

STUDENT: No, because I think she'd remember about the rocks she tripped on.

TEACHER: The other things?

STUDENT: Um-m . . . it would be a hard thing for animals to do the same thing
that they did that day again on the next day.

TEACHER: So what do you think? Are these things likely to happen the next day
in the same way? Or not?

STUDENT: M-m-m—they could. She could have forgotten about the rock.

In the next response, the child is reasonably sure that particular events "might
not" happen, and explains this by saying they "will not" happen:

STUDENT: No, because the snake might not cross the road, and she might not
fall, and the crows might not come, and mother might not bake muffins.

TEACHER: Why is it these things might not happen?

STUDENT   Well, because the snake will go away and the crows will not come.

TEACHER: Next week?

STUDENT: Well, I don't know . . . like I said, the snake will go away.

The following response suggests that the idea of chance is not yet a part of the child's thinking yet there is some hesitancy, possibly some dissatisfaction, with the conclusions presented:

STUDENT: It might. I don't know. The snake might be in the green grass . . . she could trip again on the same thing . . . she could start off like that again next week and then maybe . . . well . . . the snake could've come back, and the crows . . . wow! if she tripped again on the same stone she'd be pretty stupid.

Some of these responses suggest that a child could be ready to **begin** the search for an explanation of chance. Piaget postulates that sequences, including sequences in cognitive readiness, are to be expected in intellectual development. Sequences were observed during children's discovery of reversibility and in the ways they defended conservation. The instructional procedures suggested in forwarding this early development included rephrasing and repeating questions in alternative concrete situations and in reading. For later operations such as the discovery of chance a procedure of choice could be to ensure that operations that yield certainty on the evidence of **reversibility,** as in conservation, and operations in classification and deduction have been well established and generalized to reading. It is possible at the same time to continue to introduce materials in reading and questions that suggest the idea that events could be the outcome of chance happenings. But direct argument, demonstration, explanations designed to "push forward" acceptance of the notion of chance and probability will not be indicated. Children with appropriate preparation and given opportunities in concrete and reading situations to discover the "new reality," chance, and irreversibility, will, in doing so, be constructing their own intelligence. There is, however, another possibility to be considered in instruction. This is to link questions on operations such as chance and probability reasoning, operations that have not yet been discovered, with questions on another advanced process in thinking, for example, inductive reasoning.

F. Inductive Reasoning in Reading

In the story "Home from School" and in the story "The Cave," to be summarized further on, unexpected events occur in close succession. In the former story, it is expected that the events described will be recognized as chance happenings on the basis of children's past experiences with such events. Children, 9 to 10 years of age, apparently do consider that it would be a "hard thing" for events "like this" (events that are the outcome of multiple interacting forces), "to happen again . . . but, then again, they could." What does not yet appear to concern the children is that chance itself, the reason why it would be "a hard thing," requires an explanation.

Inductive thinking also has a basis in past experience. Before a child makes use of an inductive operation in order to account for an as yet unexplained situation, he has "acted inductively" in almost all real life situations. He has assumed that the food he ate yesterday, the dog he has known, the fire that will hurt will be "the same" in significant respects today. The question of the validity of these inferences he refers to experience: he takes his experiences to be "fair samples from a larger totality," and inferences of this kind to be "the best mode of reasoning about the unknown. . . . In his use of induction he may be said to be adopting the policy of a practicalist" (von Wright, 1965). He may be wrong. He may be mistaken in his reasoning from "all previously observed," to "this particular instance." He may not know a law of nature to which to refer observed events. But his policy is sound: he has found a way of approaching the world in both ordinary circumstances and in many critical situations. What he will need is skill in **assembling** observations: in induction "nothing is derived from a single statement, but from a conjunction of this statement with others (and perhaps with some theory or the like)" (Bocheñski, 1965). The assembling of observations is, in Bocheñski's view "the essential foundation of the whole system" of inductive thinking. What then follows is an attempt to "explain" the assembled observations by asserting a general statement from which these observations could be derived. The next step is to treat this general statement as a hypothesis to be tested against the observation statements to consider if, in fact, it might account for the assembled observations. If this appears to be the case, the hypothesis may be inserted as a premise in a hypothetical-deductive argument in order to determine its validity.

Induction "supposes at the same time a knowledge of deductive operations and of chance itself, since inductive reasoning consists precisely in sifting what is regular from what is fortuitous, organizing the regularities into a system of classes and relationships to be treated deductively" (Piaget, 1975). In the story "The Cave," these operations remain implicit; at the end of the story the resolution of the problem is not given. Inductive thinking then becomes both possible and necessary. Chance, if this understanding has been discovered, could tentatively be considered to account for the unusual incidents described in the story. An explanation in terms of chance, would be eliminated as incompatible with the evidence.

"The Cave"

Two children, climbing a mountain, discovered a secret cave. When they scrambled through an opening in the rock wall they found a huge dark cave that seemed to go on and on under the mountain.

The first day they went in only a few steps and peered into the darkness. The next day they had a real shock. Hundreds of bats flew screaming out of the cave and over their heads. Not one collided with them, but how they missed seemed a miracle.

The children got used to the bats and began to explore the cave. A little way inside they found a tiny waterfall.

"This could be the den of a wild animal," they said. But then they remembered that only rabbits, squirrels, and chipmunks lived on this mountain.

As they ventured deeper into the cave it became darker and darker. They decided to bring candles. For a month they visited the cave, waited for the bats to fly out, lit their candles, and began to explore.

One day they came to the cave and shouted as usual for the bats to fly out. Nothing happened. They threw stones to make a noise. All was silent and still. They stood where they were and lit their candles. The candles went out. They lit them again. The candles sputtered and went out.

The children turned slowly away from the cave and sat down on the rocks to think. They tossed a peanut to a chipmunk. He stuffed it in his cheek and headed for the cave. But he turned back as soon as he came to the opening and ran to the top of a rock. There was not sight or sound of the bats. The whole mountain was silent and still. An eagle soared in the blue sky over the valley. The chipmunk scooted for cover under a rock.

The events described in the story are nonrandom; they follow from the intervention of a determining agent, a constant, intervening in a previously random distribution of events. The new regularity and the nature of the intervening constant, are to be explained presumably by the operation of a law of nature. These laws are general statements, accepted as true, about how nature works. In inductive inquiry, such "laws are involved throughout the sequence of reasoning. . . : laws are not only generalizations at which we arrive after we have established the facts: they sometimes function precisely as premises . . . or as test hypotheses" (Kaplan, 1964). Kaplan describes the "assembled observations" as "data in search of a law." In the story it is not necessary for children to speak about "oxygen" or "cave gas"; it is sufficient that they postulate "something is the matter with the air in there."

Following preliminary questions to ensure the recall of events in the story, questions requiring inductive thinking are presented. Operations in induction appear to follow a logical and perhaps a developmental sequence: recognition that there is a problem; assembling observation statements; the formulation of hypotheses to account for these observations; the assertion of an inductive inference; an attempt to verify the inference by subsuming the observations under a law. The questions may be presented in an order to anticipate this sequence.

Recognition of the problem:

TEACHER: Are things really different at the cave or are the children just imagining it?

Formulating a hypothesis:

TEACHER: What do you think could be going on here? Can you find out? Go ahead and see if you can figure it out. What could have happened? How would you explain what happened?

Asserting an inference supported by evidence:

TEACHER: What could account for the unusual happenings at the cave on this morning? What does your explanation account for? How is this a good explanation? What may it not account for?

An inference supported by a law:

TEACHER: What sort of thing could have happened at the cave to make these different things happen, things like "no bats," the "stillness," the "candles going out," the "chipmunk turning away"?

Consider the sorts of responses that 9- to 10-year-old children have been found to give to such questions. A number of responses indicate that some children do not recognize that there is a problem requiring an explanation.

STUDENT: Oh, those children are just imagining things. My guess is they're just remembering they'd been told never to go into caves.

Others recognize that the situation is different but do not present an explanation:

STUDENT: Well, what the children backed out for was the candles going out . . . that never happened before. Something made them go out. And I think the bats were dead. It couldn't be just nothing was wrong . . . because two things were wrong.

TEACHER: What do you think could be wrong? What is making things wrong?

STUDENT: I don't know. . . .

Some children explain each event as having a different cause:

STUDENT: Well, I think it's quite different, because candles don't usually keep on going out. Maybe the water splashed on them. Maybe the bats just got used to the children. Maybe the bats aren't there any more, maybe they're dead. Maybe somebody is in there. It could have been. But I don't know. A lot of things seemed different.

TEACHER: What about the chipmunk?

STUDENT: Well, that would have to be the eagle or something.

In the following response there is considerable progress in thinking. As Bobrow (1975) points out, "the use of the appropriate piece of knowledge at the right time is the essence of *intelligent* mental operations." In this case it is an attempt to link at least two observations to a common precipitating factor, and this common factor, the constant, is recognized as something "in the cave":

STUDENT: Something's happened in the cave, or the children could go in and explore. Whatever it was, it made the candles go out and maybe it made the bats fly away. They wouldn't go away if nothing had happened.

TEACHER: What about the chipmunk?

STUDENT: I think he's just fooling around—maybe he hopes to get another peanut. I don't think he could tell there was something wrong in the cave.

TEACHER: You remember the story "Home from School"? Are the events in that story like what is happening at the cave, or do they seem different?

STUDENT: I think these are different, because like I said, the snake wouldn't likely come back, or the crows . . . and in the cave I don't think these things are going to change very soon.

TEACHER: How is it that what happened at the cave is not likely to change and in the other story things aren't likely to happen again?

STUDENT: Well, I don't know, but in the cave something's gone wrong, and you couldn't say any one thing had gone wrong in the other story.

A few children put it all together. They begin with a review of the incidents, try two-at-a-time explanations, then center on the candles. Implicative sentences are in their responses:

STUDENT: If the candles went out it **could** be because it was a certain kind of air. I put a candle in a bottle once and it went out. It could be that there's something the matter with the air in there. . . .

A considerable pause, then definite rather tentative implications follow:

STUDENT: If the candles went out, it wouldn't be O.K. for the bats . . . and . . . the chipmunk wouldn't go in either.

TEACHER: Could it be just a wind blowing out the candles?

STUDENT: No. A wind wouldn't blow out the bats or scare off the chipmunk. I think I read once about some kind of gas . . . it's the air all right. You'd better tell those kids not to go into that cave when you finish writing the story.

TEACHER: You remember the story "Home from School"? Do the events in that story seem much the same, or are they different from the events that happened at the cave?

STUDENT: Oh, these ones are different. They **had to** happen because the air was bad. The snake and the crows—nothing made them come just when they did, it was only luck they happened to come. There'd be almost no chance at all they'd come again like that.

TEACHER: What about the cave?

STUDENT: Things are going to stay that way as long as the air is bad.

The word *chance* occurs for the first time in this child's responses. It would seem that by considering and contrasting the two situations, and using inductive reasoning to solve a problem that involved a constant, the notion of a chance event "almost no chance at all they'd come again like that," is becoming clearer.

It appears that some 9- to 10-year-old children do not accept that if a familiar state of affairs takes an unexpected turn in a story the new situation is necessarily or significantly different, or in need of extraordinary measures by way of explanation. Other children who decide "something must be wrong" propose explanations that could "maybe" account for events taking them one at a time. These children are probably not "ready" to develop operations in inductive reasoning; further attention to basic operations in thinking—reversibility, class inclusion, inferential reasoning, with some emphasis on the relation between natural causes and their outcomes—could be indicated.

Children who consider the observations reported in the story to be related events likely to have a common explanation tend to proceed inductively to account for the new situation. They develop and test hypotheses, look for a single natural cause, and refer to past experiences. Each hypothesis is checked to determine if, in fact, it could account for all the observed events. These children could be ready for further experiences in hypothesis formulation and testing.

G. Hypothesis Formulation and Testing

Students 10 to 13 years of age may be introduced to some of the ways a scientist is likely to think in solving problem situations. A scientist will begin by considering possible solutions that can be tested **experimentally,** and then will formulate these possible solutions as hypotheses. When the hypotheses have been developed, the scientist will design experiments to test each in turn. If the results of the experiments do not support a hypothesis, that hypothesis is rejected. Other hypotheses may then be formulated and tested in new experiments.

McKinnon (1976) stresses the importance of hypothesis formulation and testing in cognitive development:

> The act of hypothesis formation followed by test is at the very heart of enhancement of logical thought, and, when these opportunities are given to students in abundance they extend to other areas as well. In other words, hypothesis formulation and the search for manipulative variables, and mental manipulation of these variables become a vital part of the cognitive structure.

The introduction to an article, "The Soaring Flight of Vultures" (Pennycuick, 1973) presents a situation that for some time eluded scientific investigation. Since the experiments that finally led to an understanding of the situation are **not** included in the introduction, the students must do as scientists do: formulate hypotheses and suggest experiments to test these hypotheses.

A part of the introduction to the article is presented here:

> Early in the morning on the East African plains one quite often meets little groups of vultures that had gathered at some small find the night before and then slept where they happened to be when night fell. If the birds are pursued, they take off, but they do not fly far before they land again. If they are forced to take off several times in rapid succession, they quickly become exhausted and can be caught by hand.
>
> Later in the morning, say after 9:00 a.m., the technique sometimes still works on a vulture that is heavily gorged with food. More often the bird will fly straight ahead for a short distance, then turn sharply and at the same time start climbing. After turning in a few irregular narrow circles and intermittently flapping its wings, the vulture settles down to gliding in steady circles. It then continues to climb, without flapping its wings and drifts downwind as it circles.

Introductory questions provide an opportunity for assembling the observations reported:

TEACHER: What is the referent of the phrase, *the technique* in the expression "the technique sometimes still works . . .'"?

What is referred to by *some small find* in "little groups of vultures that had gathered at some small find . . .'"?

The word *intermittently* describes a vulture's flight pattern, "intermittently flapping its wings." How do you picture this flight pattern?

Could the word *occasionally* be substituted for the word *intermittently* and convey the same image?

There are two implicative sentences in paragraph one. What are the implications? What are the consequences?

A question requiring a hypothesis taking into account the observations recorded is presented:

TEACHER: What do you suggest might be an explanation of the behavior of vultures observed "early in the morning," and the different behavior of the birds observed "later in the morning"?

A first hypothesis proposed is likely to be:

STUDENT: It could be that the birds are too heavy to take off right away because they've been eating most of the night.

TEACHER: How will you test that hypothesis?

An experiment suggested for testing this hypothesis may be represented by this response:

STUDENT: What you could do to find out if that was the problem, is not to let them eat anything and then see if they can take off without waiting until later.

TEACHER: Suppose you carry out this test and find that the vultures still do not take off early in the morning, but are able to do so after about 9:00 a.m. What would you try next? What would be your next hypothesis?

An alternative hypothesis and the test suggested is:

STUDENT: I'd figure they could have been sleeping for quite awhile after their feast and were only half awake. I'd try wakening them earlier, or maybe not let them sleep hardly at all and see if that made a difference. Maybe then they could fly off right away.

These are interesting hypotheses: they are supported by observations given in the text, and they are testable. They are also offered tentatively pending verification by the experiments proposed. These considerations do not appear in the following hypothesis:

STUDENT: It's because vultures are like that. They've always been like that. They run and try for a bit, and then take off.

TEACHER: How will we test that hypothesis?

STUDENT: I don't know. I guess we'd just have to know it, I mean, believe it.

TEACHER: We would like to be able to check as many possibilities as we can think of by testing them. In the explanation you suggest there is still the question: Why are vultures like that? We could be puzzled since other large birds take off if you approach them: hawks, ravens, herons. . . . Vultures take off too, later in the morning. Do you have another suggestion?

STUDENT: Well, it could be that something seems different to vultures a bit later in the morning and they like to wait till then to take off.

TEACHER: Good thinking. Suppose we explore that idea. . . .

At this point observations and experiences begin to be recalled and examined as possibly relevant; a remark such as this, for example:

STUDENT: It sounded as if the birds had just taken an elevator. A heavy bird like that could use an elevator!

The next comment introduces an additional observation reported in the text:

STUDENT: It was a funny kind of elevator they got. It went in circles.

This comment stimulates recall of an experience:

STUDENT: That reminds me. You know those things they call dust devils. You see them in a ploughed field when there's a high wind.

This comment is expanded.

STUDENT: Oh, you mean the "twisters." They twist and turn and spread out as they go up. I've seen them too. Do you suppose the vultures found a twister?

Tests for this interesting possibility are offered:

STUDENT: Sure. I bet they did. And you know what I'd do? I'd get a big balloon and see if I could go up the same way.

Caution is suggested:

STUDENT: You might go up! But it would be easier to get binoculars and watch to see if that is how the birds are going up.

A third paragraph selected from the article is presented for reading:

Soaring birds are not the easiest birds to study, partly because the bird watcher, traditionally equipped with binoculars and rubber boots, cannot watch their mobility and tends to lose track of them, and partly because one can never tell from the ground what kind of air movements a bird is soaring in . . . in fact not a great deal of progress has been made with this approach since E. H. Hankin's classic book *Animal Flight* appeared in 1913.

The children are then asked:

TEACHER: What further information are scientists interested in knowing about the flight of vultures? How might they investigate these problems today?

One child commented: "My Dad talks about updrafts. He's a pilot." Gliders and then, for safety, powered gliders are suggested as a way of following a bird in flight. The complete article, "The Soaring Flight of Vultures" may then be presented for reading and study.

Students discover that a hypothesis tested experimentally may, as in this case, raise a number of other equally interesting questions. So the process of observing, recording, formulating hypotheses, and testing goes on.

Finally, the story, "The Cave," is presented for rereading. The students contrast and compare the inductive operations they had used in solving the problem in "The Cave" with the procedures in hypothesis formulation and testing used in solving the problem presented in "The Soaring Flight of Vultures." They are asked to consider if a hypothesis could be formulated and tested experimentally in the case of the observations in the story "The Cave."

Materials for developing skill in inductive reasoning, in hypothesis formulation and testing, and in hierarchical structuring are available, for example, in *Scientific American*. Articles including "Continental Drift and Evolution" (Kurtén, 1969); "The Tropical Rain Forest," (Richards, 1973); "Communication Between Ants and Their Guests" (Hölldobler, 1971); "Bicycle Technology" (Wilson, 1973); "Early Man in the Andes" (MacNeish, 1971), and others have been found challenging. Episodes from novels, stories, and poems, and critical essays in scholarly journals are equally challenging and illustrate various approaches in presenting and solving problems. Students may "forget" much of the content of what they read. What they will not forget are the patterns in thinking and the attitudes toward thinking that they discover.

V. CONCLUSION

This chapter has explored some of the possibilities for providing children with opportunities to develop operational thinking as they learn to read in a Piagetian and language-oriented program. The topics discussed have been selected to illustrate the potential of instruction in reading for encouraging the transition to concrete operations and for developing these operations to a level that could ensure a successful transition to formal operations at early adolescence. A more complete discussion of such a program would include, for example, understandings in causality; concepts of time, in history and in evolution; responses to beauty in music, art, and literature; the child's growing awareness of the varied forms of social life, human as well as the social life of other creatures, and of social responsibility; the world of time and space and of other people, and strategies in thinking for coming to know these worlds.

In a program designed to "facilitate the transition from simpler to more complex cognitive performance" (Resnick and Glaser, 1976), essential procedures will include cognitively oriented questions designed to elicit the specific operations in thinking that a child is ready to discover or invent; and a consideration of the child's responses to these questions in the context of his continuing efforts to construct his intelligence. Responses to questions involving classification and deductive inferences, for example, could indicate a child's readiness to apply these operations in more complex situations or his readiness to discover operations in inductive reasoning; they could also suggest a child's need for time to extend his understanding of operations in conservation, in abstracting criterial properties, and in recognizing class inclusion relations.

There are many children who have difficulty learning to read, children who are identified as "reading disabled." Considering the complexity and interdependence of the thinking skills involved in learning, it would seem that caution is needed in interpreting the terms that are often used to describe these children. They are described as presenting "specific deficits": auditory-temporal processing deficiencies; visual processing disturbances characterized by performance deficits on the Wechsler Intelligence Scale for Children (WISC); lower verbal than performance WISC IQs; reversals of letters and words; directional confusions; and poor laterality. These observations are undoubtedly accurate. For many disabled readers, however, terms such as these could be an account of **symptoms** associated with delay due to difficulties that were unrecognized during an early period in the transition to operational thinking. If in these cases the descriptive terms are taken to be **explanatory,** as identifying conditions that are directly **preventing** the child from learning to read, "corrective" procedures could be incorrectly selected. Strategies in thinking that the child himself could have used to resolve his confusions may have been from the beginning, and continue to be, quite limited. Clinical and school experiences in reteaching these children (Rawson, 1978) suggest that early operations in thinking—concepts in conservation, classification, and organization, are unfamiliar even to older children in concrete experimental situations as well as in reading. A child's response as he discovers these operations is surprise and what Luria (1973) describes as "a certain level of increased alertness . . . [a] mobilization of the organism to meet possible surprises. . . ." "This mobilization," Luria concludes, "is an important basis of *investigative activity.* " Increased alertness and something that might be called a "sense of power" emerge as a child becomes aware of **how** one thinks and comes to know. Teacher and child begin to set a pace for each other that is a surprise to both of them.

Activities and materials selected for teaching children who do not read should redirect the child's attention beyond the self and the present concern to properties of the physical world, for example: floating and sinking; icebergs and glaciers; magnetism; machines; air; light; the tundras, deserts, and tropical forest of the world; to new ideas, discoveries, and adventures everywhere. High interest, low vocabulary materials are an insult to children of average or above average, even superior, potential. Books well written and well illustrated belong to all children. It is a simple matter to tell a child a word he does not recognize. The resources and procedures needed for reteaching these children are available to a teacher, perhaps only to a teacher: procedures that encourage cognitive development, organize information, set a pace, and recognize and satisfy the child's urge to know. These materials and procedures are needed by all children who are learning to think and to read. They are urgently needed by children who are experiencing difficulty. The teacher will ensure that during a period that is critical for cognitive development children are not limited to turning pages in a reader or a text, to picking up the next card, to drawing lines and circles and choosing among the few decisions available in a "work" book. Learning to think and learning to read are processes that interact and are mutually facilitative. They demand of children a degree of alertness, and "surprise" that will make a difference. For this, a teacher is indispensable.

A central purpose of education, in the view of the Educational Policies Commission (1961), "the purpose that runs through and strengthens all other educational purposes—the common thread of education" is "the development of the ability to think." The contribution of instruction in reading will be critical in the initiation and early development of the ability to think.

REFERENCES

Anglin, J. M. *The growth of word meaning*. Cambridge, Mass.: M.I.T. Press, 1970.

Becker, J. D. Reflections on the formal description of Behavior. In D. G. Bobrow and A. Collins (Eds.), *Representation and understanding: Studies in cognitive science*. New York: Academic Press, 1975.

Bobrow, D. G. Dimensions of representation. In D. G. Bobrow and A. Collins (Eds.), *Representation and understanding: Studies in cognitive science*. New York: Academic Press, 1975.

Bocheñski, J. M. *The methods of contemporary thought*. Dordrecht, Holland: D. Reidel, 1965.

Bright, J., and Bright, W. Semantic structures in Northwestern California and the Sapir–Whorf hypothesis. *American Anthropologist*, 1965, **LXVII**, 249–258.

Chomsky, N., and Halle, M. *The sound pattern of English*. New York: Harper and Row, 1968.

Clymer, T. What is reading?: Some current concepts in innovation and change in reading instruction.

In H. M. Robinson (Ed.), *The sixty-seventh yearbook of the National Society for the Study of Education,* Part II. Chicago: University of Chicago Press, 1968.

Educational Policies Commission. The Central Purpose of American Education. Washington: National Education Association, 1961.

Elkind, D. Quantity concepts in college students. *Journal of Social Psychology,* 1962, **57** (2), 459–465.

Epstein, E. Roots. *Scientific American,* 1973, **228** (5).

Fuller, W. A., and Holmes, J. C. *The life of the far north,* Toronto: McGraw-Hill, 1972.

Gerard, R. W. Hierarchy, entitation and levels. In L. L. Whyte, A. G. Wilson, and D. Wilson (Eds.), *Hierarchical structures.* New York: American Elsevier, 1969.

Grimes, J. E. *The thread of discourse.* The Hague: Mouton, 1975.

Halliday, M. A. K. Language structure and language function. In J. Lyons (Ed.), *New Horizons in Linguistics.* Toronto: Penguin Books, 1975.

Herron, J. D. Piaget for chemists. *Journal of Chemical Engineering,* 1975, **52** (3), 146–151.

Hölldobler, B. Communication between ants and their guests. *Scientific American,* 1971, **224** (3).

Inhelder, B., and Piaget, J. *The growth of logical thinking from childhood to adolescence* (A. Parsons and S. Milgram, trans.). New York: Basic Books, 1958.

Inhelder, B., and Piaget, J. *The early growth of logic in the child: Classification and seriation* (E. A. Lunzer and D. Papert, trans.). London: Routledge and Kegan Paul, 1964.

Inhelder, B., Sinclair, H., and Bovet, M. *Learning and the development of cognition* (S. Wedgewood, trans.). Cambridge, Mass.: Harvard University Press, 1974.

Kaplan, A. *The conduct of inquiry,* San Francisco: Chandler, 1964.

Kneale, W., and Kneale, M. *The development of logic.* Oxford: Clarendon Press, 1962.

Kurtén, B. Continental drift and evolution. *Scientific American,* 1969, **220**(3), 54–63.

Lloyd, D. N. Reading achievement and its relation to academic performance. Part II: Relationships of reading achievement in race, sex, socio-economic, and mental ability groups. Laboratory Paper 28. Personal and Social Organization Section, Mental Health Study Center, National Institute of Mental Health, 1970.

Lovell, K., and Ogilvie, E. A study of the conservation of substance in the junior school child. *British Journal of Educational Psychology,* 1960, **30**, 109–118.

Lovell, K., and Ogilvie, E. The growth of the concept of volume in the junior school child. *Journal of Child Psychology and Psychiatry,* 1961, **2**, 118–126. (a)

Lovell, K., and Ogilvie, E. A study of the conservation of weight in the junior school child. *British Journal of Educational Psychology,* 1961, **31**, 138–144. (b)

Lyons, J. Generative syntax. In J. Lyons (Ed.), *New horizons in linguistics.* Toronto: Penguin Books, 1975.

Luria, A. R. *The working brain: An introduction to neuropsychology* (B. Haigh, trans.). London: Allen Lane. The Penguin Press, 1973.

MacNeish, R. S. Early man in the Andes. *Scientific American,* 1971, **244**(4), 36–46.

McKinnon, J. W. The college student and formal operations. In J. W. Renner, D. G. Stafford, A. E. Lawson, J. W. McKinnon, F. E. Friot, and D. H. Kellogg (Eds.), *Research, teaching and learning with the Piaget model.* Norman: University of Oklahoma Press, 1976.

Miller, G. The magical number seven, plus or minus two: Some limits on our capacity for processing information. *Psychological Review,* 1956, **LXIII** (2), 81–97.

Murdock, G. P. The common denominator of cultures. In R. Linton (Ed.), *The science of man in world crisis.* New York: Columbia University Press, 1945.

Oléron, P. *Les activités intellectuels.* Paris: Presses Universitaires de France, 1964.

Pattee, H. Physical conditions for primitive functional hierarchies. In L. L. Whyte, A. G. Wilson, and D. Wilson (Eds.), *Hierarchical structures.* New York: American Elsevier, 1969.

Pennycuick, C. J. The soaring flight of vultures. *Scientific American,* 1969, **220** (3).

Piaget, J. *The child's conception of the world.* London: Routledge and Kegan Paul, 1951.

Piaget, J. *The child's conception of physical causality.* Paterson, N.J.: Littlefield, Adams, 1960.

Piaget, J. *Play, dreams and imitation in childhood* (C. Gattegno and F. W. Hodson, trans.). London: Routledge and Kegan Paul, 1962.

Piaget, J. *The principles of genetic epistemology* (W. Mays, trans.). London: Routledge and Kegan Paul, 1972.

Piaget, J. *The grasp of consciousness* (S. Wedgewood, trans.). Cambridge, Mass.: Harvard University Press, 1976.

Piaget, J., and Inhelder, B. *Memory and intelligence* (A. J. Pomerans, trans.). London: Routledge and Kegan Paul, 1973.

Piaget, J., and Inhelder, B. *The origin of the idea of chance* (L. Leake, Jr., P. Burrell, and H. D. Fishbein, trans.). New York: W. N. Norton, 1975.

Quine, W. V. *The roots of reference.* La Salle, Ill.: Open Court Publishing, 1974.

Quirk, R., Greenbaum, S., Leech, G., and Svartvik, J. *A grammar of contemporary English.* London: Longman Group, 1973.

Rawson, H. *Reading and cognition.* Unpublished Doctoral Thesis, University of Alberta, 1969.

Rawson, H. The function of reading in the transition to concrete and formal operations. In B. Z. Presseisen, D. Goldstein, and M. H. Appel (Eds.), *Topics in cognitive development, Vol. 2.* New York: Plenum Press, 1978.

Renner, J. W., and Stafford, D. G. The operational levels of secondary school student. In J. W. Renner, D. G. Stafford, A. E. Lawson, J. W. McKinnon, F. E. Friot, and D. H. Kellogg, *Research, teaching, and learning with the Piaget model.* Norman: University of Oklahoma Press, 1976.

Renner, J. W., Stafford, D. G., Lawson, A. E., McKinnon, J. W., Friot, F. E., and Kellogg, D. H. *Research, teaching, and learning with the Piaget model.* Norman: University of Oklahoma Press, 1976.

Resnick, L. B., and Glaser, R. Problem solving and intelligence. In L. B. Resnick (Ed.), *The Nature of intelligence.* Hillsdale: Lawrence Erlbaum, 1976.

Richards, P. W. The tropical rain forest. *Scientific American,* 1973, **229** (6).

Shank, R. C. The structure of episodes in memory. In D. G. Bobrow and A. Collins (Eds.), *Representation and understanding: Studies in cognitive science.* New York: Academic Press, 1975.

Spindler, G., and Spindler, L. The instrumental activities inventory: A technique for the study of the psychology of acculturation. *Southwestern Journal of Anthropology,* 1965, **21**, 1–23.

Sturtevant, W. C. Studies in ethnoscience. *American Anthropologist,* 1964, Special Publication, **LXIV**, 99–131.

Tower, J. D., and Wheatley, G. Conservation concepts in college students: A replication and critique. *Journal of Genetic Psychology,* 1971, **118** (2), 265–270.

Venesky, R. L. *The structure of English orthography.* The Hague: Mouton, 1970.

von Wright, G. H. *The logical problem of induction.* Oxford: Basil and Blackwell, 1965.

Whyte, L. L. Hierarchy in concept. In L. L. Whyte, A. G. Wilson, and D. Wilson (Eds.), *Hierarchical structures.* New York: American Elsevier, 1969.

Wilson, S. S. Bicycle technology. *Scientific American,* 1973, **228** (3).

Winograd, T. Frame representation and the declarative/procedural controversy. In D. G. Bobrow and A. Collins (Eds.), *Representation and understanding: Structure in cognitive science.* New York: Academic Press, 1975.

SUBJECT INDEX